Neuro-linguistic Programming Workbook

FOR

DUMMIES®

Neuro-linguistic Programming Workbook

FOR

DUMMIES®

by Romilla Ready and Kate Burton

JOHN WILEY & SONS, LTD

Neuro-linguistic Programming Workbook For Dummies®

Published by
John Wiley & Sons, Ltd
The Atrium
Southern Gate
Chichester
West Sussex
PO19 8SQ
England

E-mail (for orders and customer service enquires): cs-books@wiley.co.uk

Visit our Home Page on www.wiley.com

For general information on our other products and services, please contact our Customer Care Department within the U.S. at 800-762-2974, outside the U.S. at 317-572-3993, or fax 317-572-4002.

For technical support, please visit www.wiley.com/techsupport.

Wiley also publishes its books in a variety of electronic formats. Some content that appears in print may not be available in electronic books.

British Library Cataloguing in Publication Data: A catalogue record for this book is available from the British Library

ISBN: 978-0-470-51973-8

Printed and bound in Great Britain by TJ International Ltd, Padstow, Cornwall

10 9 8 7 6 5 4 3

About the Authors

Romilla Ready works as a trainer and executive coach. Having realised that the common denominator in any interaction – whether that causes stress or gives pleasure – is people, she developed and delivers Relationship Wizardry® in Business. These are workshops where her clients learn to build profitable relationships by understanding the psychology of communication. Romilla also offers a potent blend of NLP and metaphysics in her Breakthrough Coaching for executives who experience fast, powerful results. Some of the positive 'side effects' experienced by Romilla's clients are a reduction in stress and an increase in personal effectiveness. Romilla also plays matchmaker at her public workshops, Relationship Wizardry® for Singles where people learn about creating their dream relationship.

Kate Burton is an executive coach and trainer who is passionate about enabling individuals and teams to communicate effortlessly and tune up their careers to be healthy and sustainable. She brings 30 years' experience to her international work with services-based businesses and professional firms. Her own career began in corporate advertising and marketing with Hewlett-Packard.

Today she thrives on supporting people in boosting their motivation, self-awareness, and confidence. Her belief is that people all have unique talents, abilities, and core values. They just need to be focused in the best direction.

Kate also co-authored the bestselling *Neuro-linguistic Programming For Dummies* with Romilla Ready and *Building Confidence For Dummies* with Brinley Platts.

Authors' Acknowledgements

From Romilla: NLP has been an amazing journey for me so far. It's allowed me to learn not just about family, friends, and clients but most importantly, about myself. The greatest lesson I have learnt is to appreciate each and every person whose life intersects with mine because, no matter what, they enrich my life through their love or the lessons I needed to learn. With that in mind, I would like to thank the founders of NLP for their gift and the brilliant people who have taught me along the way. The more I learn and practice, the more I appreciate the fantastic grounding that David Shephard and Tad James gave me.

I would like to thank Kate for partnering me on this project and our team at Wiley, especially Alison for giving us this opportunity; Rachael, you have been a delight; and Kathleen, you have opened my eyes.

Sometimes it's easy to take for granted those closest to us so I would like to say thank you to my family, particularly Derwent for holding up the metaphorical mirror and keeping the technology going; Mum for her 'Go for it' attitude; Derek for sharing half his life with me; Angela for keeping me on the straight and narrow; and Os for being. Thank you Carol, as always. Rintu, my NLP knowledge would be the poorer for not having you there to explore with.

A special thank you to our fabulous readers around the world for your feedback and for taking the time to get in touch and say hello. It's heart-warming to hear from you.

From Kate: With the support and encouragement of so many people I've been bitten by this book-writing bug and you now have the finished workbook in your hands. I appreciate all the thousands of buyers of the original *Neuro-linguistic Programming For Dummies* and *Building Confidence For Dummies*. Thanks to you, our friends at Wiley issued yet another invite to write.

My special thanks go to Romilla for more fun and enthusiasm as my co-author on this sequel and to all our editors including Alison, Rachael, Kathleen, and Christine for patiently smoothing out our words.

I'd also like to acknowledge Bob, Rosy, and Jessica for their love and loyalty – writers are seldom domestic goddesses too. And to my parents, Gina and Tony, who instilled the core values that I cherish. Finally, I have been privileged to work with hundreds of fabulous clients, colleagues, and trainers who continue to inspire me. I trust that this collective wisdom will spread and prove valuable as you travel through this workbook.

Publisher's Acknowledgements

We're proud of this book; please send us your comments through our Dummies online registration form located at www.dummies.com/register/.

Some of the people who helped bring this book to market include the following:

Acquisitions, Editorial, and Media Development

Project Editor: Rachael Chilvers

Commissioning Editor: Alison Yates

Development Editor: Kathleen Dobie

Copy Editor: Christine Lea

Technical Editor: Anne-marie Halliwell

Proofreader: David Price

Content Editor: Nicole Burnett

Publisher: Jason Dunne

Executive Project Editor: Daniel Mersey

Cover Photo: © GettyImages/Johner

Cartoons: Rich Tennant (www.the5thwave.com)

Composition Services

Project Coordinator: Erin Smith

Layout and Graphics: Claudia Bell, Beth Brooks, Stacie Brooks, Carl Byers, Alissa D. Ellet, Brooke Graczyk, Shane Johnson, Erin Zeltner

Proofreader: John Greenough

Indexer: Broccoli Information Mgt.

Brand Reviewer: Zoë Wykes

Publishing and Editorial for Consumer Dummies

Diane Graves Steele, Vice President and Publisher, Consumer Dummies

Joyce Pepple, Acquisitions Director, Consumer Dummies

Kristin A. Cocks, Product Development Director, Consumer Dummies

Michael Spring, Vice President and Publisher, Travel

Kelly Regan, Editorial Director, Travel

Publishing for Technology Dummies

Andy Cummings, Vice President and Publisher, Dummies Technology/General User

Composition Services

Gerry Fahey, Vice President of Production Services

Debbie Stailey, Director of Composition Services

Contents at a Glance

Table of Contents

Introduction

*N*euro-linguistic Programming (NLP), like hypnosis, is now widely accepted, thanks to the work of Milton Erickson, having moved off the stage into the world of therapy and into the consciousness of everyday folk as well the business community. From its beginnings in the early 1970s, the first wave of people to take NLP on board were trainers and therapists – using NLP in a specific field in a very focused way. More recently there has been new-found interest in NLP, with both adults and children wanting to find out what NLP is all about.

The following conversation between Dave, his daughter Charlotte, a very bright ten-year-old, and their neighbour, an NLP trainer and coach, illustrates the current interest in NLP perfectly.

> **Dave:** So what is this NLP? Charlotte's been asking me.

> **Neighbour:** 'Neuro' means the neurology that is common to humans. You're only able to see a picture, hear a sound, recognise someone's touch, or feel an emotion because of the neural pathways in your body. 'Linguistics' refers to language. But NLP is much more than being concerned with words. NLP also means the body language that you display and, finally, 'programming' is the way you repeat behavioural patterns that give you your good and bad habits.

> **Dave (tongue in cheek):** Yup, that's what I told Charlotte. Wasn't it Charlotte?

> **Charlotte (deadpan):** Actually Dad, what you said was more like, 'I haven't a clue'.

The reason NLP is becoming more and more popular is because it allows people to understand human psychology in a way that is easy to apply to different aspects of their lives, and to bring about changes in the way they live their lives.

About This Book

Our reason for writing *Neuro-linguistic Programming Workbook For Dummies* is to help you gain a basic understanding of NLP in a format that you can easily work with and understand.

To crib a saying attributed to Confucius, *You forget what you hear; You remember what you see; You understand when you do.*

In this workbook, we explain the principles of NLP through anecdotes to bring home particular points, and explain, using examples, how you can tackle the exercises. Now if this seems a little like W-O-R-K (which some consider a rude, four-letter word), replace it with another four-letter word most of us use from a very young age: P-L-A-Y. Arm yourself with coloured pens or pencils, don your favourite learning hat, and play with the exercises.

Learning for the sake of learning is very commendable. But if you want to actively learn and achieve results, make the content of the workbook belong especially to you by coming up with your own real-life scenarios and using them in the exercises.

Foolish Assumptions

You're probably well aware of the need to question everything and not to assume anything because it makes an *ass of u and me*. Well, we're sticking our necks out because we're assuming that at least some of the following, if not all, applies to you:

- ✓ You're literate.
- ✓ At some point you've said to yourself, '*Neuro-linguistic Programming*, what a mouthful, but what does it mean and how can it help me?'
- ✓ You want to know how understanding human psychology can bring clarity to your thinking.
- ✓ You want to improve your relationships with the people around you.
- ✓ You have areas in your life that can do with improving.
- ✓ You want to be healthy, wealthy, and wise.

So in the spirit of our foolish assumptions, we're offering you a toolkit that has changed our lives for the better, and we hope it does the same for you.

Characters in This Book

We don't have a disclaimer like you get at the end of a film that goes something like: 'The events depicted in this film are fictitious. Any similarity to any person living or dead is merely coincidental.' In *Neuro-linguistic Programming Workbook For Dummies* a number of the anecdotes and examples belong to real people, but their identities have been heavily disguised, in most cases, to protect the innocent.

How This Book Is Organised

This workbook is split into five main parts, each part consisting of chapters relating to the overall concept of NLP.

Part 1: Setting Up Your NLP Journey

Part I starts you off by getting you to think about your reasons for buying *Neuro-linguistic Programming Workbook For Dummies* and how you are going to use this workbook to learn and apply NLP to your everyday life or in the world of business. As with any journey, you want to know where you're setting off from and how you're going to get there. The purpose of this part is to get you thinking about how you're living your life, and bringing your lifestyle to your conscious mind so that you can make choices about the paths you want to take.

Part II: Connecting with the World

The chapters in this part get down to the basics of understanding how you, and other people, think. You find out how you create your thoughts in terms of pictures, sounds, and feelings. This understanding allows you to connect with yourself and take charge of your thinking. Once you get to grips with ways of connecting, you can start communicating more effectively with other people – for example, by developing your personal rapport in all areas of your life. Discovering how to listen to other people and adapting your language patterns to theirs makes it easier to connect with, and understand, other people's style of thinking.

Part III: Honing Your NLP Toolkit

This is where you get down to the nitty-gritty of the NLP toolkit. For example, in Chapter 9 we show you how to manage and change your emotions, regardless of what is happening to you, and how you can change the way you perceive 'bad events' from the past. Chapter 10 demonstrates ways of recording and managing your experiences, turning the difficult experiences into positive experiences. Chapter 11 gives you a model for getting you aligned with your sense of purpose and meaning. You find out in Chapter 12 how to use the tools for understanding your own behaviour, how to change annoying habits, and how to model successful people from all walks of life. And finally, in Chapter 13 you discover the pattern for creating and recalling memories. You also find out about your time line and how to put it to good use to make your goals irresistible.

Part IV: Riding the Communications Escalator

Part IV is all about communicating effectively. You find out about the magic of words and making language work for you. We show you how to dig deep into the psyche by going into the detail of how a person thinks and how to get your message across and be heard. Finally, we consider ways to hone your storytelling skills, for use in business situations and in your everyday life.

Part V: The Part of Tens

In The Part of Tens we suggest ten ways of introducing NLP into your workplace. We also offer you tips on developing your NLP skills and taking them further by practising and expanding your skills. Of course, you have a section on resources so that you can find out more about NLP – on the Internet, in books, and through other people and organisations.

Icons Used in This Book

To make some information stand out for you we have placed icons in the left-hand margins. You'll see the following icons in this workbook:

This icon is used to tell stories and relate incidents to clarify the application of NLP processes.

You see this icon when an explanation of a term that is very specific to NLP is used; otherwise the term may sound like gobbledygook to you.

This icon tells you when it's time to put theory into practice and start doing an exercise.

This icon is used as a friendly reminder and a recap of NLP principles and practices.

When we're trying to be particularly helpful we use this icon to bring to your attention tips and tricks we've picked up to help you shortcut your learning process.

Where to Go from Here

Neuro-linguistic Programming Workbook For Dummies is, as the name says, a workbook and doesn't have the space for a lot of in-depth explanations. Like any work, the best way to learn is to dive in and simply get started. You find out more as you go along. Naturally, some of you will want to begin at the very beginning and go through the chapters in sequence. Others of you may prefer to start wherever takes your fancy. (Maybe, like us, you tend to read the last page of a novel first!)

If you're currently very confused about various areas of your life, you may want to head straight to Chapter 3 where you can take a personal assessment of how satisfied you are with work, money, relationships, health, and other important aspects of your life. If you're going through a time of change at work or home and want to plan your best approach, you can read Chapter 11 first and then work back to the beginning. If you've heard about the classic NLP language models and want to practise those, try Chapters 14 and 15 and experiment with the Meta and Milton Models as well as spinning a few stories with the help of Chapter 16.

Now we're biased, but we also recommend that you read _Neuro-linguistic Programming For Dummies_, and use this workbook as a means of building on what you've already found out about NLP. There are also NLP courses you can attend and more books you can read relating to NLP – you can check resources out in Chapter 19. But of course, nothing beats working one-to-one with an NLP coach.

After trying out the exercises in this book, you may surprise everyone, perhaps yourself most of all. When you do find those magical _aha_ moments, please drop us an e-mail – our contact details are in the resource section – so we can celebrate your success too!

Part I
Setting Up Your NLP Journey

The 5th Wave   By Rich Tennant

"I've tried Ayurveda, meditation, and aroma therapy but nothing seems to work. I'm still feeling nauseous and disoriented all day."

In this part . . .

We help you to figure out how you can apply Neuro-linguistic Programming to your everyday life, whether in the business or personal arena. You discover your starting point for your journey of discovery and get your destination in mind. The whole purpose of this part is to get you thinking more clearly about how you're living. This part enables you to recognise what drives your thinking and behaviour so that you can increase the choices you have in future.

Chapter 1

Where Are You Right Now?

In This Chapter

▶ Figuring out what you want from NLP

▶ Discovering the power of your thoughts

▶ Keeping track of the gems you uncover

▶ Making a personal commitment to your learning

▶ Having fun on the journey

Are you at a set of crossroads in your journey through life? Questioning where you are and what you want to do next? 'Shall I go this way or that?', you may be asking yourself when faced with choices. Or, 'I'm sure it doesn't have to be this hard', when you're getting overwhelmed. Whether you're facing choosing a job, tackling a project, or committing to a relationship, you're not quite sure what you should do for the best when such opportunities present themselves. You may have picked up *Neuro-linguistic Programming Workbook For Dummies* because you want to do things differently or improve a situation in your life. Perhaps things are a bit flat at the moment and you want more ZING, or your life is manic and you want time to 'smell the flowers'. Or, you're simply curious about this NLP word, wanting to know what NLP can offer you and how it can help you to interact with other people – if so, that's just great.

In this first chapter, we take time to help you get firmly grounded in NLP. You begin by taking stock and getting yourself in the right state of mind to ask what it is you want from this workbook. A basic assumption of NLP is that 'the map is not the territory' – you find out more about basic assumptions (we actually call them 'NLP presuppostions') in Chapter 2. You may currently have a 'map' – an idea of what you want, or of how life is, yet as you travel the road you find the 'territory' isn't as you expected. 'Stuff happens', as the saying goes. Your world view changes as you journey along.

As you get drawn into NLP, you find yourself taking your learning further – into more and more areas of your personal life and the world of work. You discover how to create your own 'maps' of what you want, rather than navigating with an outdated map or using someone else's.

Curiosity is a great starting point. Clear out any loose thinking about NLP. Come with an open mind and make it your intent to start paying attention to what you want to attract into your life. We promise that you'll be exploring this in more detail very soon.

Explaining the Basics of NLP

Einstein said that there are two ways to live: you can live as if nothing is a miracle or you can live as if everything is a miracle. Really it's up to you. The thoughts you have determine the results that you get in your life. Have you ever stopped to consider the quality of your thinking? NLP can be the starting point to get you thinking in a new way and get you curious about the power of your own thought process. After you know how you think, you can translate that into chosen actions with the help of the NLP tools we share with you in this book.

At first, the concept of NLP can be hard to get a grip on – like grappling with jelly. NLP is defined as 'the study of your subjective experience'; it's about how you communicate with others and with yourself. In NLP the more you pay attention to *how you think* as well as what you think about, the more you will achieve the results that you want.

NLP is based on the idea that you experience the world through your senses and translate sensory information into thought processes, both conscious and unconscious. Thought processes activate the neurological system (hence the *neuro* part of NLP) that affects physiology, emotions, and behaviour.

The *linguistic* aspect of NLP refers to the way your language helps you to make sense of the world, capture and conceptualise your experience, and communicate that experience to others. Body language is important here as well as the spoken word. The *programming* part addresses how you code or mentally represent your experience. Your personal programming consists of your internal processes and strategies (thinking patterns) that you use to make decisions, solve problems, learn, evaluate, and get results.

Lining Up at the Starting Block

NLP offers tools and models to help you solve problems in different ways. For example, take the 'logical levels of change' model from Robert Dilts that we explore in Chapter 11, which breaks down your experience into manageable parts, from looking at the environment in which you operate through to your overall sense of purpose as you go about your daily business.

You also have the classic linguistic models that the co-creators of NLP came up with in the early days: the Milton model, derived from studying Milton Erickson at work, and the Meta model, which enables you to gain greater clarity by going beyond language and digging deeper into the meaning underlying words. We show you how to filter your thinking according to your deepest values and beliefs without even consciously knowing that you do it. NLP is like opening a huge window onto your thought processes, so you have a huge treat in store.

You may already have a few ideas of what you want to get out of *Neuro-linguistic Programming Workbook For Dummies* – using NLP to be a more effective teacher, presenter, coach, parent, or business person?

Perhaps you're looking for the latest thinking. As you read and work through this workbook, you're likely to find more territory than you anticipated, discovering new ways of applying NLP that you hadn't even thought about – until today.

Worksheet 1-1 is a simple exercise in placing your feet on the NLP starting block and being poised to get the most out of this workbook. That means starting with what NLP calls your 'desired state'. Get your running shoes on and begin right now.

NLP talks about present state and desired state. The clearest way to describe these places is as a journey. Your present state is where you are now, today. Your desired state is where you'd like to get to; your goal or outcome for the future.

In Worksheet 1-1, we invite you to look at your present state as you begin to play with the ideas in this book. One of the purposes of the exercise is to make you stop and think about what you want to gain from reading this book, because as you do so you set yourself off on a proactive route, being curious (which is a great state to be in for learning) and taking responsibility for your learning. Consider whether you're simply interested in NLP as part of an academic lesson, or if you have something specific happening in your life where you want help. Are you struggling with career choices, your health, your relationships, or do you feel that life could be more fun or more rewarding?

By making some preliminary notes, you place a marker that you can revisit in the months to come to observe your progress.

Worksheet 1-1　　　　　　　　　**My NLP Starting Block**

What is your main reason for buying *Neuro-linguistic Programming Workbook For Dummies*? And what do you want to gain from this workbook?

To understand the concepts so I can apply them to coaching/walking business

Is there something very specific that you want to get from this workbook – either for yourself or for others? For example, has a particular event triggered change for you recently that's made you question what's important for you in a particular aspect of your life?

As a result of being off in 2013 I need to find a way to be outside more & be able to earn

Are you facing a particular challenge right now? For example, in finding a job, completing a project, or in feeling your most confident and healthy? Have you had a setback? Are you running out of time, money, or energy for the things you want to get done?

- Pressures on time & work/life balance are challenges

If this book proves to be exceptionally helpful for you, what would you really like to be different for you (perhaps in terms of quality of life or achieving better results in a specific field)?

Have more tools available to deal with my own issues & to help others

What is the one area of your life where you would like to apply NLP to yourself? For example, in coaching, training, managing others, personal development, in making changes in your career or your personal life?

Coaching career

Worksheet 1-1 is followed up in Chapter 18 where you're asked to assess how confident you are with NLP, after having worked through the book.

Beginning with Your Intent

In NLP you hear a lot of talk about setting intents and the reason for this is that when you set your intent, this is where you place your focus. Perhaps you meet someone and set your intent to have a long-term friendship with her. That dictates how you think about that person and behave towards her. By contrast, if you decide immediately that you'd be happy never to see her again, that intent affects how you relate to her from day one.

An intent isn't as specific as a goal, but about how you are; a way of being that informs your action. When we run training or coaching sessions and set our intents, they're usually fairly broad concepts such as, 'We're going to share knowledge', 'We'll listen supportively and challenge appropriately', or 'We'll be open to whatever comes up for our clients.' You can often summarise intent in one or two words such as, 'Be present', 'Share', 'Listen'.

'Do you think you're really up to this job, or would you prefer to shift down a grade and reduce the pressure on yourself?' Maddy was having a tough time at work and felt pressurised to the point of physical exhaustion. She'd taken a new job as a client services director in a financial institution and her first annual pay review had come at a time when the business was going through a lean time; business leaders were pushing ahead to take operations abroad and cutting down on the cost of staff to compete more strongly. Maddy's boss was suggesting that she might like to take a less stressful job at a lower salary even though she had met her performance targets. That same year, Maddy's mother had been taken seriously ill. Maddy was taking the train home to support her father on alternate weekends in the west of the country. To cap it all, she returned late one Sunday to discover that her boyfriend had been seeing another woman while she was away. He announced that he wanted to get out of their five-year relationship, sell their flat, and split their belongings. She found herself crying on the tube to work and ready to throw in her job. Maddy became interested in NLP after a girlfriend invited her to come along to an NLP seminar on relationships where Maddy learnt that she could manage her emotions, even when under stress. That seminar led to others, to more reading and listening to CDs, which in turn gave her the encouragement to make significant changes in her job and home life.

When Maddy went on her first personal development workshop, her aim was to reduce stress in her life, to live and work with less hassle, and to rediscover her natural ability to enjoy life once more. Worksheet 1-2 shows her personal intent for her NLP learning plus one word that reminds her of what she wants.

Worksheet 1-2	Maddy's Setting Personal Intent
My intent is:	Achieving a calm sense of focus
The word summarising my intent is:	Perspective

In Worksheet 1-3, write down a statement of your intent for your learning through this book and then summarise it in one word that applies to you.

Worksheet 1-3	My Setting Personal Intent Worksheet
My intent is to:	
The word that summarises my intent is:	

Intents are a powerful way to focus your attention and quieten your mind. Write your 'one word' in colour on a card or piece of paper where you can see and refer to it easily. Try writing your one word on the front page of your diary, office wall, computer, fridge door, or your bathroom mirror.

Taking Responsibility for Your Learning

Not everyone learns in the same way. Some people love to have to have theory, others need to try out a new idea; some need to be sure the idea is practical and useful, and others need a chance to think it through. You'll learn about NLP in different ways that work for you and this book is part of that journey. One of the key concepts of NLP is to be flexible in your behaviour, so think about your learning in this way and be willing to experiment with new ways of learning.

You can develop your NLP expertise in various ways by:

- Diving straight in, and doing the exercises in this workbook.
- Finding opportunities to practise your skills, and applying them to everyday situations.
- Studying around the subject and researching NLP's underlying theories.
- Allowing time to regularly step back and reflect on any areas where NLP tools and exercises can make a difference for you and for others.
- Checking out how and with whom you learn best. Do you, for example, learn best with a buddy, or by taking yourself off to a quiet place to learn?
- Choosing for yourself your own method of learning, supported by this workbook.

At the age of 14, Clare found school life boring and dull. Feeling restricted by the demands of the curriculum, she played truant, finding it much more satisfying to meet up with friends in a local café rather than to go to lessons that she couldn't understand, and be criticised for her pierced earrings and messy school uniform. For Clare the lessons were pointless and all the fun of being at school had gone out of the window. She left school at the earliest opportunity and took a job as a trainee hairdresser where she became a firm favourite with the customers. Ten years later, when she decided to live and work abroad, Clare enrolled in Portuguese language classes. She had a sense of purpose – being highly motivated to learn so that when in Portugal she would be able to speak to the locals in their own language. Clare went about finding the best way of learning the language quickly and easily. She looked up the names of everyday objects in her home, at work, and in the car, and placed colourful labels on the objects so as to remember the equivalent Portuguese words. She also bought children's books written in the language and listened to foreign pop songs and radio programmes on her iPod. Clare found that one of her clients was Portuguese and when she went to her client's house to cut her hair and that of her circle of friends, Clare got them to chat to her in Portuguese. She realised that she could learn quickly when she wanted to. For Clare it was all about finding the style of learning that suited her best, together with taking ownership of her learning – no one else could do it for her.

You learn at your best when you're motivated for your own reasons rather than when someone tells you to. So if someone has given you this workbook, or told you to work through it, find your own reason why this workbook will be helpful for you. Put your-self first, and connect with your own sense of purpose.

In Worksheet 1-4, you use three examples from different times through your life when you had a great time learning something new. Go back to those experiences, capturing what worked best for you.

Worksheet 1-4	My Learning at My Best
As a child, I learnt to:	
I did this by:	
As a teenager, I learnt to:	
I did this by:	
As an adult, I learnt to:	
I did this by:	

When you do the exercises in this workbook with an open mind and a willing heart, you're the person who benefits most.

Noting the Nuggets as You Go

While reading a book, you may come upon a word or phrase on the page that makes you stop and think – you go: 'Aha, that's good, I must remember that.' We hope that you find many such nuggets in this NLP workbook. Feel free to track your journey through this book by making notes on the pages using coloured pens and sticky gold stars – anything that catches your eye. Photocopy exercises, stick them on your wall, cut them out – whatever works for you. After all, you can always buy another copy if you want to keep the book 'clean'! Get into the mindset that this is *your* NLP journey and you can travel it in any which way you choose.

What we like to do is to keep our own special notebooks and diaries for jotting down our thoughts and ideas relating to NLP. Try carrying a small notebook around with you when you're on the move – one that fits inside a pocket or a bag and that can be kept handy on your beside table – for recording the real gems from this workbook that catch your attention. When writing down your nuggets make a note of your intent at the very beginning, then capture landmarks as you go – rather like a map in *Treasure Island*; you may like to draw your own NLP work map seeing how key themes join up for you.

Having Fun Is a Must

This is the only time we say 'must'. Fun is one of our core values and we'd like to share that with you, and Dummies books make learning fun. When we set out to write the first *Neuro-linguistic Programming For Dummies* book, we agreed the writing process must be fun. We were delighted when readers wrote in to tell us that our fun-loving attitude came through in the stories and ideas we shared. Similarly, in this workbook the process of sharing and learning together through writing about NLP in practice has been fun. Humour may not come through so loudly in the written word as it would if we were to meet and laugh in person, but rest assured that an essential ingredient of NLP training is to have fun.

Do whatever you need to make your own learning fun. Take the workbook to the beach or to the zoo. Dance around the kitchen, draw silly faces, and play with bendy toys. Make yourself a chocolate milkshake, a smoothie, or have a glass of your favourite tipple as you do the exercises. Look out for humour even in serious situations – yes, if you look, you can always see the bright side of life.

So, with mind and body fully present and correct, you're all set to take NLP action.

Chapter 2

Getting Your Mindset Right with NLP

Have you ever had the feeling that the whole world is plotting against you: Everything that is going wrong is happening just to you? Oops! And maybe you are wallowing a teeny-weeny bit in self-pity? Poor you. Then again, there are times when you feel blessed at having been born in the right place at the right time. Lucky you. Guess what? These experiences that you carry about with you in your head are normal. It was the great psychologist Carl Jung who came up with the concept of 'perception is projection': People project to the outside world what is going on inside their heads. Jung said that the world is like a mirror and that if you change what goes on inside your head, then the world changes for you.

Vikram, a 12-year-old Indian boy with a wise head on young shoulders, emigrated to Australia, where he was asked by his new school teacher, 'Don't you find people here prejudiced'? His response was, 'No, not at all, but then I'm too excited adjusting to a new life here to look for prejudice.'

The point of the story is that because Vikram is confident in himself and he is not prone to harbouring prejudice against others, Vikram doesn't have prejudice reflected back, so is seldom on or at the receiving end of discrimination and is a popular young person.

With NLP tools you can take responsibility for controlling what goes on inside your head and not getting overwhelmed by emotions flying all over the place. It's simple when you know how. The examples in this chapter lead you through how NLP tools work.

Surveying Cause and Effect

The assumption you can make is that *every effect has an underlying cause*. What this means is that the results you get today are caused by something that either you did previously or somebody else did. For example, if you're finding that your jeans are feeling tight today, it may be because you've had a few too many good dinners lately! Or, if you're finding yourself lonely and alone, something you've done (such as turning down invitations to socialise) may be causing the problem.

The 'effect' may not always be due to your direct earlier action. If you find yourself being made redundant because you work in a company that's moving your job abroad, for example, the underlying cause rests within market forces over which you have no control. You get back to 'cause' by taking action over your own career choices.

In NLP terms, people are said to be 'at cause' or 'at effect' as follows:

- **At cause:** When you operate 'at cause', you don't make excuses. You take responsibility and ask 'What do I need to do? Or what lessons do I need to learn?' You are in charge of your destiny.

- **At effect:** When you are 'at effect', you have lost power, you make excuses, offer justification, and blame others. You can't see that you have any options or choices and are likely to be taking the role of victim or passive observer of your experiences.

Where are you in different situations you face right now? Are you 'at cause' or are you 'at effect'? The game plan in this workbook is to allow you to be at cause for more aspects of your life – empowering yourself and others on the way.

John booked a last-minute holiday in Spain with three of his old school friends. He's naturally a quiet and artistic character and likes to visit old buildings and art galleries. His friends are more outgoing and persuaded John to stay in a coastal resort with bars and nightclubs where they drank beer late every night and slept for much of the day on the beach. John spent the whole week feeling cross that he'd agreed to go with their choice of location and wishing that he'd argued more convincingly for going to Barcelona where he could have enjoyed the architecture and met up with the lads later for the nightlife. He was at effect by not stating his own holiday needs more powerfully.

Table 2-1 shows some of the things to notice and check when you're at cause or at effect.

Table 2-1	Cause and Effect Signals
At Cause Signals	**At Effect Signals**
You feel that you are in a comfortable environment.	You feel stressed in this environment.
You can say and do what seems right and natural to you.	You feel that others are controlling what you can say or do.
You are acting with a level of competence.	You are questioning your ability and may be panicking.
You know it's okay to be yourself.	You are asking: 'Am I good enough?'
You are making choices based on what you want.	You are doing what you 'should' or 'ought to' rather than what you want to.
You take any difficulties in your stride.	You find it hard to say 'no' and are trying to please others.
You have a sense of ease and feel healthy and energetic.	You look tired, overwhelmed, and have low energy.

In Worksheet 2-1 you have the chance to observe when you act at cause and when you act at effect.

1. Track an example of when you felt you were at cause and an example of when you were at effect.

2. Choose particular situations where you were with other people. You can select either a social context with friends and family or a professional one with work colleagues, advisers, or suppliers.

3. In both your at cause and at effect examples, check against Table 2-1 and notice what specifically has happened that places you at one or the other end of the cause/effect spectrum. Do certain people affect you in a negative or positive way? Does how much time you have affect your energy levels? Perhaps you feel you have certain skills, or feel incompetent.

4. What can you discover from these situations that will be helpful in future circumstances to put you even more at cause?

In John's example earlier, John realised that he'd booked his holiday in a hurry when he was busy at work. He decided he needed to plan his breaks earlier, select trips that appealed to his interests, and tell his friends what kind of holiday he wanted to take. Also, he needed to be willing to decline an invitation that wasn't right for him and know that he could retain his friendships. Then he'd be 'at cause' again.

Worksheet 2-1	**My Observations of a Cause and Effect Situation with Other People**
At cause situation:	*At effect situation:*
How do I know I was at cause – what were the signals?	*How do I know I was at effect – what were the signals?*
What can I learn from this situation to help me in future?	*What can I learn from this situation to help me in future?*

Tuning into the language

To hone your skills in pinpointing the ways in which you can detect cause and effect in other people, *listen* to the words they use. In Worksheet 2-2, think about each statement and decide whether the speaker is 'at cause' or 'at effect'.

Worksheet 2-2	The Cause and Effect Quiz	At Cause	At Effect
Statement			
1. Not now, I'm giving myself time to consider my reply.			
2. You make me so angry. No wonder I'm stressed out!			
3. Sorry, guv. He made me do it.			
4. Thank you, I'd love to come to the party. I just need to find out about the train times.			
5. I have to spend my weekends visiting my parents because they make me feel guilty if I don't.			
6. I'm going to take a holiday as soon as I've finished this project.			
7. I've a large mortgage to pay, so I have to do this job – it's the only way to pay the bills.			
8. It's a sunny day, so I'll sit in the garden to read my papers.			
9. I didn't leave until I was ready, even though the children were impatient with me.			

In statements 1, 4, 6, 8, and 9, the speaker is at cause. In statements 2, 3, 5, and 7 the speaker is at effect. Notice that when the speaker is at cause that person takes control of the situation and makes choices about what he wants to do and when. You hear statements such as 'I want to', 'I can', 'I choose'. Conversely, when the speaker is at effect, control has shifted away from the speaker and you hear phrases such as 'I should', 'I ought to', 'I have to'.

Examining internal dialogue

Do you ever lie awake at night with conversations going on inside your head? Perhaps you go over the day's events chattering to yourself about what you could have done or planning out what you'll do and say tomorrow? As a normal human being, you live in a private world of internal dialogue as well as the external world of language and conversations with other people. This capacity for internal dialogue develops as a child with the creation of imaginary friends, and is intimately connected with your *'what if' reasoning process* – the ability to mentally rehearse different scenarios.

You uphold your own private world with such self-talk. The 20th-century mystic Carlos Castaneda argued that we repeat the same choices over and over, because we keep on repeating the same internal talk over and over until the day we die. This noisy chattering takes an inordinate amount of energy and is hugely distracting if you're running internal dialogue about situations in which you're at effect.

Listen to your internal dialogue, thank it for its positive intention, and then interrupt the pattern and quieten the words so that you can think calmly and access your more creative intuitive self – that part of you that can come up with new choices. You can break the dialogue through activities such as breathing exercises, meditation, or writing into a daily journal, and by repeating positive phrases to yourself. Simple affirmative phrases such as 'I am good enough', 'I live in a healthy body', and 'I choose my own life' can help you break the cycle. Replacing the noisy chatter with a clearer, simpler at cause internal dialogue can get you back in control.

In Worksheet 2-3 you see that Andrew has a difficult manager to please. His manager puts pressure on him to work late and likes to have very detailed reports produced quickly. Notice the difference in Andrew's internal dialogue when he replaces his negative at effect statements with at cause ones that put him in the driving seat.

Worksheet 2-3	Andrew's Cause and Effect Internal Dialogue
'At Effect' Internal Dialogue	*Replacement 'At Cause' Internal Dialogue*
I can't leave the office until 7 again because he'll make me re-work the numbers.	I've worked hard and I deserve to leave on time.
He only has to look at me and I feel a big weight on my shoulders.	I'm the best person to do this job. I choose to work here.
I can't wait for him to go on holiday so I get a breathing space to get the end of the month figures done.	I can create space to think clearly whenever I want to.

Think of a situation that you find challenging and examine what you say to yourself – your internal dialogue. Notice three things you might be thinking if you are at effect and three things you might be saying to yourself if you are at cause. Try this out in Worksheet 2-4, just picking up on a situation and changing your own words. As you do so, notice the effect the situation has on you.

Worksheet 2-4	My Cause and Effect Internal Dialogue
'At Effect' Internal Dialogue	*Replacement 'At Cause' Internal Dialogue*

Revisiting the NLP Presuppositions

NLP offers a number of basic assumptions or convenient beliefs known as *presuppositions*. Try these assumptions on for size to find out if any strike a chord with you. You won't find written evidence proving the presuppositions are true, but just play with the ideas as if you held the assumption:

✔ **The map is not the territory.** The world in your head is a strange place, much of it uncharted. Your map of the world is not the same as someone else's and it may be only a partial map. For example, you go into a new job with a job description (the map) and it turns out that the words on the paper only reflect part of what you need to do (the territory). You may have mapped out a plan on paper of how you want your wedding celebration to be, yet when you arrive, the event is more than you ever imagined because all the guests bring their own energy and joy to the special occasion. Or perhaps you're working on a house-building project and find that on the actual site the architectural drawings have to be adapted.

✔ **People respond according to their map of the territory.** Whenever you find that someone else behaves differently to you, recognise that he may have a different map for the same territory. You notice different things and have different experiences. Respect that map and aim to find out what the world is like from the other person's perspective. If you're a teacher or parent, step back for a moment and consider what it would be like to be five years old or a teenager again.

✔ **There's no failure – only feedback.** Imagine that you don't actually get anything wrong; everything is a learning experience. Notice what a different light that sheds on times when you feel you've made mistakes in the past, and on times when you experiment with something new in the future. Knowing that you simply can't fail may give you the courage to try something adventurous and overcome limiting beliefs about yourself. It can also make you less critical and judgemental about other people's efforts.

✔ **The meaning of the message is the response it draws out.** This assumption places full responsibility on you as the communicator of a message to get the right point across. If you've ever been misunderstood, the implication is that this was your responsibility to get it right, rather than the other person being difficult. Looking forward, if you have something very important to say where you need to get the message across loud and clear, think about who you're talking to and what will help that person to receive your message as you intend it. Start with thinking about what that person's needs and interests are before you work out what to say.

You communicate non-verbally too. Your words account for only a small part of the message compared with your gestures and tone of voice.

✔ **If what you're doing isn't working, do something different.** Are you banging your head against a brick wall by carrying on doing the same old things in the same old way? Sometimes you can get so involved in a situation that you don't notice the habits you've got into or can't recognise that old hurts cause unhelpful, emotional behaviour. You get stuck in a rut, repeating the same old mistakes or just reacting to your hot buttons. What are some of the situations that are not working for you where a change would be welcome – perhaps a new job or group of friends is called for?

✔ **The person with the most flexibility influences the outcome of any interaction.** After you begin to make changes, hey presto, other people do too, and you break patterns of behaviour. Look out for examples of people who behave with flexibility and so bring about change. Perhaps someone's willing to work abroad for a while to get a better job, or take on some extra responsibilities to gain experience. Maybe you quit moaning at your family about whose job it is to mow the lawn and hire a gardener instead.

✔ **You cannot *not* communicate.** Saying nothing is still communicating. The very fact that you keep quiet and smile sweetly or walk away is still a message.

✔ **You have all the resources you need to achieve your desired outcomes.** Resources can be internal beliefs, energy, and personal skills as well as people, possessions, and money.

✔ **Every behaviour has a positive intent.** This assumption applies to all behaviours – even bad habits you'd like to change such as smoking or procrastination. This presupposition is particularly valuable if you think of times when you behave badly or do something that you don't want to do, yet still do it. Ask yourself what the positive intent of this behaviour is. What are the positive things I get from doing this – maybe smoking gives you some time out from work or the kids for example? NLP calls this the *secondary gain*. (You come across secondary gain in Chapter 3 when you set your well-formed outcomes.) When you work out all the positives you get from the behaviour, you can come up with new and creative ways to get your needs met. For example, the smoker can find new ways to get thinking space or a five-minute break from the children.

✔ **People are much more than their behaviour.** When you see an actor on TV, you know that he's only acting a part and is likely to be very different in private. You may make judgements about a person based on one aspect of his behaviour and miss other very important aspects of that person. This is particularly important if, as a manager, for example, you give critical feedback on someone's performance. Just because one of your employees struggles with an aspect of his work doesn't make him a bad person.

✔ **The mind and body are interlinked and affect each other.** Neuroscientists have discovered that emotion can be detected by changes in the molecular structure of our bodies at the level of neurotransmitters. Become more aware of how your mental state affects how your body feels, and vice versa. For example, when you think about someone you really like or dislike, how does your body react? Notice whether particular events and activities seem to give you energy or drain it away. People who struggle with poor eating habits are often so distracted by their internal dialogue that they don't pay attention to what they're eating and drinking.

✔ **Having choice is better than not having choice.** This is a useful presupposition to remember when you're feeling at a loss. You may hear yourself or others saying, 'I have no choice, I have to do it.' Remember that you always have choices, such as chucking in your job or moving abroad. You make that choice based on evaluating the risks and consequences of taking action.

✔ **Modelling successful performance leads to excellence.** When NLP was originally created by Richard Bandler and John Grinder, they used outstanding people as role models. NLP assumes that if someone does something well, he's reached a level of being *unconsciously competent* – he can't easily explain how he does it. You can learn from an outstanding person by paying close attention to what he does and how he operates – from how he breathes, through his behaviour, to his values and beliefs.

Worksheet 2-5 shows you ways that the NLP presuppositions can alter your thinking and ultimately the results you get. The following three steps will help you to fill in the worksheet:

1. **Read the summary of each presupposition to check your understanding.**

2. **Think about times when this assumption would have been useful for you in the past and could be useful for you in the future, and write these situations in the appropriate columns.**

3. **Write down specific ideas inspired by the presupposition.**

If you can't think right now of an example for every presupposition, that's okay. You can come back to Worksheet 2-5 later as you read on in the book or work through other worksheets and new ideas occur to you.

Worksheet 2-5	NLP Presuppositions Playtime		
Presupposition and Related Questions	*Past Applicable Situation*	*Future Applicable Situation*	*Further Thoughts*
The map is not the territory. Where are your incomplete maps?			
People respond according to their map of the territory. How do you respect other people's maps?			
There's no failure – only feedback. What would you do if you simply couldn't fail?			
The meaning of the message is the response it draws out. How can you get your point across more clearly?			
If what you are doing isn't working, do something different. What are some of the things that aren't working for you where a change would be welcome?			
The person with the most flexibility influences the system. How do you show flexibility or inflexibility?			
You cannot *not* communicate. What might you be communicating unintentionally?			
You have all the resources you need to achieve your desired outcomes. Think of something you are trying to achieve and note the resources you already have, being sure to list your personal qualities that serve you well.			
Every behaviour has a positive intent. What is the positive intent behind your 'bad' behaviour?			
People are much more than their behaviour. What judgements do you make about people?			
The mind and body are interlinked and affect each other. Does your breathing change?			

Presupposition and Related Questions	Past Applicable Situation	Future Applicable Situation	Further Thoughts
Having choice is better than not having choice. If you feel limited in your choices around money, relationships, jobs, or commitments to family and friends, ask yourself what your real options are.			
Modelling successful performance leads to excellence. Who has special qualities you can model?			

Charting the Maps

In this section, you explore more fully the NLP presupposition that 'the map is not the territory' as applied to your daily life. In particular you'll open your eyes to the idea that the words you speak are a limited description of your experience, just touching the surface of what's really going on for you. You'll also become more aware of the limited maps you currently have, how they differ from other people's, and how you can make your own maps more complete and a more valuable guide.

Spotting the different maps

NLP highlights the language you use and reminds you that any word can bring more than one image to the mind. A word does not represent *all* the facts in a given situation. Writing down your own experiences of the word 'ball' in Worksheet 2-6 will help you to understand this idea.

Worksheet 2-6	My Words Representing 'Ball'

Take a simple word like 'ball', think of your experience of a ball, and write down what comes to mind:

_____

_____

_____

Now ask somebody else what comes to mind when you say the word 'ball' and write down his response:

_____

_____

_____

(continued)

Worksheet 2-6 *(continued)*

Note the difference between your responses:

_____

_____

_____

_____

Typically you will find that everybody has a slightly different interpretation of just one simple word. The word 'ball' can represent all manner of images and memories – a tennis ball, a ball of string, a ball of knotted elastic bands, a ball of mud, or thousands of little white polystyrene balls in packaging. Or it may be none of these things at all.

Now, if you take another word like 'money', a wealth of different descriptions surface and maybe emotions start flying around. This is where you discover that your map of the territory and the other person's are completely different.

Travelling through the territory

Armed with the idea of the map not being the territory, you can raise your own awareness of where you may be missing vital information. Because the words are just part of the story and you don't have the full picture, you have an incomplete map.

Think of something you'd like someone else to do and leave that person a map of what you want. First state the context – the specific situation that you have in mind. Then write out one simple statement that summarises your instruction. Looking at the words you have written, add more detail, making the map more specific. Then look at the map again and add further detail to make the map even more specific. Zoom in on the map and make your words say what you really mean; like when you're looking for something on a Web site and adding more and more specific words to get you a hit.

In the example, Jon is a manager in an office and leaves his assistant a note on a client file. Worksheet 2-7 shows his map.

Worksheet 2-7   **Jon's Map Charter**

Context: Delegating work to my assistant

Map 1 statement: Sort this out for me.

Map 2 statement: Please go through the file on my desk and see what needs to be done before Friday.

Map 3 statement: Frank, please go through the file for ABC company and type up the notes I've taken, ready to distribute at the board meeting. Prepare three PowerPoint slides for me on the figures, the issues, and our timetable that I can present to summarise the situation.

Now write your own map in Worksheet 2-8.

Worksheet 2-8 **My Map Charter**

Context:
_____

Map 1 statement:
_____
_____
_____

Map 2 statement (be more specific – what, when, where):
_____
_____
_____

Map 3 statement (be even more specific on your meaning):
_____
_____
_____

Observe how easy or difficult you find it to be very specific about the words you use and hold that thought for when you practise working with the Meta Model and Milton Model in Chapters 14 and 15.

Changing Focus through Your Projections

If you've been in a relationship for any length of time, you've probably gone through moments when you couldn't stand the sight of your partner. Your internal dialogue may have gone in a downward spiral of, 'Why can't *he* put oil in the car for a change'? Or 'For goodness sake, what does it take to squeeze the toothpaste from the bottom of the tube?' And all you can think of is divorce courts and living in separate continents. Until consciously or unconsciously you remember the roses or the unexpected cuddle, and suddenly you reconnect to why you are together. All that happened is that your focus shifted from noticing all the negatives about your partner to noticing the positives.

The same principle applies to friends, bosses, and colleagues. In tricky situations, it can be helpful to always keep in mind the outcome that you want, or would prefer to have.

Much of NLP is about holding up the mirror closely to yourself and looking at your own thoughts and behaviours. Only then can you understand that what you perceive to be the case and what you focus on may just be a projection of your needs onto another person rather than a complete map of a situation. Your projections can often provide valuable clues as to what you focus on and how this reflects what your true needs are, which you may not have articulated.

Kate went to see a beauty therapist who greeted her at the salon saying, 'You look nervous. There's no need to be.' Kate was surprised by the comment until she realised that the young woman had only recently set up in business and was herself very tentative. The comment was really the beautician expressing her own need to feel more confident in her work.

The psychoanalyst Jung thought the process of projection was very important because we tend to blame the other person for what we don't like or don't recognise in ourselves. He said, 'Projections change the world into the replica of one's own unknown face.' As mentioned earlier, Jung coined the phrase 'perception is projection', which means that what you perceive in others is often what you are looking out for or holding in your own map of the world as an aspect of your personality. For example, if you find yourself complaining about 'Sunday drivers', is it because *you* are sometimes guilty of driving slowly and without due care and attention?

Table 2-3 offers some ways in which you may express your needs through your behaviour with people around you. Notice that each behaviour has a positive intention but what's missing in these behaviours is any open expression of your needs. You need to practise stating your needs by telling other people what you want rather than getting your needs met through projecting them onto other people, especially if this involves judging and criticising.

Table 2-3 Examples of Projecting Your Needs onto Others	
Behaviour	*Possible Underlying Need*
Complaining to your colleagues that your boss doesn't like you because he doesn't acknowledge your contribution	You want to feel valued and recognised
Telling your friend that he spends too much money on clothes	You want financial security
Reminding your girlfriend that you love her by sending her a text message every few hours	You want to be reassured that you are loved too
Pointing out to your mum that she eats too much chocolate	You want to be healthy
Noticing that the IT support guy isn't giving clear instructions	You want to be a clear communicator
Working late at the office and expecting others to as well	You want job security

Talking about mirrors reminded us of Kate's young friend Bill and his trip to the local shop to buy fittings for his new bathroom. He was something of a novice handyman and in a great hurry to fix up the bathroom before his friends from America came to stay. He'd been working on installing the new bathroom suite and had allocated a weekend to complete the job with new tiles and mirrors. In a hurry late one evening Bill ordered over the Internet all the tiles and mirrors that he thought he needed. When he went to collect them, he found that the wrong ones had been reserved for him. The customer service representative apologised for the error and said she'd get the right ones in the following week. Bill went away disappointed and frustrated but returned on the following Saturday as agreed. This time the mirrors had arrived but they were much smaller than he wanted. Bill blew a fuse – went red in the face, shouted 'You're just useless' at the customer service representative, and stormed out of the shop in a temper. Only when he got home and checked the order he had placed did he see that he had made a mistake and ordered the wrong sizes. Bill was projecting all the sense of the uselessness he felt about himself as a novice handyman onto the customer service representative. Bill would have behaved more resourcefully if he had remembered that what he wanted was to get his bathroom finished quickly, focusing on adapting his behaviour towards this goal.

Reflect on something that has gone wrong for you and how you can apply the assumptions from any of the NLP presuppositions to gain a greater understanding of what went wrong and how you may act differently in future.

- ✔ **Think of a situation that caused you to get upset.** For example, you had an argument with someone, gave a presentation that wasn't well received, made a mistake in choosing a place to live, felt foolish on a date, maybe got rejected by someone you cared about?

- ✔ **What result did you get?** What was the worst thing that happened for you? Make a note of how you felt at the time or the impact it had on other people.

- ✔ **What were you projecting onto someone else?** For example, how much of your reaction was due to a need in you to feel accepted or confident, or to manage your finances, time, or energy well?

- ✔ **What would be a more useful mindset to get into to get better results?** Read through the list of NLP presuppositions in the earlier section 'Revisiting the NLP Presuppositions'. Select two or three of the key ones that seem particularly relevant to your situation and make a note of any ideas that occur to you that can shed new light for you.

Worksheet 2-9 takes you step by step through the lessons that Bill learnt from his trip to the DIY shop.

Worksheet 2-9	Bill's Mirror Worksheet to Change Focus
The Situation:	At the shop, I lost my temper.
The Result:	I went away empty-handed and very angry and then went to have two cigarettes to calm down in the car park even though I said I would give up smoking.
The Projection:	It's your entire fault. You're useless.
Useful Mindset:	Bill has three mindsets to think through.
There's no failure – only feedback.	From this I can learn that I need to check the order more carefully in future and check with the store that they have the same details. I won't make this mistake again.
The mind and body are interlinked and affect each other.	When I get angry, it affects my body and then I start smoking, which I don't want to do. My mental state definitely affects my health.
Every behaviour has a positive intent.	The customer service rep meant well. She's only young and didn't do this on purpose. She's only one part of the team and didn't deserve to be shouted at by me.

Now, turn your eye towards your own behaviour and fill in Worksheet 2-10.

Worksheet 2-10   **My Mirror Worksheet to Change Focus**

The Situation:

_____

_____

_____

The Result:

_____

_____

_____

The Projection:

_____

_____

_____

Useful Mindset (include any presuppositions that are helpful for you):

_____

_____

_____

_____

Picking Your Mindset

You can choose the mindset that supports you in being the very best you can be. You deserve to excel, to be your very best, and that begins when you choose your mindset. From the following list of words, circle any that stand out for you that may inform your attitude and behaviour. If you feel you could benefit by being more curious about other people, circle that one. Or maybe you run so fast that you stop noticing what's happening around you, maybe ignoring your family or friends because you're so busy at work. If so, set your aim at being fully present in the moment for today and see how this can change your experience for the better.

- ✔ Curious
- ✔ Flexible
- ✔ Fully present in the moment
- ✔ Interested
- ✔ Keen to learn
- ✔ Listening to others
- ✔ Open
- ✔ Optimistic
- ✔ Resourceful
- ✔ Spiritual
- ✔ Wanting the best

Add any other words that reflect the positive mindset that would be useful for you.

Play around with these words and add others of your own that describe a useful mind-set to adopt. Choose one at a time and make it your aim for the day, for example, being 'keen to learn' in all your tasks and interactions. If you're keen to learn when faced with a boring task, such as your tax return, see if that increases your enjoyment in the moment.

Use your mindset to help you stay at cause rather than getting knocked off track and being at effect. Make a note of anything that gets in the way of you holding this mind-set. Do particular times or people trigger a poor reaction in you? Who can support you? Think of a role model or someone who operates with the mindset you'd like. What kind of hints and tips would they give you?

Find an inspiring picture, quote, or object to touch that can act as a memory jogger to keep on track with your positive mindset? Finally make a note of anything that improves for you when you change your mindset. Perhaps you have better-quality conversations. Or you have fewer fallings out with people and a pleasanter journey when you travel, regardless of poor weather or delays?

Observe the difference that the mindset has on you when filling in Worksheet 2-11.

Worksheet 2-11 **My Choice of Mindset**

My choice of mindset is:

_____

_____

What key words summarise this mindset for me?

_____

_____

What are some useful ways to remind myself of this mindset (for example, a Post-It Note, a note in my diary, picture on the wall, or small stone)?

_____

_____

When and where am I most likely to go off track and get caught up in negative thinking?

_____

_____

Who or what else can support me in order to have the most treasured mindset?

_____

_____

What else improves for me when I take on this mindset? Make a note here of the benefits you notice along the way by choosing your mindset.

_____

_____

Chapter 3

Planning Your Road Map

. . . .

In This Chapter

▶ Seeing your starting position

▶ Daring to dream bigger dreams

▶ Adopting the well-formed outcome for success

▶ Trying on the Cartesian questions

▶ Tracking the milestones

. . . .

*W*elcome to one of the most important chapters in this book! Here we help you assess where your life is at the moment and get you thinking about where you want to take it. We finish with the practicalities of setting sound goals to get you where you want to be.

This chapter is where you start travelling and doing some really great work – and it's just for you. So, if you've got to the point of knowing that some things aren't so hot in your life anymore or never were in the first place, here's where you start listening to yourself saying what you really want. Cool stuff.

You find your own way by using your own map. Because you're the creator of the clearest, most colourful maps ever, you become both navigator and driver in your own life.

We show you, step by step, how to decide where you want to take your life. We offer you simple NLP tools to follow in your own way and to come back to time and time again, including the smarter than smart well-formed outcome and the Cartesian questions.

Mapping Your Life Journey

If you've ever driven to a holiday resort, did you know exactly where you were going, have all the stops planned, and did you stick to the plan precisely? Then, when you arrived at your destination, did you realise that if you'd taken more time to appreciate the beauty of the countryside, you might have discovered a hidden, historical gem along the way that you really would have loved to have seen?

Your life is also a journey and you need to step back from time to time to review where you're travelling to and how. Soon we'll be asking you to take a snapshot of your life journey so that you can recognise and appreciate what's good in it and perhaps include more of those good things. You'll also start noticing the things and people that energise you and begin to identify the things you want to change or let go

Working with the metaphor of your life as a journey, consider the following – you capture your ideas in Worksheet 3-1 soon:

- ✓ **Your map.** Some people have a clear idea of where they are today and where they're going. For example, they may have plans for jobs, holidays, retirement, how to spend their leisure time and explore intellectual and spiritual interests. Other people simply mosey along, seeing what happens. Do you have a detailed map or a rough sketch?

- ✓ **Your preferred route.** You route is about how you get to where you want to go, and the choices and options open to you. Will you take the direct motorway link or meander through the back lanes?

- ✓ **Your vehicle or mode of transport.** Would you like to travel by bicycle, an open top sports car, or a rugged four-wheel drive? Do you like to let the train take the strain so you can really enjoy the view? Or maybe a combination of all of these at different times?

- ✓ **Your speed.** Not everyone wants to travel in the fast lane. For some it's important to take time and enjoy the travelling. Yet at times you may need to put a spurt on and get moving.

- ✓ **Your travelling companions.** What kind of people would you like to travel with or meet along the way? Having teachers, guides, and supportive companions can be helpful but at times you may simply want to be alone.

- ✓ **Your distractions and treasures.** What else makes your journey distinctive? Do you get knocked off course by certain events or demands from other people? What are the things you really appreciate, the 'treasures' along the way? Maybe you appreciate time to have meaningful conversations or enjoy a special view or place.

As you begin to travel, ask yourself the warm-up questions in Worksheet 3-1 to see how they relate to you. Notice your reactions.

Worksheet 3-1	Considering Your Life as a Journey

Do you have a clear map that you're following as your guide?

_____

What kind of route are you travelling on and in what type of vehicle?

_____

Are you meandering along? Or are you rushing headlong to get there on the fast track? What decides your speed?

_____

When and where would you like to pick up with other people on your travels?

_____

What makes you get lost and lose your sense of direction?

What hidden treasures do you notice on the way?

Hopefully, this exercise gives you a sense of how your life is going, and you can use Worksheet 3-1 as a starting point for the worksheets throughout this chapter.

Assessing where you are on the journey

Your assessment in Worksheet 3-1 is defined in NLP as the Present State, the first step needed before you can move to the Desired State – what you want. *Present State* means the current conditions you find yourself in; the reality check of what's going on right now.

Gerri is a popular and cheerful 45-year-old with a sought-after job and a smart riverside flat in a trendy part of town. She's divorced and has lived a single existence for the past couple of years. People at work admire her lifestyle – she seems to go from one successful project to the next, weaving upwards through the organisation, getting awards and recognition. She arrives at the office driving a new upmarket open-topped convertible car, sunglasses on her head, and with no apparent cares in the world.

Gerri's NLP coach has been working with her on her team strategy and vision. Sensing that Gerri works crazy hours, one day her coach suggests she might like to do a quick assessment of seven things in her life that are working for her and seven that can be improved. Worksheet 3-2 shows Gerri's notes as she grabs a coffee and croissant.

Worksheet 3-2	Gerri's What's Working/What's Not Assessment
What Is Working for Me Right Now?	*What Isn't Working So Well?*
I've been promoted to a senior account director. It's a fantastic job and I get to work on exciting projects.	I last had a proper date two years ago. It would be good to have someone special in my life.
I'm staying in some great hotels with wonderful food.	My flat's in a bit of a mess – I'd be ashamed to invite anyone back. The paperwork is falling off the dining room table.
The money I'm earning is good – I got a really strong bonus this half-year.	I'm spending lots of time travelling, which means I don't see friends very often.

(continued)

Worksheet 3-2 *(continued)*

What Is Working for Me Right Now?	What Isn't Working So Well?
My mum has had an operation on her hip and she's recovering well.	I've put on 14 pounds in weight this year — I have a bit of a tummy on me.
I have two great nieces. I'm proud of them and they love their school activities.	I didn't manage to get to see my niece Alice in her school play because I was in the US and she was really disappointed in me.
The company has sponsored me to do a Masters degree.	I had to give up my personal gym training.
I've booked to go on an adventure holiday in Iceland next month.	I haven't read a novel since last summer.

When Gerri and her coach look at the 'what's working/not working' worksheet, they group Gerri's thoughts into a few key areas. Typically, these key areas include physical environment, money, romantic relationships, friends, family, work, health, personal development and learning, community, and spiritual life.

In Worksheet 3-3, Gerri sets a preliminary score as to how satisfied she is in each area on a scale of 0 to 10, with 0 being 'I'm really unhappy about this right now' and 10 being 'It couldn't be better'.

Worksheet 3-3   **Gerri's First Assessment Scores**

Gerri's Key Areas	Score
Family	5
Health	6
Job	8
Money	9
Romantic relationship	2

When Gerri comes up with her scores, her coach is curious as to what she's missing on her life's journey. Her coach asks, 'What are some of the other things you'd like to have in your life as well as success at work?' 'When did you last play the saxophone that you learnt while you were a student or went to an evening class or the cinema?' 'What're you missing out on by all this travelling and working hard?' 'When did you last see a friend?'

Gerri says that she's missing out on in-depth friendships. Ultimately, she'd like to meet someone special and she'd also like to make more time in her schedule to relax with family and old friends.

Now, it's your turn to have a go. If you're not sure where this is going just now, that's OK. This may be the first time you've taken a moment to reflect on your own life, especially if you've been busy making everyone else happy. You saw how Gerri started hers off; look at the columns in Worksheet 3-4, ask yourself the questions and jot down how you think your life is doing today.

Worksheet 3-4	My What's Working/What's Not Working Assessment
What Is Working for Me Right Now?	*What Isn't Working So Well?*

Now group your answers into broad categories (NLP calls this *chunking*) and rate your degree of satisfaction with each in Worksheet 3-5, using the same scale Gerri used in Worksheet 3-3.

Worksheet 3-5	My First Assessment Scores
Area of Life	*Score*

Okay! So this is how your key areas look to you at the moment. But have you really thought about everything? Just in case, we put some of our ideas in the boxes in Figure 3-1 and left some others blank for you to make any further additions you want to use when updating Worksheet 3-5.

Here are some more labels that may be helpful for you to fill in when you think of some things that you may want in your life. The blank boxes are for you to write words that are meaningful to you.

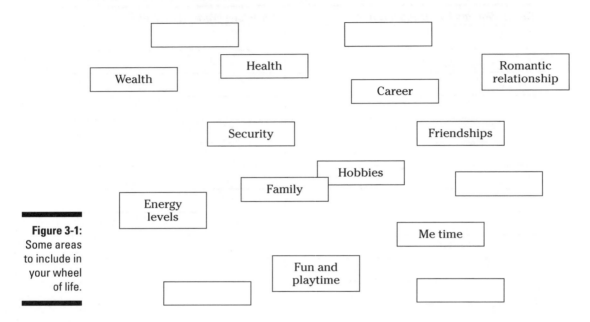

Figure 3-1:
Some areas
to include in
your wheel
of life.

Boxes shown: Wealth, Health, Career, Romantic relationship, Security, Friendships, Hobbies, Family, Energy levels, Me time, Fun and playtime

Assembling your wheel of life

Often, you can get so focused on making one area of your life work that other, important areas fall by the way. It's so easy to get caught up in the minutiae of day-to-day 'busyness' that it's valuable to have the big picture of your dreams and aspirations to create a smoother ride.

Which brings us to the analogy of a wheel. The idea is that you divide a wheel into segments representing the areas of your life that you're assessing. Then, by plotting values along the spokes of the wheel and joining them up in an arc, you can see whether your wheel of life is in balance and will give you a smooth ride. Of course, if the values differ widely, you may be in for a bumpy ride.

Gerri discovers that the wheel of life – hers is shown in Figure 3-2 – is a useful illustration to help decide where to focus her attention for the months ahead. She notices just how unbalanced her life has become when she gives herself a score for different segments of her life's wheel, because she's enjoyed being successful at work and throwing herself even deeper into international projects after the break-up of her marriage.

To support her overall wellbeing in the long term, Gerri's NLP coach works with her to set a simple and clear agenda to begin to redress the balance and to get specific about the changes she wants to make. This is easy to work through yourself, step by step, and you'll find even more help in setting your own agenda clearly when you reach the 'Designing your well-formed outcomes' section.

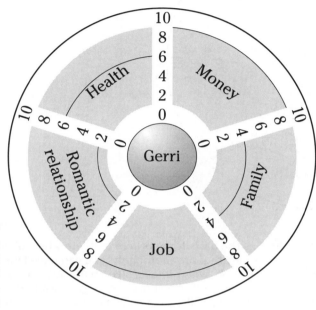

Figure 3-2:
Gerri's
Wheel of
Life.

What segments seem most useful to you right now in your personal wheel of life?

We offer you a maximum of eight areas in the sample wheel of life in Figure 3-3 because your conscious mind can process anywhere between five and nine bits of information. (It's also easy to divide a circle into eight sections!) If you remember the NLP approach – that for you to process information it needs to be in chunks of the right size for you – then it makes sense to view your life in segments.

Fill in the wheel in Figure 3-3 labelling the parts that are meaningful to you.

If you want to, use a geometry protractor to draw perfect arcs and coloured pencils to fill in each slice. Likewise, if you want more or fewer sections, use multicoloured pens to mark out the number of parts you do have, then join the numbers from one segment to the next.

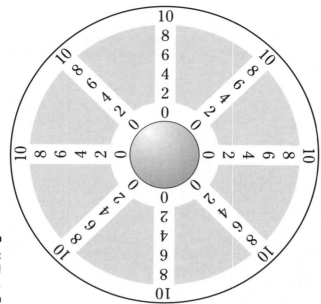

Figure 3-3:
My Wheel
of Life.

You can use any segment of the wheel as the basis for another complete wheel of life. For example, if you want to review your health more thoroughly, you can have labels for tracking exercise, healthy eating, nutrition, water intake, sleep patterns, sports coach, weight, and so on. Of course, choosing to put a spurt of energy into a particular area for a fixed length of time is okay – as long as it's a conscious choice and you're aware of the impact the choice is going to have on all other areas of your life. You may decide to let one area where you're very successful run at an unconscious level to get a greater balance in other areas.

Looking at the wheel and the scores you have given, is it a bumpy ride or are you rolling along smoothly?

Shooting for the Stars

The saying goes: 'Shoot for the moon. Even if you miss, you'll land among the stars.' Do you ever find yourself playing small and safe while the others have fun? Or are you like Crank, an endearing automaton in the film *Robots* who says, 'Never try, never fail. Those are the words I live by.'? Here's your chance to be more adventurous.

In Worksheet 3-6 write quickly – so that the conscious mind doesn't spoil the fun – what your 'Shooting for the Stars' dream is.

Worksheet 3-6	What is your 'Shooting for the Stars' dream?
What I really want is:	

_____

_____

_____

_____

_____

_____

So you have a dream, which some may think is totally out of the question and even you may have only a glimmer of belief in your dream, or perhaps even in yourself.

Hold onto your dream, nurture your dream.

One of the fantastic things about NLP is that it enables you to excel; after all NLP was created by modelling excellence, taking what works, studying it, and reproducing it. The evidence that we have experienced in our work as NLP coaches and trainers, as well as the resounding reader feedback from the original book *Neuro-linguistic Programming For Dummies*, is that NLP enables people to have a stronger sense of what is truly possible.

Robert Dilts, the great, early pioneer of NLP used NLP modelling on Walt Disney's approach to business. If Disney had not allowed himself and his people to dream as well as to manage budgets, then the world of entertainment would have missed out on much joy and fun. The *Concise Oxford English Dictionary* defines 'realistic' as 'having a sensible and practical idea of what can be achieved'. All too often your conscious mind and limiting beliefs and assumptions get in the way of your dreams. Quit sensible for now. Let it go!

Behave 'as if' you know all the right people who trust you totally and can help you in your endeavours. Believe that you have all the resources you need and you can only succeed. When you start to behave 'as if' you already have what you want, change naturally happens because you attract new opportunities and people to you. For example, if at work you behave as if you're already doing your dream job, you can find ways of expanding your skills and placing yourself in line for that kind of work.

The 'as if' NLP frame is excellent for exploring possibilities that may not have occurred to you. Behave 'as if' the dream (your desired state) is true and has already happened, and looking back to now (your present state) enables you to envisage steps along the way.

Checking for Smarter than SMART Goals and Well-formed Outcomes

In NLP, goals are generally referred to as 'outcomes' and an outcome is the answer to the NLP question 'What do you want?' An outcome is something that you intend to accomplish or attain. Traditional goal setting in business talks about SMART goals – ones that are Specific, Measurable, Realistic, Achievable, and Timed. NLP adds extra dimensions through the process of setting well-formed outcomes that make achieving the outcomes you want more likely. You see how this works in the following few pages.

Choosing your focus

Think now of a something that you have not succeeded in achieving yet. If you hear an argument going on in your unconscious mind about the outcome you're creating, allow yourself to let go of the realistic and critical voices and niggles. Create an inspiring, exciting outcome, one that makes you tingle just by looking at it, let alone feeling it.

Before you work through the seven steps to a well-formed outcome in the next section, consider the points here that can make your existing ideas even 'smarter than SMART' and help you to gain clarification about what you really want.

✔ **Do an ecology check:** An ecological goal in NLP terms means that the outcome works in all areas of your life. For example, if your dream is to be a millionaire but doing so means neglecting your emotional needs or ignoring your family, then chances are the goal isn't really ecological.

✔ **Set the context:** In making sure you have a well-formed outcome, getting the context right is very important. What setting the context means is that you drill down and focus on exactly when, where, and with whom you want this goal. So for example, if you have a dream of being a famous actor, it most likely means leaving home and heading to Hollywood to hang out with the big-screen movie-makers. Or your aim may be to make your name on stage in London or New York instead. You have to see your outcome in context.

✔ **Look for secondary gain:** In NLP, a secondary gain relates to a behaviour that appears to be negative or to cause problems, but which in fact serves a positive function at some level. An example is a smoker who knows that smoking is harmful to her health, yet appreciates the secondary gain of the peace and quiet of sitting outside for a cigarette and feeling calm and solitary. When you identify secondary gain, you can remove blocks to your success.

Designing your well-formed outcome

Setting yourself a well-formed outcome helps you to get from where you are now – having a glimmer of a dream – to achieving your dream. Worksheet 3-7 shows the steps to reach a well-formed outcome, tips on how to design your own outcome, as well as an example of how one imaginary dancer used the steps.

 Joanna is a 32-year-old mother of two and business manager for an international freight company. Since she was a small child she has always loved dancing and her 'Shooting for the Stars' dream is to set up a dance studio of her own. Everyone tells her she mustn't give up her well-paid job and Joanna believes them. Joanna doesn't think giving up her job is an option until she tries the NLP well-formed outcome exercise and discovers a route for moving forward on her journey.

Worksheet 3-7	Joanna's Well-formed Outcome	
The Steps for a Well-formed Outcome	**What Makes a Well-formed Outcome**	**My Outcome: To Have My Own Dance Studio**
1. Positively stated.	You want your unconscious mind on board for this to happen easily and the unconscious mind works more effectively with the positives.	I want my own dance studio.

The Steps for a Well-formed Outcome	What Makes a Well-formed Outcome	My Outcome: To Have My Own Dance Studio
2. Is it initiated by you and can you maintain it yourself?	Are you doing this because you want to do it or is it because someone else will be pleased or is putting on the pressure? Is the achievement of having a dance studio dependent solely on you or can you achieve this only if someone else takes responsibility for all or part of this?	Yes, it's for me, but I will need the support of my husband if I'm going to chuck my job in.
3. Appropriately contextualised.	Where are you when you achieve your goal? When do you expect to achieve your goal? With whom will you be working/playing/sharing when you have got your outcome?	I'd like it close to my house in the centre of town. By 22 April 2010. I want my husband and children involved, and my friend Clara who's also a keen dancer.
4. Describe the evidence procedure.	How will you know that you're getting the outcome you want? What will you be doing when you get it? What will you see, hear, and feel when you've achieved your outcome?	I can picture daytime tap classes for the three and four year olds, and evening classes in salsa, Ceroc, and Argentinian tango. I can hear the clippety-clop of the little tap shoes and the sounds of the Milonga playing — lots of chatter and voices. I'll be teaching some tap classes and can see Clara and other teachers too. It'll feel so right — very calm and focused, yet energetic too.

(continued)

Worksheet 3-7 *(continued)*

The Steps for a Well-formed Outcome	What Makes a Well-formed Outcome	My Outcome: To Have My Own Dance Studio
5. Identify the resources needed.	What resources do you have now? Do you need further resources and if you do, what are they? Have you evidence of having achieved this before?	I have some savings and dancing skills but I'll need more money and need to learn how to teach others. I've good business experience from all the budgeting and planning I've done at work. The business management is very straightforward after what I have done here.
6. Check if your goal is ecological.	What is your *real* purpose for wanting this outcome? Is there a secondary gain lurking in not achieving this outcome? Is there a situation where achieving this goal might be harmful to you or others? What will you lose or gain if you have your outcome?	I love the joy on people's faces as they master a dance. I feel alive as I dance. It would be safer not to do this as ultimately it means giving up my job which pays very well — so maybe I need to do it as a partnership to share the risk. I want to hold onto our family life and not work silly hours. I'll gain lots of personal satisfaction — just to see the name 'Dashing Dance Studio' in lights. It's essential for me to be passionate about my work so it'll be no loss to give up the day job.
7. What is the first step?		I need to start my research today on the competition and call Clara to have a chat. Can't wait to get hold of her.

Phew! Get the idea? That's a lot to think about. Joanna took a while to work out her well-formed outcome but once she thought it through, she had a clarity of vision and purpose that gave her the tools to sell the idea to her husband and Clara.

How is a well-formed outcome different from other goal-setting processes? Some of the bonuses of using well-formed outcomes are:

✔ You get to understand the hidden reasons behind your desires and fears relating to this specific outcome.

✔ You recognise resources you have, such as skills or people to help you, and also resources that you may need to develop or find.

✔ Most importantly, by engaging all your senses, the goal becomes so compelling that you can only achieve it.

So, find yourself some quiet time, away from your nearest and dearest and the telephone, invite your unconscious mind to the party, and get cracking at designing the next phase of your wonderful life. If you're going, 'Hrumph, where am I ever going to find the time?', just ask yourself what the secondary gain is for you in avoiding doing this exercise.

Doing the exercise in Worksheet 3-8 can make the impossible suddenly possible. You can do the exercise by yourself or by talking it through with a friend or coach. The exercise is also a terrific way for teams and families to assess major plans and decisions affecting everybody.

Worksheet 3-8		My Well-formed Outcome
The Steps for a Well-formed Outcome	**What Makes a Well-formed Outcome**	**My Outcome:**
1. Positively stated.	You want your unconscious mind on board for this to happen easily and the unconscious mind can't process negatives. So it's important to keep your outcomes positive.	
2. Self-initiated and maintained.	Are you doing this because you want to do it or is it because someone else will be pleased or is putting on the pressure? Is the achievement of this dependent solely on you or can you achieve this only if someone else takes responsibility for all or part of this?	
3. Appropriately contextualised.	Where are you when you achieve your goal? When do you expect to achieve your goal? With whom will you be working/playing/sharing when you have got your outcome?	
4. Describe the evidence procedure.	How will you know that you're getting the outcome you want? What will you be doing when you get it? What will you see, hear and feel when you have achieved your outcome?	

(continued)

Worksheet 3-8		My Well-formed Outcome
The Steps for a Well-formed Outcome	*What Makes a Well-formed Outcome*	*My Outcome:*
5. Identify the resources needed.	What resources do you have now? Do you need further resources and if you do, what are they? Have you evidence of having achieved this before? If you were to act 'as if' you had achieved this goal, how would you be acting and what would be happening for you now?	
6. Check if your goal is ecological.	What is your *real* purpose for wanting this outcome? Is there a secondary gain lurking in not achieving this outcome? Is there a situation where achieving this goal might be harmful to you or others? What will you lose or gain if you have your outcome?	
7. What is the first step?		

Congratulations. You now have a framework to help you shape any goal in your life into a well-formed one.

If the well-formed outcome still looks a bit overwhelming when you apply it to your big dream, break the outcome into a series of smaller outcomes, taking one step at a time.

Overcoming your own resistance

Star Trek fans will be familiar with the Borg and their penchant for using the phrase, 'Resistance is futile'. In earthling terms, resistance may not be futile but it certainly creates a lot of stress and unless you take measures for learning to relax (Chapter 4 shows you an easy process) you may feel the side effects of such stress. Swimming against the current is very stressful, which is what you're likely to do if you're trying to resist what you don't want rather than going for what you do want.

Try this simple exercise that demonstrates the destructive effect of stress on enabling you to get what you want. Notice how staying relaxed enables you to have greater control than when you tense up.

Place a tablespoon of water in the palm of your hand. As long as your hand is relaxed, the water rests there and you can control it – for example to pour it into a cup. But if you imagine tension building up in your hand and your hand closes into a fist, you lose the control as the water squirts or leaks out from every crease. How you feel about your goals is like having the water in your hand. Are you moving steadily along or are your teeth gritted and are you uncomfortable with the determination to achieve your goal?

In Chapter 8 you read about the NLP metaprograms of 'Toward' and 'Away from'. In motivation terms it's like going towards a carrot or away from a stick. Sometimes when you think you're aiming towards what you want, actually you have a hidden 'Away from' driver. For example, 'I *must* get my pay rise' may be more powerfully driven by the unconscious fear of failing to get the additional money. In this case your wonderful, co-operative unconscious mind is going to oblige fully by helping you 'fail' to get that desired increase! Your mind is so concerned about what it's moving away from that this is what you end up paying attention to – your fear of failing. That pay rise moves further and further out of reach. After you recognise what's happening, you can start focusing attention on the positives of what you do want, and let go of the negatives of what you're moving away from.

Progress in achieving your outcomes can be hindered by a *limiting decision* that you made unconsciously at some point in your life. Examples of limiting decisions are 'If I get ill, I'll get my mum's attention' and 'Wealthy people exploit others'.

Limiting decisions are formed because of how you interpret the events that you have experienced in your life and are formed for a good reason at the time. Yet they can hold you back in achieving your own outcomes. For example, you may have observed someone very wealthy exploiting everyone in her path and decided that to be super-rich is not what you want: You don't want to turn into a manipulative, exploitative person. However, one of the goals you have is that of financial independence. But because of the limiting decision you made, you may self-sabotage your attempts at becoming wealthy.

By doing the well-formed outcome exercise and in particular, answering the question in Step 6 in Worksheet 3-8 relating to ecology, you can uncover some of the reasons you didn't achieve your goal.

By examining the consequences of getting your goal, you may decide it isn't for you and move on to something that you do want. You can clarify this even further in Chapter 4 where you can work through the exercises that help you articulate your values.

Questioning Cartesian Style

By answering the following four simple Cartesian questions, you quickly recognise the difficulties you're facing in making your decision. And answering the questions is a great way of uncovering secondary gain issues. The term Cartesian comes from the mathematical Cartesian Co-ordinates developed by René Descartes. Just as you may be familiar with the X and Y axes in maths problems, the NLP Cartesian questions provide a framework in which you can explore actions and possible outcomes in answer to the 'what if?' kind of decisions you face.

When you're hesitating over a decision and want a further check on your well-formed outcome, ask yourself:

1. **What will happen if I do this?**
2. **What will happen if I don't do this?**
3. **What won't happen if I do this?**
4. **What won't happen if I don't do this?**

Kate couldn't decide whether to accept an invitation for a conference speaking engagement. The conference conflicted with a busy working period in the run up to Christmas when she wanted to spend time with her family. She kept putting off making a decision on accepting the invitation. When Romilla reminded her of the Cartesian questions, Kate got speedy confirmation that she really didn't want to over-pack her diary in December. So she offered the opportunity to a colleague who jumped at the chance.

Staying on Track for Your Journey

So you've set your well-formed outcome and you have an idea of the end that you have in mind, but how do you keep sight of your destination, particularly when a project is so big that it comprises several goals in their own right? Traditional project planning works in a set order through tasks. The NLP approach is to 'Begin with the end in view', to quote Stephen Covey's famous suggestion. On your journey, you plan the pit stops and crossing the finishing line by using the following steps. Notice that the steps do not match the chronological timeline: at each stage let your imagination flow as to what moving towards your outcome and away from where you are right now will be like. Allow yourself to imagine all the sights, sounds, and feelings you're likely to have at each stage as if you're there right now.

You can do this exercise in your mind's eye or you can put pieces of paper on the floor to represent each stage and stand on them to consider what every stage will be like for you.

1. **Go to the desired state 'as if' the outcome is completed.** First of all imagine what it will be like when you have achieved your outcome. Enjoy all the sights, sounds, and feelings you get.

2. **Come back to the present.** Notice what the situation is like for you right now. It may feel quite daunting. If so, don't stay here long.

3. **Go to the mid-point of the project completion.** Again, imagine what reaching this halfway mark will be like.

4. **Go to the point three-quarters of the way to completion.** Notice your experience of imagining this next stage where you have nearly achieved your outcome.

5. **Take the first step from today.** Notice how that first step is for you and any extra help you need to take it. For example, do you need people around to support you, or extra skills?

You have your turn to lay out your map in Worksheet 3-10 but, as the worksheet may seem a little complex, have a look at how Fran and William tackled their project.

Fran and William decided to carry out a massive rebuilding project on their house, converting an old, disused church into a spacious family home. It's a three-year project with numerous people involved, from the local planning department to the church conservationist, architect, bank and builders. Fran and William have to hold onto their dream as they get stuck into the nitty-gritty of building work.

In Worksheet 3-9, Fran and William break their outcome into five main project sections, so that each becomes a smaller, or sub-outcome. At each stage they consider how this project looks, sounds and feels using the principles of engaging their senses, NLP-style. In particular Fran and William consider the emotions they will experience at each stage and where they may lose their nerve; also, where things may go over budget and how they will deal with that.

Here's what Fran and William talk about happening at each stage. By working in this order they see that the first step – shifting from where they are today, the present state – and making the commitment to action is the hardest but feel that they can hang onto the dream, as they have a strong sense of the excitement of completing it.

Worksheet 3-9		**Fran and William's Milestones**		
Present State Step 2	**First Steps Step 5**	**Mid-point Step 3**	**Mid-point to Completion Step 4**	**Desired State Step 1**
Today, we're excited and apprehensive about the commitment we've taken on. There's so much to think about and we're in discussion with many suppliers questioning them about their building products.	The first few months are the scariest part. We haven't used these builders before and we're not sure what we might discover as we start to pull apart the interior of the old building. We're having many discussions with each other and the builders about our dream and there's going to be some serious demolition noise.	We're halfway through the project. By now we have the shell of the building completed and the new roof on. It'll still be very noisy with all that banging and workmen around the site.	We're heading towards completion. We expect to be working flat out with plasterers, carpenters, and electricians to fit out the new building. We're choosing the fittings and planning to move out of our temporary mobile home. It sounds more like industrious, quieter work at this stage	Three years from now. Our dream home is complete and we're moving in. We can't wait for this moment when the builders have finally gone and we have our dream home to ourselves and family. We can hear ourselves saying: 'At last, this is just wonderful!' Champagne corks are popping.

Worksheet 3-10 offers you the opportunity to immerse yourself in your dream.

Worksheet 3-10		My Milestones		
Present State Step 2	First Steps Step 5	Mid-point Step 3	Mid-point to Completion Step 4	Desired State Step 1

Your journey to achieve your dreams – getting from your Present State to your Desired State – can be a daunting experience with setbacks along the way. Remember that in NLP terms 'there is no such thing as failure, just feedback' (read about the NLP presuppositions in Chapter 2), so if things don't work out just as you expected and you get it wrong, take in the lessons and move on. Maybe the reason for your setback will become crystal clear in time.

Rolling Smoothly Along

In our NLP coaching sessions and Romilla's 'Going for Goal'™ workshops, we encourage you to use all the resources you have to make every journey run smoothly and be fun. The workshops begin with setting the intent and choosing the best NLP presuppositions (Chapter 2 covers presuppositions) to strengthen your mindset for success, and continues as we help you uncover limiting beliefs and other unconscious barriers to achieving your desired results. As you develop your outcomes using your own wheel of life and well-formed outcomes, you engage all your senses and build harmony between your unconscious and conscious mind to make reaching the goal effortless.

One popular device is to create an *illustrated personal dream diary*. This is a book, journal, or file that you find beautiful to look at and which heightens your sense of anticipation and excitement from the feel, or perhaps the smell, when you pick it up. It's another way of keeping your unconscious mind in harmony with your conscious mind, looking out for creative ways to help you achieve your outcomes – whether that is a business plan or a personal one. You can build your dream diary by putting your goals in wonderful colour and beautiful writing, using pens you keep just for writing in the diary. You can also use your dream diary as a scrapbook to keep pictures, photos, and records of your various accomplishments. Keep it close to hand, up to date, and look at it and enjoy it when life gets too much to handle. You may be surprised at how much of it comes true in time.

Holding the dream unconsciously

In your diary create a separate section for each major outcome you're moving towards resulting from your wheel of life exercise and hold a short summary of your well-formed outcomes. Write it in the present tense as if it's complete, and engage all your senses. Worksheet 3-11 gives an example from Danielle's diary where she's writing 'as if' her outcome for a new garden is completed. She's writing about a future date when her dream has come true.

Worksheet 3-11   **Danielle's Outcome Summary**

It's 1 May: I am walking from the kitchen into the new garden that I designed in the backyard. It's hard to recall how the backyard was just a patch of rubble a year ago. It is spring and I see the pale pink blossom of the crab apple tree, the camellias, and auriculas as well as the narcissi bulbs I had for my birthday. There are a couple of busy robins pinching worms for their young. John and Tim from work have come over to help me put up the greenhouse and they are laughing and teasing me: 'What would you do without us to help?' as I try to get the barbecue alight and hand them a can of beer each. It feels amazing to have my own garden at last after years of living in a flat. I love the sense of gardening in my shorts and watering the potatoes in the vegetable plot. I can feel in my bones that it's going to be fun having friends over this summer.

Now use Worksheet 3-12 to write your own outcome. If you prefer to use the space to simply draw a picture or compose a personal slogan for yourself, that's fine too.

Worksheet 3-12   **My Outcome Summary**

Collecting photographs and pictures to illustrate each outcome and including these in your diary can make your vision even stronger. You may want to include something tactile such as a small piece of fabric, wood, or metal, or you can spray the pages with a particular perfume that brings to mind your success. Maybe there's a holiday you want to take or restaurant you want to go to when you're ready to celebrate your success – include a picture of the team of people to invite or the menu, to hold the end in mind.

Staying on course

So now you have your dream diary and oops! a few days have passed since you looked at it – minutiae, 'busyness' – and the excuses go on but the consequence of all this is that you discover you've lost your motivation.

To get back on track make use of the following bedtime ritual:

- ✔ Spend a few minutes savouring your dream diary and your dreams
- ✔ Make a note of five actions that you're going to take tomorrow to stay on track
- ✔ As you're dropping off, invite your unconscious to help you with your dreams and outcomes

In the morning, as you're waking up, *stay in bed for a few more minutes!* while setting the intention that 'today is going to be a fabulous day' and mentally rehearsing the successful completion of your actions.

Making the Difference

This chapter is full of ways in which you can take charge of different aspects of your life, working out what you like just now and how you can make it even better in the future. After completing the exercises in your own time and way, take a piece of paper or journal and write down your thoughts on the one most important thing you've uncovered for yourself in this chapter.

Chapter 4

Working with Your Unconscious Mind

In This Chapter

▶ Understanding that both bad and good habits have hidden benefits

▶ Resolving internal conflict

▶ Calming your mind in order to communicate with your unconscious

Are you a sweet or a savoury person? How did you find out that you preferred sugar to spice? Did someone sit down alongside you with a list and you ticked 'yes/no'? Very unlikely! But what *is* very likely is your unconscious mind saying to you, 'Oooh! chocolate – heaven'.

Your unconscious mind can be compared with the hidden 9/10ths of an iceberg and is on duty 24/7 with no time off for good behaviour. Your unconscious mind tells you to eat, drink, sleep, and to perform numerous other actions.

The purpose of this chapter is to show you how you can turn your unconscious thoughts into deliberate conscious thinking and behaviour, by finding out what triggers your thoughts and behaviour and then adjusting your behaviour, before letting your unconscious mind take over again.

Recognising Conscious and Unconscious Behaviours

Remember the last time you munched your way through a whole packet of crisps without realising it or snapped at someone without thinking? These are examples of *unconscious behaviours*, actions you carry out while on automatic pilot.

When acquiring any new skill, you go through a learning curve. Take writing for example. To start with, you did everything painfully and consciously, from laying out the book and sharpening the pencil, to carefully positioning the point of the pencil just right within a set of lines. Your only unconscious action was letting your tongue stick out while you were deep in concentration. Now you write almost without giving it a thought, you just grab a piece of paper and get writing. Or, look at the scenario of snapping at someone. That person probably unwittingly pushed one of your buttons and triggered your unconscious response. A *trigger* is a stimulus that sets you off on a pattern of behaviour over which you may have very little control.

Because you can only consciously deal with a few thoughts at a time, your unconscious mind is left to deal with everything else: Your unconscious tells you to breathe or to scratch that itch and protects you from physical and emotional pain. However, at times your unconscious can get things wrong. In trying to protect you, your unconscious may bring into play fears that stop you doing things. Because of this you have to be willing to bring your unconscious thoughts to your conscious awareness, analysing them and tweaking them if necessary, and then sending them back to the care of your unconscious.

Jacob noticed that his bathroom scales showed that his weight had gone up alarmingly. So he started recording what he ate and when. He found that he ate healthily except on the days when he had a really bad day, which sent him heading off to the pub to meet up with his buddies and drown his sorrows in drink. At the pub he would down a minimum of six pints and eat several packets of crisps in one sitting. The worst of it was that he didn't even notice the taste of what he put in his mouth or remember what he'd eaten. As Jacob and his pals unwound, they got talking about how bad things were at work, with their partners, with their cars, and so on. Instead of feeling better and cheering up, Jacob always ended up feeling worse. In an attempt to turn the situation round, Jacob decided to list his conscious and unconscious behaviours, as you can see in Worksheet 4-1.

Worksheet 4-1	Jacob's Chart of Conscious/Unconscious Behaviours	
My Behaviour	*Conscious or Unconscious*	*My Thoughts on Changing*
If I have a difficult day, I want to meet the boys for a drink.	Unconscious trigger	I will use the trigger to go for a run instead of going to the pub.
Once I go past the three-pint mark, I am no longer in control.	Unconscious behaviour	When I do choose to go for a drink, I am consciously going to switch to soft drinks after two pints.
I eat without thinking.	Unconscious behaviour	I am going to think about each crisp as it goes into my mouth. To stop myself eating, I am going to talk instead of eat. Burns more calories.

Take the opportunity presented in Worksheet 4-2 to think about the way you behave and whether you're acting consciously or whether your unconscious is *making* you behave as you do.

Worksheet 4-2	My Chart of Conscious/Unconscious Behaviours	
My Behaviour	*Conscious or Unconscious*	*My Thoughts on Changing*

Searching for Hidden Messages

Does life sometimes remind you of the Simon and Garfunkel lyric: 'Slip slidin' away/Slip slidin' away/ You know the nearer your destination/ The more you're slip slidin' away'?

If you made a conscious decision to take a course of action and you didn't get the results you were hoping for, you're likely to put the whole thing down to experience, and consciously decide on another course of action. However, often it is your unconscious behaviour that is affecting your conscious decisions. Wouldn't it be fantastic if you could just step back and get answers to your problems quickly and effortlessly?

You make a conscious decision to move to a new job, but the job doesn't work out. You may consciously decide that now's not the time to make another change or that your current job is the best you can expect. A likely cause of your job failing to meet your expectations is your unconscious decision not to go to the networking meeting to get help and advice on your job move. You made the excuse to yourself at the time that you were too tired. You allowed your unconscious mind to get in your way because your previous experience of networking wasn't pleasant and your unconscious was trying to protect you from further pain.

Understanding how your unconscious mind works is a great tool for helping you achieve positive results. By communicating with your unconscious, you can get on with the business of enjoying life, happy in the knowledge that your unconscious is beavering away in the background taking care of things for you. For example, you have taken to comfort eating – you can't stop stuffing yourself with chips and chocolate – until your unconscious mind points out to you that you're overeating because you're feeling unloved, giving you the opportunity, with very little effort on your part, of starting to eat healthily again.

A way of communicating with your unconscious mind is by using a *pendulum*, a small weight on the end of a string, to draw out 'yes/no' answers from your unconscious mind. The principle is that a conscious thought provokes an unconscious muscular response, called an *ideomotor movement*.

The pendulum is simply a tool. If you find you're successful and getting good results, you may find yourself becoming dependent on the pendulum. Please remember you have plenty of other NLP tools. Pulling out your pendulum in the middle of a meeting and saying 'I'll give you an answer in a moment' probably isn't an effective strategy. By the same token, if you aren't immediately getting satisfactory results, try persevering with the pendulum until you can use this tool successfully.

A pendulum can be anything from a bath plug tied to a piece of string to a beautiful crystal on a necklace or a favourite pendant hanging on a chain.

If you want to try working with a pendulum, follow these steps:

1. **Sit at a table.**

2. **Think about what you want to find out and write down the questions you're going to ask.**

3. **Rest the elbow of your pendulum arm on the table, with your wrist at right angles to your forearm.** This stops your arm from getting tired and allows the pendulum to move freely.

4. **Ask the pendulum to give you a signal for 'yes' and another one for 'no' at the start of every session.** You don't have much control over the movements the pendulum chooses to make. The signals are usually the same, and you become familiar with them over time, but be sure to ask every time.

5. **Ask questions and watch for responses.**

   The response you get may not always be clear – you may get yes and no responses to the same question. Sometimes you find that the pendulum hardly moves or only moves half-heartedly. This indicates that your unconscious mind doesn't understand the question or doesn't want to give you an answer. You may need to ask, 'Is there a reason you don't want to give me an answer?' If the response is 'yes', you can ask, 'Are you afraid I won't like the answer and will get upset?' You can then work your way through another set of questions.

Jack is a trainer and had been offered jobs with two companies. Despite his best efforts he was in a quandary as to which job he should accept. He'd made his list of pros and cons for both jobs and they were coming out about equal, except that 'company A' was offering Jack a 10 per cent higher salary than 'company B'. Jack decided to work with the pendulum.

Jack: Can I have a signal for yes please?

Pendulum moves in a clockwise direction.

Jack: Thank you. Now can I have a signal for no please?

Pendulum moves in a line from north to south.

Jack: Thank you. Should I accept 'company B'?

Pendulum gives a yes.

Jack: Thank you. Should I accept 'company A'?

Pendulum gives a no.

Jack: I should accept 'company B' even though 'company A' is paying more?

Pendulum gives a yes.

Six months later, Jack discovered that the financial director of 'company A' had been embezzling funds and the company was laying people off. In this case it may seem that working with the pendulum equated with working with the paranormal. But the simple explanation is that Jack had picked up on the subtle signals that the directors of 'company A' were sending out, that they were having doubts and uncertainties regarding the future of the company.

Worksheet 4-3 shows you how you can use a pendulum. But before starting, here are two points to bear in mind:

✔ Your unconscious mind is like that of a young child, so the questions you ask need to be simple and direct.

✔ Sometimes a 'no' response can hide an 'I don't know' or 'I don't want to tell' type of answer and you have to ask for clarity. If you're suspicious of the response, you can always ask, 'Do you know the answer?' and if the response is yes, you can ask, 'Do you want to tell me?' After gaining experience of using the pendulum, you can fine-tune your questions and your intuition.

Worksheet 4-3   **Using a Pendulum for Communicating
with My Unconscious Mind**

---

1. Plan your questions so that you only get a *yes* or *no* response.

---

2. Find a quiet place and set the intention that you're going to make an honest connection with your unconscious mind, giving you truthful answers.

For example, tell your unconscious, 'I truly appreciate all the care you take of me and want to ask you to help me get some honest answers to this problem I am experiencing.'

---

3. Place your elbow on the table and dangle the pendulum. Decide on your 'yes' and 'no' movements of the pendulum:

       Ask, 'Please can you signal a yes?' Remember to say 'Thank you'.
       Stop the pendulum swinging.
       Ask, 'Now can you signal a no?' Remember to say 'Thank you'.

---

4. Ask your questions, remembering to stop the pendulum after each response.

Use Worksheet 4-4 to write down a problem that you're wrestling with and the yes/no questions you want to ask your unconscious mind.

Worksheet 4-4   **My Issue and Questions Worksheet**

My issue: _____

_____

_____

My questions for my unconscious mind: _____

_____

_____

_____

_____

You may not get the results to your questions straight away, but when you do, fill in Worksheet 4-5.

Worksheet 4-5   **My Results with the Pendulum**

Results: _____

_____

_____

Areas that I need to explore further: _____

_____

_____

_____

_____

Not getting the results you want may well be because a belief is standing in the way of your questions. Perhaps at the back of your mind you believe that getting answers through a pendulum is a bit weird. Or you lack confidence in your ability to communicate with your unconscious mind and that using a pendulum is what other people do, and something that you can't do. The last belief can become self-fulfilling as it causes you to 'fail' with each attempt. So, if you're having problems using a pendulum, confront any negative beliefs you're holding about the pendulum and try to work out the positive benefits.

Discovering Fears You Hadn't Spotted

While searching for the word *fear* on the Internet, we came across this terrific acronym: FEAR, False Evidence Appearing Real. Obviously this doesn't apply to life-threatening situations such as being held up at gunpoint or being attacked by a scorpion. However, there are times when you can let a minor worry grow into an overwhelming fear and you need to take steps to lessen your fear so that it becomes just a storm in a teacup.

Are you allowing false evidence to appear real and stop you from fulfilling your potential? A fear can hold you back from doing something simply because you haven't given enough thought to what you want to do and achieve. Because the threat isn't physical, you can take it for granted that the fear is generated by your unconscious mind. So for the purpose of uncovering your thinking about fear, please treat your unconscious mind as a separate person from yourself.

Chapter 9 describes a process you can use to uncover your thinking around emotions, including your fears.

Charlie was in the process of being made redundant. He wasn't sure whether to set up as a consultant or whether he wanted the safety net of working for another established company. Because of his fear and uncertainty about what to do next, he was avoiding the issue by using his gardening leave to garden instead of looking for jobs or researching what he needed to do as an independent consultant. Charlie decided to focus on his problem and bring it into perspective by using the 'movie-director' technique outlined in Chapter 9. For the movie, Charlie took on the role of the Observer with his conscious mind acting as the Protagonist and his unconscious mind acting as the Antagonist, closely viewed by the movie director through his lens. As the characters acted their roles, Charlie discovered that while he wanted the stability of a secure job, his unconscious mind wanted him to have the variety and excitement of a consultancy. Charlie had got himself in trouble with his previous employer because he was bored, and his unconscious mind had equated boredom with trouble and was trying to protect him from getting into difficulties again. Once Charlie's fear had been brought to his conscious awareness, he was able to accept a permanent job. However, Charlie made doubly sure during the interview that the new job would stretch him intellectually and give him plenty of variety!

Integrating Your Separate Parts

Do you catch yourself saying something like, 'Part of me wants to go, but I'm not sure?' You may be experiencing conflict in response to an event that had a significant emotional impact. Ideally, your nervous system works as a unit. But on your journey through life, you experience events, some of which are painful, and you create new parts of yourself to protect yourself from further stress or pain. At times these parts don't always communicate effectively with the rest of your nervous system.

In this section, we describe a process of working with two separate parts, allowing each part to have the same common purpose and integrating each part into a whole. You can integrate more than two parts at a time but for the sake of simplicity, we recommend only two at a time.

Keeping the idea of integration well to the forefront of your mind, follow the process for integrating conflicting parts:

1. **Find yourself a quiet place to sit where you won't be disturbed.**

2. **Identify the parts of you that are in conflict.**

   You can identify conflicting parts by looking at an issue you want to resolve. For example, if you're saying, 'I need to get my dissertation finished but something is stopping me', conflict exists between 'Part A' that wants to get the dissertation finished and 'Part B' that's sabotaging the process. Or, you may be saying, 'I love her but I'm scared of commitment'. 'Part A' wants to commit; but 'Part B' doesn't, resulting in a conflict within you that can lead to difficulties in your relationship.

3. **Imagine each part as two separate people. Imagine what each person looks like, sounds like, and what feelings each person has.**

4. **Ask the part that you think of as the problem part to come out and stand on one hand.**

   In the examples in Step 2, the problem parts (B in both cases) are the ones stopping you from achieving your goal. Parts may be in disagreement for years and you don't notice until you decide to focus on why you aren't getting what you want. Then you realise that the disagreement is actually a conflict between what the two parts are trying to achieve.

5. **Now ask the part that you think of as not being the problem part to come out and stand on the other hand.**

6. **Starting with the part you consider to be the problem part, ask each part, 'What is your positive intention and purpose?'**

   Although a part is sabotaging your efforts, that part's intention is for a positive result. The 'problem' part B in the examples may not want you to complete your dissertation because it is protecting you from the knocks you will inevitably receive when you go out into the big world. Not letting you commit is Part B's way of protecting you from future emotional pain. (See Chapter 3 for lots more on positive intentions and secondary gains.)

7. **Repeat Step 6 for the non-problem part.**

8. **Repeat Step 6 for both parts until they both realise they have the same intention at which point the hands can come together, integrating the parts into the whole.**

   On the face of it, it seems unlikely that both parts have the same intention, but as you work through the exercise, both parts will come together with a common, positive intention.

9. **Ask each part what resources it has that the other part may find useful in reaching the positive intention and purpose of each.**

   Resources, in this context, may be the ability to plan, keep time, be visionary, motivate others, or the tendency to be utterly pig-headed and not let other people throw you off your track.

Integrating your separate parts is particularly useful because while it allows each part to recognise that both have a common purpose, each part also gains an appreciation of the strength and capabilities of the other.

Tim had gone bankrupt, after working as a freelance trainer. The whole process of his business failing and his filing for bankruptcy had a huge impact on him. Although he quickly found a job working for another company, he was demotivated and his training courses were ill-prepared. This was having a negative impact on his career. Tim thought maybe he was experiencing a conflict between a part that wanted him to be successful and another part that wanted him to fail. Worksheet 4-6 shows the process Tim used to integrate the two parts.

Worksheet 4-6 Steps	Tim's Integration Worksheet Part A	Part B
Identify two parts of yourself in conflict	I want to be a really good trainer.	I'm never quite prepared with the material.
Imagine each part as a person. Describe what each person looks like, sounds like, and feels. Ask each person to come out and stand on each hand.	Both parts are versions of me but this part, on my right side, is big and has a halo around it. The sounds are people clapping. I can see people smiling and standing up to clap because they've had such a fantastic time. I feel this glow in me and I'm bursting with energy.	Part B is standing on my left side and feels small. It's much smaller than me, and the room is dark. There are very few people in the room and the energy is very low.
Ask, 'What is your positive intention and purpose?'	I want to be successful.	If I don't succeed, I won't have the confidence to do new things.
Ask, 'What is your positive intention and purpose?'	I will have lots of delegates.	I want to stay within my comfort zone.
Ask, 'What is your positive intention and purpose?'	My company will give me challenging jobs.	I'll always stay in my present job.
Ask, 'What is your positive intention and purpose?'	I will increase my knowledge.	I'll be safe.
Ask, 'What is your positive intention and purpose?'	I will earn lots.	I'll have financial security.
Ask, 'What is your positive intention and purpose?'	I will have security.	I won't need to worry.

Steps	Part A	Part B
Ask, 'What is your positive intention and purpose?	I will be happy.	I'll be secure.
Ask what resources each part has to offer the other.	I am enthusiastic and can drive my dreams forward. I know how to communicate and I have a lot of energy.	I am cautious so I can make sure that all the pros and cons are looked at. I am the voice of reason.

Notice that, although Parts A and B use different terms, further questioning shows that both parts have the same intention. Although Part A uses 'earn lots' and 'security' and Part B uses 'financial security' and 'secure', the terms aren't really that important. This exercise isn't about the words that each part uses, it's more about getting to the same result at the end – being happy.

Now, following the same steps as Tim, try integrating two parts of yourself. Write your thoughts down in Worksheet 4-7.

Worksheet 4-7	My Integration Worksheet	
Steps	**Part A**	**Part B**
Identify two parts of yourself in conflict		
Imagine each part as a person. Describe what each person looks like, sounds like, and feels. Ask each person to come out and stand on each hand.		
Ask, 'What is your positive intention and purpose?'		
Ask, 'What is your positive intention and purpose?'		
Ask, 'What is your positive intention and purpose?'		

(continued)

Worksheet 4-7 *(continued)*

Steps	Part A	Part B
Ask, 'What is your positive intention and purpose?'		
Ask, 'What is your positive intention and purpose?'		
Ask, 'What is your positive intention and purpose?'		
Ask, 'What is your positive intention and purpose?		
Ask what resources each part has to offer the other.		

To have even greater impact, try tying the process of integrating your separate parts into a whole with your time line (we tell you about 'time lines' in Chapter 13). After you learn how to travel along your time line with the new, integrated you, you can navigate even more successfully through life.

Getting Centred

Quietening your thoughts is an ideal way of getting in touch with your unconscious mind. One of the best ways of doing this is by building some quiet time into your life in order to meditate or contemplate.

A great way of training your unconscious mind is to have a ritual in place. Setting up a ritual of lighting candles, dimming the lights, and turning on music to relax and calm your overactive brain is a great way of getting into the process of meditation. To get yourself started, cordon off a space in a room, or if you're lucky, an entire room that your unconscious mind associates with quiet time.

The meditation steps you find here aren't the 'standard' format you find in more conventional teachings. The purpose of this 'active' meditation is to help you to focus your unconscious mind on an issue that you would like to resolve for yourself because the help of a coach or therapist isn't available.

1. **Decide where and when you're going to set aside time for meditation.**

For example, clear a corner in a room and move a recliner or other comfortable chair there together with a side table for holding a candle, notepad, and pen.

Meditation is a great way to slow down before going to bed. On the other hand, some people prefer to start the day with some quiet, focused meditation.

Start by meditating 10 minutes a day on a regular basis, building it up to 20 minutes when you find you can fit it in. After a time you may choose to extend your period of meditation to an hour or build in two 20-minute slots at each end of the day. Be easy on yourself. It's no use setting unrealistic targets of an hour a day from the start and giving up after a few days.

2. **Think about an issue you're wrestling with.**

   If you aren't wrestling with anything right now, go to Step 4.

3. **Choose a statement that expresses the result you want. Say it in the positive, as if you have already achieved the result.**

   Table 4-1 offers examples of positive statements.

   Deciding on the length of time you want to focus your attention on an issue is helpful. You may decide to work on an issue for a week and extend it a week at a time, depending on how satisfied you are with the results.

4. **If you don't have any issues at the moment and are generally happy and content, thank your unconscious mind or speak about something for which you're grateful. For example:**

   • Unconscious mind, I acknowledge your help and thank you.

   • I am grateful for Derry.

   • My T-cells are plump and healthy.

5. **Get your ritual going for settling down and getting comfortable.**

   Rituals are very important in training yourself to be disciplined. You may find that when you start meditating, most of the 10 minutes you've put aside for meditating can get taken up with getting into the right frame of mind and calming your brain. As your ritual becomes second nature, you find that you slip into a meditative state quickly and smoothly.

6. **Take a breath in through the nose. As you breathe out softly from the mouth, speak your statement.**

   Repeat this step for the length of your meditation time.

Keep a notepad and pen to hand and write down any thoughts that occur to you while you're meditating.

Table 4-1	Turning Issues into Positive Statements
Issue	*Positive Statement*
I am feeling unloved because I don't have a partner.	I am blessed with friends and family who love me. or I am happy and know I will meet the right person at the right time.
My eyesight is poor.	I have perfect 20/20 vision.
I don't own my own home.	I own my own flat and I love it.
My boss refuses to promote me.	I am thrilled with my present job.

If you don't like the thought of meditation because you're afraid that you may not be able to come out of a deep trance, fear not. All that happens is that you go into a deep, restful sleep, and wake up naturally, when your body is rested.

Keep track of your progress. At the end of your meditation time, write down the changes you've experienced.

If you find your results aren't as good as you expected, extend the time that you focus on your goal or simplify your statement. Try breaking your statement into smaller steps or shifting your focus to something different and letting your unconscious mind come up with alternative answers. Sometimes when you want something desperately, you can actually push it away with the fear of not getting it. Moving your focus somewhere else allows you to draw other needs into your life.

Worksheet 4-8 is for recording the positive results of your meditation.

Worksheet 4-8	My Positive Results

Your unconscious mind is doing its best to give you what it thinks you want and attempting to guide you. Learn to listen to what your unconscious mind is saying and if your unconscious mind sometimes gets the wrong end of the stick, direct your unconscious mind *gently* to get it to do what you want. You can do this by using the well-formed outcome process (which you can find out about on the Cheat Sheet and in Chapter 3). You can then have the *positive* outcome you want. By going back again and again to your well-formed outcome, you train your unconscious mind to work with you in achieving your goal.

Saying a 'thank you' every so often to your unconscious mind helps you to develop faith and trust in your unconscious.

Chapter 5

Recognising How You Filter Your Thinking

In This Chapter

▶ Looking at the NLP communication model

▶ Applying your internal/external metaprogram filter

▶ Checking your values

▶ Changing decisions and behaviours

▶ Stirring up memories

Do you have the bad luck of knowing someone who, just by thinking about them, makes you want to heave? Okay, maybe she isn't that sickening – nevertheless you find your hackles rising whenever your paths cross. And then there's that person on the phone whose voice warms the cockles of your heart – someone you really look forward to meeting. Chances are, in the case of the first person, you're simply not on the same wavelength, and poles apart in your thinking – whereas with the second person you probably have similar values, speak the same language, and have common interests.

Yes, the old cliché says that opposites attract, but in practice it's definitely easier to get on with a person you can communicate with comfortably because of shared values, interests, and traits.

In this chapter we give you the tools for reaching a better understanding of how you and the other person are thinking and behaving, getting your message across and accepted, and increasing your influence and rapport.

Checking the Communication Model

This section introduces you to the NLP Communication Model. Essentially, this model deals with the fact that your brain is inundated non-stop with huge amounts of information crying out for your attention. The way your mind deals with this information overload is to filter the incoming messages through your metaprograms, values, beliefs, decisions, and memories. As a result of this filtering, you create your own internal representations from the filtered message, which has elements of deletions, distortions, and generalisations.

Internal representation is the term used to refer to the pictures you see, sounds that you hear, or the feelings that are generated within you in response to the information you take in from the world around you. Basically, internal representation is the interpretation you make from what's left of the information after passing through the filters.

NLP enables people to understand human psychology. One way of reaching this understanding is to recognise how the NLP Communication Model filters affect your internal representations, which in turn affect your state of mind, your physiology, and ultimately your behaviour. Understanding these filters gives you the power to change them to alter your internal representations, which in turn changes your state of mind, your physiology, and finally your behaviour. When you can understand how someone else is deleting, distorting, and generalising, you can communicate with that person with even greater rapport because you understand that person's psychology and can alter your language and behaviour to match hers.

This chapter focuses on the first three steps of the Communication Model. Chapters 14 and 15 explain the process of how you 're-present' your internal representations to the world verbally.

The Communication Model has five steps

1. **Gathering information about an event through your five senses:**

    Visual – Pictures

    Auditory – Sound

    Kinaesthetic – Touch

    Olfactory – Smell

    Gustatory – Taste

2. **Passing the information through the following filters:**

    Metaprograms (Chapter 8 tells you about metaprograms)

    Values

    Beliefs

    Decisions

    Memories

3. **Resulting in an internal representation of the event within you.**

4. **Creating in you a state of being which is a combination of your mental and physical states.**

5. **Stimulating a physical response, from speaking to shaking hands, from cuddling to kissing.**

Ruling out deletions

Allowing your conscious mind to ignore a mass of incoming information has the benefit of letting you cope with the remaining messages. The downside is that you may be ignoring information that is important.

Take a good look at your surroundings. Then, without taking a second look, make a note in the first column in Worksheet 5-1 of what you can remember. Look again at your surroundings and write down in the third column the things you didn't notice first time round.

This exercise is designed to help you recognise how your filters determine what you pay attention to when you process your incoming messages. For example, in your office you take notice of the commemorative plaque hanging on the wall because it reminds you of an occasion that holds a special memory for you. However, you ignore your bunch of keys lying on your desk because they're only important to you when it's time for you to go home. This shows that filters can be as simple as remembering items that have meaning, value, or immediate use to you and deleting items that you don't have an emotional connection to or immediate use for. What has meaning or value for you is determined by your experiences and your environment.

Worksheet 5-1	What I Remember about My Surroundings	
What I remember		
Possible reason for remembering		
What I deleted		
Possible reason for the deletion		

Sorting out distortions

A *distortion* is a false representation of what is happening, or misinterpreting what is being said. In relation to the NLP communication model, distortion is one of three things that can happen when you filter data that comes through your senses (the other two are deletions and generalisations).

Distortions allow you to fit the incoming information to what you believe to be true and are created as a result of your life experiences. Distortions can work for you, or against you. Take the example of someone who believes that there's no such thing as an alternative to conventional medicine because she tried hypnotherapy but it wasn't very successful for her. So now when she finds articles on the benefits of a herb, she may not bother reading the article because she equates herbs as being 'quack medicine'. Or the person who is asked to move to a different job and decides it's because her boss doesn't like her and wants her out of the way. In fact, her boss knows she's not very happy and has offered her an opportunity for her to shine by using skills that have been wasted in her current job. If these people were aware of these unhelpful distortions, they could change their thinking.

One summer, Drew felt the arachnids had really got it in for him. Despite being a strapping adult, he drove his mother to distraction with stories of his nightly encounters with spiders. After a hectic day, Drew's mother decided to regain her sanity by wallowing in a hot, scented bath. As she lay in the bath, she noticed an enormous spider under the sink. While she soaked, she fretted about how she was going to get rid of the spider. Then she realised that it wasn't a spider at all, but hair that she had shed from her clothes after her visit to the hairdresser. Not being particularly maternal, she couldn't stop giggling as she debated whether to leave the 'spider' for her son to discover or do the motherly thing and clear it up. When a clump of hair becomes a spider, you definitely have a distortion of reality!

Write down your experience of a distortion in Worksheet 5-2. If you can't think of any real-life ones, films are a good source for material to start training your mental muscles. Surrealist paintings can be thought of as a distortion, where the result doesn't truly represent the picture of the world the artist saw but is affected by aspects of the artist's imagination, psychology, and philosophy. Government statistics are seen as a distortion by the opposing party, who would agree with Aaron Levenstein's quote that 'Statistics are like a bikini. What they reveal is suggestive but what they conceal is vital.'

Worksheet 5-2	My Distortion

Another example of a distortion is when you try reading a person's mind and end up getting the wrong end of the stick. Hurry on to Chapter 15 to explore the mind-reading issue.

Making generalisations

When you group and name a range of happenings under one heading, you're making a *generalisation*. Generalisations can relate to things and people, as well as events.

Generalisations are one of three NLP communication filters you use on the information that you receive from your environment. Generalisations are very helpful when it comes to something like learning because they stop you from having to go back to basics and enable you to build on what you already know. The time a generalisation can hold you back is when you have an unpleasant experience and decide similar experiences are also going to be unpleasant. For example, after a bad experience at a Japanese restaurant, you decide never to eat Japanese food again.

Isms, such as sexism and ageism, are classic examples of generalisations. Someone who has had one unhappy relationship may decide that 'all men are selfish' and have trouble finding a suitable partner.

On a positive note, generalisations can also create the hooks for you to grab hold of as you climb the ladder of learning or achievement.

Sarah was already an experienced trainer when she started learning NLP. As she listened to what was being said, she was constantly thinking of ways to apply NLP in her presentations. You could say she was generalising because she was building on the experience she had gained as a trainer. As a result, Sarah had 'hooks' on which she could hang her new-found learning and so outstripped her fellow students who were still working on ways of pulling the new information together.

Roma decided she didn't like going to art galleries because, apart from some paintings by Jacob van Ruisdael of Dutch windmills and clouds and Canaletto's views of Venice, she found most other paintings pretty dull. For that reason, she nearly refused an invitation to view the works of Tamara de Lempicka. Luckily for Roma, she didn't, because she found Lempicka's paintings utterly enthralling. So her generalisation about all art galleries being dull may well have made her life the poorer. She then discovered she enjoyed some Mogul art after giving herself the chance to open up her mind. You can see in Worksheet 5-3 that Roma changed her behaviour as a result of gaining insight into how she generalised in the context of art. Hopefully, she can take this awareness to other areas of her life. Roma can stop to assess when she realises she's generalising and consciously decide whether to go with the generalisation or make an exception.

Worksheet 5-3 shows how Roma examined her generalisation.

Worksheet 5-3	Roma's Examination of Her Generalisation
My generalisation	I decided art galleries were dull.
Experience(s) that my generalisation is based on	As a child I was dragged around galleries in the hope of broadening my horizons.
How my generalisation may be limiting me	I might have missed the Lempicka pictures and never discovered about Art Deco.
Exceptions	Jacob van Ruisdael, Canaletto, some Mogul art.
How I may behave differently	I won't say No! instantly when asked to visit a gallery. I know which artists I don't like so will be choosy about the invitations I accept.

Find a quiet time to think about how you generalise.

- Do you make time for someone just because the person's an actor and you believe all actors are interesting?
- Do you avoid the woman who says, 'I'm just a housewife', thinking her only topic of conversation is her husband and kids?
- Are you an ageist, believing anyone over the age of 45 is ready for the scrapheap?
- Or are you a youngist, dismissing young people's opinions as not worth listening to?

What are your 'isms' and other generalisations? Worksheet 5-4 gives you an opportunity to explore this side of you.

Worksheet 5-4	Examining My Generalisations		
	Generalisation 1:	Generalisation 2:	Generalisation 3:
Experience(s) my generalisation is based on			
How my generalisation may be limiting me			
Exceptions			
How I may behave differently			

Combining deletions, distortions, and generalisations

Deletions, distortions, and generalisations don't happen in isolation. Elements of each are in the internal representation that you create after you filter the information that you take in from your environment. Pick an example of a behaviour that you'd like to examine, or go with our example and notice how you read a newspaper. As you find yourself skimming the headlines and moving on, stop and work out the deletions, distortions, and generalisations that prevent you from paying attention to that article. Is it because you think *all* (generalisation) politicians are bad because they're dishonest and *never* (generalisation) tell the truth so you won't read what *any* (generalisation) politician says? You've deleted the fact that there may be many honest politicians and distorted one aspect of their persona in one context – dishonesty – and decided that anyone who is a politician is bad.

Generalisations are easy to spot because of key words such as 'all', 'never', 'always', 'must', 'should'. You can spot distortions when you come across statements where one thing is interpreted as meaning something else, as in the case of the politicians being bad because they're dishonest or being dishonest because they're politicians. Some words that give clues to distortions are 'causes', 'results in', 'if', 'then', 'because'. When you're looking out for deletions, listen for words like 'better', 'best', 'worst', 'more', 'less', 'most', and 'least' because these give you an indication of what is being left out. For example, the statement, 'Politicians are better liars' implies that worse liars exist but who these worse liars are has been left out of the statement. Similarly, you can read between the lines of certain statements, such as, 'Politicians make me angry'. In this case, you can read between the lines and identify that politicians' actions make you angry.

Dot is a 39-year-old singleton, desperate to find a partner. Some of the words in her story are in italics, showing you how to recognise generalisations in her everyday language.

I'm *never* going to find a man to share my life. *All* the men I meet these days shy away from making a commitment or are workaholics, and *all* the guys I meet think I am pretty ugly.

The reason Dot is being very hard on herself is because at an unconscious level she doesn't really believe that she has time for a relationship. Worksheet 5-5 shows Dot's deletions, distortions, and generalisations.

Worksheet 5-5	Dot's Deletions, Distortions, and Generalisations	
Deletions	*Distortions*	*Generalisations*
There are no eligible men I don't see men as potential friends	With my looks, I won't get a boyfriend	Never going to find a man All men are reluctant to make a commitment or are workaholics All the guys think I'm pretty ugly

Now that you've practised working out your deletions, distortions, and generalisations and read the anecdotes and examples, pick one issue in your life that you'd like to learn from. Note down the deletions, distortions, and generalisations that you recognise yourself experiencing in Worksheet 5-6.

You can find much more detail about understanding and working with deletions, distortions, and generalisations in Chapter 14.

Worksheet 5-6	My Deletions, Distortions, and Generalisations	
Deletions	*Distortions*	*Generalisations*

Transmitting for Reception

Communication is a two-way process. In the context of the communication model, you can maximise your ability to communicate by

- Recognising the filters of the person with whom you're communicating
- Understanding your own filters so you can adjust them
- Adapting your language to reflect the other person's filters

The rest of this chapter shows you how each filter – metaprograms, values, beliefs, decisions, and memories – affects you, and how you delete, distort, and generalise as a result of applying these filters to information you receive from the world around you. The following section picks a subset of the metaprogram filter to illustrate how a filter works specifically in deleting, distorting, and generalising incoming data, and its effect on your behaviour. You can amend your filter in order to change the results you're getting, or leave it unchanged if you're satisfied with the results.

Looking in and out of the internal/external metaprogram

You have customised filters called metaprograms for filtering your various experiences. Most metaprograms work on a sliding scale and you can find yourself operating on different points of the scale according to your situation. (To find out lots more about metaprograms look at Chapter 8 'Influencing with Metaprograms'.) The internal/external metaprogram dictates whether you prefer to trust your own judgement (internal) over that of other people (external) or whether you're willing listen and defer to someone else's point of view. The importance of the internal/external metaprogram lies in recognising how you filter the information you're receiving.

In other words, you may be deleting valuable information and dismissing feedback as unimportant. When you're aware of this tendency, you may find it useful to remember to keep an open mind. A simple exercise is to make a conscious note to weigh up the pros and cons of the information you're being presented with, instead of dismissing it out of hand. One way is to use someone you trust as a sounding board and ask her to play devil's advocate in examining both sides of the argument. This person may be able to point out if you're distorting the information you're given simply because you think you're always right (*generalisation*), and that it may lead to a misunderstanding.

If you find yourself on the 'external' end of the scale you're likely to regularly seek out other peoples' opinions and rely on their feedback. Coming to a decision is harder for you because you're listening to too many people. You can turn this state of affairs around by making a note of the times when you've come to a decision successfully on your own and use this as a launch pad to build trust in yourself, allowing you to sift the good advice from the bad.

When you're aware of your internal/external tendencies, you can train yourself to keep an open mind. Try getting into the habit of always weighing up the pros and cons of the information you're receiving, instead of dismissing the information out of hand.

When you're on a learning curve or in a new situation, you may find yourself displaying rather a lot of 'external' tendencies – until you find your feet, when you may switch over to having more 'internal' tendencies because you've learned to trust yourself in the new field.

Cassy had been working as a legal secretary at a large firm for six months and although she got on very well with her bosses and colleagues, she felt unsettled as she didn't really know whether she was doing well or not. After reading the chapter on metaprograms in *Neuro-linguistic Programming For Dummies*, Cassy realised she wasn't able to judge how she was getting on because her manager hadn't been very forthcoming with feedback. Cassy recognised that she was on the external side of the internal/external scale and relied heavily on feedback to assess her performance. Her manager most likely operates more on the 'internal' side of the scale and he didn't feel it necessary to talk to Cassy about how well or badly she was doing.

The following activity enables you to recognise that metaprograms can affect your behaviour, which can change depending on the situation in which you find yourself. Worksheets 5-7 and 5-8 give you the opportunity for some self-examination and understanding, and this, in turn, gives you a choice over how you behave.

Take this opportunity to fill out Worksheet 5-7 with:

✔ The context in which you're thinking about your internal metaprogram. For example, are you at work where you know your job and feel confident, or at home, where you rule the roost because you feel safe and in control?

✔ Your observations as to why you think your behaviour is more internal. Is it because you find yourself not listening or ignoring what you're told?

Then fill out Worksheet 5-8 after thinking about where you display more 'external' tendencies:

✔ Circumstances where you're more on the 'external' end of the sliding scale. Do you, for example, find yourself operating at the external end of the scale by allowing people to overrule you when you're at work, where you may have started a new job and don't know the ropes?

✔ Your observations as to why you think this is the case. Think about what causes you to behave differently and how you recognise this aspect of yourself. You may be behaving in a more 'external' way because you've put someone on a pedestal or you value someone's experience over yours. You notice your behaviour is different because you're quieter, as you choose to listen rather than talk.

In doing these exercises, recognise some of the positive and negative effects of your internal/external metaprogram on the way you process information and behave. The way you determine whether the effect is positive or negative is by measuring the results you get against the results you want. For example does it take you longer to come to a decision because you're listening to too many people (negative) or do you switch off and discount people's feedback (negative)? Perhaps by being more 'internal' you make decisions quickly (positive) or by telling instead of listening you get the results you want more quickly (positive). So for each, assess whether you think the behaviour you're exhibiting as a result of the metaprogram is good or bad.

Worksheet 5-7	**My Internal Tendencies**
The context:	
Where I am on the scale:	Internal External
My observations for making this statement are:	
I judge this tendency as good/bad because:	

Worksheet 5-8	My External Tendencies
The context:	
Where I am on the scale:	Internal ———————————— External
My observations for making this statement are:	
I judge this tendency as good/bad because:	

Just for fun and to give yourself a bit more practice, pick someone you know well and fill out Worksheet 5-9, this time noting what *you* observe about the person you've chosen.

Worksheet 5-9	My Observations of Internal/External Tendencies
The person and the context:	
Where the person is on the scale:	Internal ———————————— External
My reasoning:	

If you want your message to be listened to and you're talking to a person showing 'internal' tendencies, use expressions like:

- ✔ Ultimately only you can know
- ✔ Judge for yourself
- ✔ Weigh up all the facts and decide
- ✔ The decision rests on your shoulders

A person with more of an 'external' bent may be better persuaded by what you're saying if you use expressions like:

- ✔ The general consensus of opinion is
- ✔ This has thousands
- ✔ The Joneses have just bought this super-duper gadget
- ✔ Research shows

Discovering your values

Dina believes passionately in animal welfare and hates the thought of experimenting on animals. Her cousin, Tim, works for a pharmaceutical company and practises vivisection. Although Dina and Tim were inseparable as children, things have moved on and family get-togethers can become interesting, to say the least, as the debate between the cousins is often heated and acrimonious. Other members of the family can't understand why each reacts with such passion. 'Values', you say? Yup. Dina and Tim clearly have different values concerning vivisection and animal welfare.

- ✔ Values influence behaviour
- ✔ Values are used to check whether something is good or bad
- ✔ Values can motivate or demotivate

Your values are created at different stages in your lives by outside influences such as culture, family, friends, and what you experience in life. Value words include honesty, truth, honour, fun, wealth. Some of these values can change across contexts but you take your core values with you in whatever role you find yourself playing. If fun is one of your core values, you want fun to permeate all aspects of your life, be it work, rest, or play. Core values are non-negotiable and if you're forced into a situation that isn't fun, you're probably thoroughly miserable. However, if you value fun but it isn't a core value, you may be willing to sacrifice fun for a while to achieve a particular outcome.

In the case of Dina and Tim the cause of conflict between them arose from a difference in values. Battling against your own conflicting values can lead to a great deal of stress and unhappiness. Conflicts of values can grow out of trying to live up to other people's expectations and values, which don't always fit in with yours.

Tara was a highly paid accountant. She had a very busy social life and brilliant prospects. Her parents were very proud of her and liked telling their friends and family about their high-flying daughter. Then Tara fell ill. She felt unfulfilled, tired and listless, and spent a lot of time in tears. In desperation, Tara hired a coach, who, among other things, helped Tara work out what her job and career values were. Tara discovered she had been trying to live up to her parents' values. She decided to take a sabbatical, during which time she planned her career move. Tara is now working as a freelance accountant with a charity. She is fulfilled, fit, and happy, and believes the work she is doing is really making a difference. She isn't earning as much as she did, and she doesn't have the responsibilities she had before, but because a big salary and a high position weren't motivating factors in her life, she is unaffected by their absence. Sadly, her parents aren't impressed and don't have much to say about her new job and lifestyle.

You may find yourself holding different values depending on the area in your life. For example, it may be important for you to be loved in your romantic relationship but not at work, where achieving success may be more important and the need for love doesn't even come into the equation.

Here's a simple method for detecting your values in a particular area of your life.

1. **Think of an area of your life that you want to improve.**

2. **Make a list of what is important to you in this context.**

For example, in a work context, your values may be things like job security, money, career prospects.

Certain values may spring to your mind very quickly. As you sit and think a little more about what is important to you, you may find another set of values surfacing.

3. **List your values in order of importance.**

You may well find that the values that surfaced later now have a greater significance for you.

If you're having trouble deciding where to rank each value in your list, imagine that you're in a life raft that is taking on water fast. You need to lighten the load in the raft and each value is marked on a heavy bag. In what order would you throw the bags overboard?

Have a go at working out your values, using the method above. Fill in the swag bags in Worksheet 5-10 with the values that come to mind when you think about what is important to you in your chosen area of life. You can write the importance of each value in the top of the bag.

Worksheet 5-10	Working Out My Values

The area of my life:

The brainstorming from Worksheet 5-10 may end up looking a bit messy. So in Worksheet 5-11 recap by writing your values in the order of most important to least important.

Worksheet 5-11	Ranking My Values
1.	
2.	
3.	
4.	
5.	
6.	
7.	
8.	
9.	
10.	

Your values act as a filter, resulting in you deleting, distorting, or generalising about aspects of your life. Dina and Tim, for example, often end up not hearing each other (deletion) or misunderstanding what the other is saying (distortion). Dina's generalisation may go something like, 'Oh there he goes on his old tack of how medical interventions can save lives', which stops her learning about Tim's new research into the application of herbal remedies to animal welfare. Consider how the values you have bring deletions, distortions, and generalisations into your life.

By gaining greater understanding of your own or another person's values, you increase the choices you have in your life. Work out in what area of your life you may be limiting yourself and how you can turn things around. For example, you may not be over-friendly with that acquaintance leading a bohemian lifestyle, but by getting to know her better and appreciating her way of life, you're weaving new strands into your way of thinking.

Use Worksheet 5-12 to consider your values and how you use them to delete, distort, and generalise.

Worksheet 5-12	Deletions, Distortions, and Generalisations Created by My Values
How and what I delete because of my values:	
How I can choose to behave differently:	

(continued)

Worksheet 5-12 (continued)	
How and what I distort because of my values:	
How I can choose to behave differently:	
How and what I generalise about because of my values:	
How I can choose to behave differently:	

Recognising Blocked Filters

Recognising the impact that filters have on the way you process the huge amount of information you're receiving isn't always easy. Some of your filters can have an empowering effect – for example, where a recent success gives you the confidence to spread your wings and soar a little higher. But what about the filters that keep you rooted to the one spot, stifling your dreams and aspirations? Wouldn't it be great to silence the voice that says, 'Last time you did something like that you got hurt' or change the focus of your thought from 'failure' to 'lessons learned'? This section is intended to help you understand how blocked filters, such as decisions and beliefs that limit you, can stop you from seeing the potential in a situation.

Some events that happen in your life can cause your unconscious mind to create a belief or make a decision on your behalf that can limit your behaviour. A decision that constrains you in some way is called a *limiting decision*. A belief that has a negative impact on your life is called a *limiting belief* – for example, 'money is the root of evil' is a belief that can keep you trapped in poverty. The event that created the limiting decision or belief is in your memory but hidden from your conscious awareness. You may need to seek professional assistance to help you if the memory has created some issues. Not all limiting decisions or beliefs need clearing out. Does it really matter if you love or hate Marmite?

If you need to resolve an issue, you can help yourself by reading Chapters 10 and 13, which show you how to access forgotten memories and release the hold that some limiting beliefs and decisions have on you.

Lena has a process for choosing friends. She has long-term friends, people with whom she'll socialise when she's retired, and inconsequential friends who are just passing through her life. Perhaps her conscious decision is dictated by an unconscious decision that is hidden deep in her memory. The point is that Lena could be deleting people as friends because she has a distorted view of them and has put them into the 'inconsequential friends' pigeonhole as a result of her generalisation. This may sound quite negative to someone who likes a lot of acquaintances, but it suits Lena who has fewer friends and can enjoy meaningful relationships with them.

This book is all about gaining a better understanding of people, primarily yourself. Worksheet 5-13 helps you to evaluate how a decision you've made impacts your life. If you consciously analyse a decision and decide the results you're getting aren't satisfactory, you can choose to behave differently, based on a more empowering decision.

Worksheet 5-13	Deletions, Distortions, and Generalisations Created by My Decisions
My decision is:	
How I delete as a result of this decision:	
How I distort as a result of this decision:	
How I generalise as a result of this decision:	
The effect of the decision on my life is:	
I will change the decision to:	

Tara believes that because obesity runs in her family, she has no hope of being a normal size. When she hears about success stories of weight loss, she dismisses them (deletion) because she doesn't believe they'll work for her. Her distortion is that her genetic makeup predisposes her to be fat and her generalisation is that diets don't work for her. Because she sees lifestyle changes as diets, she deletes these as well.

If you can recognise how a belief is affecting your life, you have the option to change it if you're not getting the results you want from it (refer to Chapter 10 for more). Use Worksheet 5-14 to consider how your belief affects the way you delete, distort, and generalise.

Worksheet 5-14	Deletions, Distortions, and Generalisations Created by My Belief
My belief is:	
How I delete as a result of this belief:	
How I distort as a result of this belief:	
How I generalise as a result of this belief:	
The effect of the belief on my life is:	
I will change the belief to:	

Shifting Memories

You may remember Vincent Price, an actor with a wonderfully distinctive voice, perfectly suited to his roles in horror movies. One of his young fans sat through all his films covered in goose pimples. In fact the movie star had such an effect on her that later when she was an adult, she couldn't even watch his TV cookery programmes without feeling the same shiver of fear she'd experienced several years before.

Memories can be powerful filters affecting the way you experience your world, the way you behave, and the results you get. Memories are inextricably linked to other filters such as your beliefs and decisions.

As with other filters, memories can cause you to delete, distort, and generalise too. Think about caravanning. If you remember your first caravan trip as being cold, wet, and claustrophobic, chances are you're likely to delete a caravan site from your catalogue of holiday destinations. The distortion may be that caravan holidays are unpleasant because you only focus on the cold, wet, and claustrophobic and from the one holiday, generalise that all caravan holidays are to be avoided.

If, on the other hand, all you remember is the camaraderie, the games, and time with your family, you might delete other holiday destinations, having distorted the memory by forgetting the bad weather and focusing on the fun and generalising that caravanning is fun.

Recognising that your memories affect your behaviour gives you the choice to consciously make an exception or not, depending on the results you want in your life. The purpose of Worksheet 5-15 is to give you an opportunity to examine a memory – happy or otherwise – and evaluate how it affects the way you delete, distort, and generalise data coming in through your senses. If your memory is a happy one, you may decide that you need to change your behaviour to think of the memory more often, or when you're stressed or sad.

Worksheet 5-15	Deletions, Distortions, and Generalisations Created by My Memory
My memory is:	
How I delete as a result of this memory:	
How I distort as a result of this decision:	
How I generalise as a result of this memory:	
The effect of the memory on my life is:	
I will change my behaviour:	

According to Sir Francis Bacon, 'knowledge is power' and in this chapter we have given you the knowledge you need to change your way of thinking and behaving. The next time you find yourself having difficulty in getting your message across, consider whether your filters and the other person's filters are in collision. Remember, you can afford to be magnanimous in your dealings with others, as well as wield your new-found expertise with strength and elegance.

Part II
Connecting with the World

The 5th Wave   By Rich Tennant

"I sense that you're becoming more defensive and unapproachable lately."

In this part . . .

You're developing your understanding of your personal preferences in terms of how you create your thoughts in pictures, sounds, and feelings. As you communicate more effectively with yourself, you develop your personal rapport building skills. In particular, you end up listening more effectively and adapting your style to connect faster with colleagues, friends, and family.

Chapter 6

Seeing, Hearing, Feeling

*'V*ery little is needed to make a happy life. It is all within yourself in your way of thinking.' So wrote Marcus Aurelius, Roman Emperor, in his *Meditations* back in the year AD 161. Wise words, yet thoughts are sometimes slippery little things to keep in check.

In this chapter you find out the best ways of controlling your thinking and recognising how small changes can make a huge difference for you. By getting to grips with your thoughts you can build amazing relationships with people as well as feel better in yourself.

We also help you get to the bottom of one of the fundamentals of NLP – your *sensory acuity* – how you take in information through your senses and the quality of your awareness about what you are sensing.

Uncovering Your VAK Preferences

NLP, which is about the study of your inner experience, makes the assumption that your experiences are a result of what you see, hear, feel, smell, touch, and taste. NLP suggests that you develop a favourite *representational system*, which is likely to be predominantly *Visual* (seeing), *Auditory* (hearing), or *Kinaesthetic* (feelings, movement, or touching). In NLP this is called your VAK preference.

Are you ready to discover your VAK preference? Begin by taking yourself off to a comfortable space where you can sit back and relax. In this exercise your mission is to become consciously aware of your senses and simply to enjoy the pleasure of connecting with them.

Using Worksheet 6-1, think back to the last time you were in a busy public place. Choose somewhere with action going on – an office reception area, a train or petrol station, a doctor's waiting room, a shopping centre. Call to mind the place as vividly as you can, bringing each of your senses into full play:

✔ **Look** at the images that come to you. See the colours and shapes. Allow the pictures to come alive.

✔ **Listen** to the sounds. Tune into noises you hear, such as voices or music, heavy drilling and banging, as well as the sound of your own voice in your head.

✔ **Feel** what it's like to be back in the place you are visualising. What's the temperature, the textures of seating or surfaces that you are touching? Notice the physical activity. Are you experiencing any emotional connection to that place?

✔ **Sniff** the air to notice the smells.

✔ **Notice** if the place is giving you a particular **taste** in your mouth.

Be mindful of what's special about each of the senses, jotting down your observations in turn in Worksheet 6-1. Next, write down any other important thoughts occurring to you. Do your additional thoughts trigger other memories or make you think about taking a particular action?

Worksheet 6-1	My Sensory Awareness Worksheet
Event recalled:	
Sights:	
Sounds:	
Feelings, touch, and movement:	
Smells:	
Tastes:	
While experiencing the action of the place, note your strongest sense, if any:	
Other sensations you're aware of:	

Armed with this heightened awareness of your senses, you can begin to notice which, if any, sense is easiest for you to access – this is an indicator of your VAK preferences. For example, do you find it easy to notice the sounds but struggle to notice the sights?

The aim of enhancing your sensory awareness is for you to expand your powers of observation and so improve your experiences by flexing your other preferences. You can overcome ways in which you may limit your experience and skills by concentrating on one sense to the exclusion of another. For example, when you play tennis, if you never notice the sound of the ball as it hits your racket, then you may be missing out on the one aspect that can improve your game.

Worksheet 6-2 helps you to take a speedy check on your primary VAK senses to decide how you prefer to access and mentally store information. For each question consider whether you would answer 'never', 'sometimes', 'often', or 'always', and give yourself a score on a scale of 0 to 10 where 0 is 'never' and 10 is 'always'. After you've scored yourself on each question, total your scores for the Visual, Auditory, and Kinaesthetic sections.

Worksheet 6-2   **My VAK Preference Ratings**

Visual

Walking into a room, how aware are you of the colours, the design of furniture, pictures on walls?   _____

How important is it to you to have an attractive appearance so that you look good, paying particular attention to your clothes, hair, and skin care?   _____

If you think of a colleague or acquaintance, how clearly can you picture him?   _____

When planning your work do you like to see it on paper?   _____

Overall visual score: _____

Auditory

How good are you at detecting someone's mood from the tone of his voice?   _____

Do you notice sound levels in your environment?   _____

How often do you like to talk through ideas with other people rather than reading an electronic message or document?   _____

When you are working do you like to read reports, books, and papers?   _____

Overall auditory score   _____

Kinaesthetic

Do you notice the textures and feel of materials and surfaces around you?   _____

How much do you like to get hands-on with practical projects?   _____

How often do you check out your gut feelings on an issue and go with your feelings?   _____

How good are you at recognising your own moods and the moods of others around you?   _____

Overall kinaesthetic score   _____

If you discover that your VAK preferences ratings are low in one or more of the three VAK areas, think of ways of building your awareness in the area in question. For example, if you realise you're not good at judging how someone is feeling from his tone of voice, practise by listening carefully to the person speaking during your next conversation. If your job involves talking for most of your day, think consciously about how you are physically moving – maybe take up dance classes to help your body language.

Use Worksheet 6-3 to set yourself three actions to develop your lower-scoring VAK preferences.

Worksheet 6-3	My Developing Other VAK Preferences Worksheet

My top three actions to develop my less dominant VAK preferences are:

1.

2.

3.

Strengthening your connections through VAK preferences

You may be asking 'why all the fuss about VAK?' The answer is that once you get to grips with your VAK preferences, you have the ability to form bonds with people quickly and communicate effectively.

Your preferred system is echoed in the way you choose words, so language offers clues to VAK preferences. For example:

✔ Having a Visual preference, you are likely to say: 'Let me take a *look.'*

✔ Having an Auditory preference, you are likely to say: 'Let me *talk* it through.'

✔ Having a Kinaesthetic preference, you are likely to say: 'Let me get a *feel* for this.'

Tuning into VAK is the first step to understanding your own and other people's preferences – you *match* preferences. You can become an ace communicator by adapting your language patterns to connect with other people. An NLP presupposition (refer to Chapter 2) is that *the person with the most flexibility can control the outcome of any interaction.*

Although you may have a preference for one sense over another, nothing can stop you accessing your other senses. By trying different angles, you get different – and often pleasantly surprising – results. Albert Einstein said that we don't solve problems with the same thinking that created them. One way of changing your thinking lies in raising your awareness of your different senses and practising other preferences. Try raising your awareness and making amazing breakthroughs in your thinking.

Looking at language preferences

Clues to your preferred representational systems lie in the language you commonly use. Table 6-1 lists some familiar-sounding sensory-specific words and phrases, known in NLP as *predicates*. Take a look through Table 6-1, checking which words look, sound, or feel right for you. As you notice which ones you're most likely to use yourself, you add to your understanding of your own preferences and you also can begin to notice how other people use language.

Table 6-1	VAK Words and Phrases	
Visual	*Auditory*	*Kinaesthetic*
Bright, blank, clear, colour, dim, focus, graphics, illuminate, insight, luminous, perspective, vision	Argue, ask, deaf, discuss, loud, harmony, melody, outspoken, question, resonate, say, shout, shrill, sing, tell, tone, utter, vocal, yell	Cold, bounce, exciting, feel, firm, flow, grasp, movement, pushy, solid, snap, touch, trample, weight
It appears that	The important question we are all asking is...	Driving an organisation
A glimpse of reality	So you say	We reshaped the work
We looked after our interests	I heard it from his own lips	Moving through
This is a new way of seeing the world	That strikes a chord	It hit home
Now look here	Clear as a bell	Get a feel for it
This is clear-cut	Word for word	Get to grips with
Show me what you mean	We're on the same wavelength	Solid as a rock
Tunnel vision	Tune into this	Take it one step at a time
Sight for sore eyes	Music to my ears	Pain in the neck

 Many words in your vocabulary are 'neutral' and therefore don't give you any indication of VAK preferences. Words like 'think' or 'idea' are neutral yet all words may trigger pictures, sounds, or feelings in different people you speak to according to the meaning they make from your words. You may get clues as to another person's preference by seeing how his body language changes as a result or finding predicates in his response, as you see in the later section, 'Detecting Patterns'.

A great way of familiarising yourself with sensory-specific vocabulary is by tuning into the news on the radio and sitting quietly with pen and paper noting down any sensory-specific words and phrases you hear. In this way you build your skills to listen more attentively to anybody you want to communicate better with. Try listening to the news for a week, or any of your favourite radio programmes, or just listen to the TV with your eyes closed (as long as you don't start snoozing!). In Worksheet 6-4 write down the sensory-specific words and phrases you notice, highlighting the words you want to add to your vocabulary to help you to relate to people having different VAK preferences. The next section 'Matching and Moving through VAK Preferences' talks about relating to the whole range of preferences.

Worksheet 6-4	The News Quiz Skillbuilder
VAK Words and Phrases	**My Favourite Words and Phrases**
Visual:	
Auditory:	
Kinaesthetic:	

Use your favourite words and phrases to broaden your VAK range of preferences. During meetings, play with dropping words and phrases relating to all VAK preferences into the conversation to include the preferred style of everyone present. Try using VAK words and phrases when writing e-mails, letters, or documents to vary your approach. Keep your list of words in Worksheet 6-4 in a handy place when making phone calls to help you tune into and connect to people productively.

Notice which representational system comes most naturally to you and feels most comfortable. Then consider how you can widen your VAK vocabulary further to make yourself into a more rounded communicator. Keep referring to and adding to your list of words and phrases so that when you have an important meeting or communication coming up, using your VAK vocabulary will make a real difference for you.

Matching and Moving through VAK Preferences

Do you ever find when talking to friends, colleagues, or loved ones, that sometimes they are listening intently and respond to what you say whereas at other times you feel as if you are talking to a blank wall? Or, in the past that one teacher captured your imagination allowing you to grasp a point immediately, while another teacher, although an expert in his subject, left you feeling he was from another planet when attempting to get his message across? What's going on here?

NLP places great store on the principles of *pacing* and *leading*, meaning you need to pace somebody in his way of behaving before you can lead him to what you want him to hear and respond to. *Pacing* involves paying keen attention not just to what people are saying but to how they are expressing their thoughts through their language patterns, gestures, and tone of voice.

One great way of pacing people is through observing their predominant representational system and feeding back your response using the same system. This pacing is a form of matching; you can read more about matching in Chapter 7 as you find ways of developing your rapport skills.

Pacing through matching is like using the same computer programs as the person you are communicating with. Perhaps you come from a financial background and like to have documents in a spreadsheet format, but your colleague comes from a literary background and prefers word-processed documents. If you want to connect with your colleague quickly, you send information in word-processed documents initially. You need to pace where he is before you can lead him onto your preference for spreadsheets.

After seeing how to match one VAK preference, you can try *mismatching* by looking at the difference when you bring language into play from the other VAK preferences.

When you mismatch by shifting your words to a different representational system, you can stay in agreement with the person you're speaking too and yet start to politely loosen the connection with him. This can be helpful when you want to end a conversation without appearing rude, or if you simply want to test out whether you've correctly guessed his VAK preference.

For example, in the statement, 'The weather looks bright and sunny', notice the visual words of *looks, bright and sunny*. A matching visual sentence is: 'When I look outside I can see that it's clear' (visual).

By contrast, a mismatching statement is: 'It feels like it'*s too hot to breathe*' (kinaesthetic–moving or feeling).

A second mismatch is: 'Everyone's *talking about* the sunshine. Even the bees are *humming* happily' (auditory).

Worksheet 6-5 gives you an opportunity to practise matching and mismatching preferences. The exercise heightens your flexibility in the different ways of using VAK language and widens your scope for communicating effectively.

Worksheet 6-5　　　　Matching and Mismatching Language

Auditory Example: It sounds as if we've talked about all the key points.

Matching statement:

Mismatch statement 1:

Mismatch statement 2:

Kinaesthetic Example: I can't get a grip on how the system crashed again.

Matching statement:

Mismatch statement 1:

Mismatch statement 2:

(continued)

Worksheet 6-5 *(continued)*

Visual Example: My perspective on this has changed as more evidence has come to light.

Matching statement:

Mismatch statement 1:

Mismatch statement 2:

Desensitising VAK

As you get more expert in applying NLP, you come to realise that thinking in terms of your senses has many valuable applications. Once you discover how to play with images, sounds, and feelings you can raise your problem-solving ability, change your behaviour, improve your relationships, and make choices about how you think in every area of your life.

For some years Gina has been suffering from a mild form of tinnitus, a medical condition that results in a constant ringing or other noises in the ear. The condition gives Gina a lot of restless nights. Like most sufferers Gina has learnt strategies for coping with tinnitus but no obvious medical cure exists. When Kate asked Gina to describe what tinnitus is like for her, she said: 'It's worse at night when it's *quiet* or at times when there's a lot of *noise* around me. It's best when I *turn a blind eye* to it or *focus on doing* something else. Then I *feel* okay.' (Gina's predicates indicating VAK preferences are in italics.)

Notice from the predicates Gina adopts how she switches between the representational systems (to remind yourself what predicates are, see the earlier section 'Looking at language preferences'). She talks about the worst experience of the tinnitus in Auditory words (quiet, noise), which is appropriate for a hearing condition. Then on better days, Gina switches into Visual (blind, eye, focus) and Kinaesthetic language (do, feel). Clues as to how she can ease her symptoms are contained within the language she is using. In fact, as Gina becomes aware of her natural strategy of shifting to the visual field, she develops more visual activities to desensitise herself to the unpleasant ringing noises.

For now, play at switching between the three main representational systems to dissociate or distance yourself from a problem. When you've acknowledged that a problem exists, dissociation is valuable in NLP to remove the painful intensity of a problem and get a better sense of balance quickly when overwhelmed. There's no value in dwelling too hard or long on the painful aspects of it and reinforcing the negative experience.

To benefit from VAK desensitising, think about a problem you're having. It may be a recurring health problem like Gina's, a minor irritation, or an area in your life where you are stuck. You then describe what is happening for you, noticing whether you are experiencing the problem in a predominantly Visual, Auditory, or Kinaesthetic way. You then look to the preference you used the least to highlight possible solutions without using the other, more dominant senses. This can help enable you to find new perspectives that may not have occurred to you before.

In Worksheet 6-6 you can follow Anna's solution to desensitising her problem. At work she found herself getting into a panic whenever her boss asked her to put her ideas onto paper. Every time she heard his voice asking her to put ideas into writing at work, she got hot and flustered and unable to write or type.

Worksheet 6-6	**Anna's VAK Desensitiser**

The problem situation: Documenting ideas at work

Which representational system triggers the problem?

Auditory: The sound of Anna's boss's voice and hearing the request triggers the negative feelings, setting off the kinaesthetic response of feeling hot and flustered and being unable to use her fingers to type or write.

The least used representational system:

Visual: There's no sense of any strong visual images here.

Anna's three possible solutions in the least used representational system of Visual:

1. Start by drawing a diagram or looking for pictures that illustrate the message.

2. Take myself to a quiet space, put sticky notes on the flip chart, and colour-code the notes to get my ideas in order.

3. Invent cartoon characters with amusing faces and draw the story as a cartoon strip.

Now use Worksheet 6-7 to come up with possible desensitising solutions to your own problem.

Worksheet 6-7	**My VAK Desensitiser**

The problem situation:

Which representational system triggers the problem?

The least used representational system:

Three possible solutions in the least used representational system:

1.

2.

3.

Turning Up the Passion

Have you ever observed how something interesting happens to the language people use when they get passionate about a subject and are fired up on all cylinders? The person's language automatically becomes richer, and brimming over with those wonderful sensory-specific words – such as action-packed verbs and vivid adjectives – known in NLP as *predicates*.

Our favourite example is Martin Luther King's famous 'I have a dream' speech, which he delivered on the steps of the Lincoln Memorial in Washington DC on 28 August 1963. Every paragraph boasts VAK predicates. The speech contains phrases such as: 'great *beacon light* of hope to millions of Negro slaves, who had been *seared in the flames of withering* injustice' and 'when we allow freedom *ring*, when we let it *ring* from every village and every hamlet, from every state and every city.'

The next time you hear a speech or see one reported in the newspaper, listen or look carefully at the language. Decide for yourself whether having lots of predicates makes the speech more convincing.

Jonathan is passionate about tropical plants. Over the years, he has designed and planted many stunning gardens for his clients. Recently, Jonathan took on the challenge of managing the planting of a show garden for one of the UK's most prestigious horticultural shows. For many year he'd refused invitations to get involved with such events as he felt it would be incredibly stressful to have to grow and nurture hundreds of plants to display in peak condition at show time. This time around, Jonathan was surprised at the energy he was gaining from the experience, finding himself on an adrenaline 'high'. 'It was as if I was taking some kind of illegal substance!' he said. 'All my senses were raised to a completely different level of awareness after three days of planting and *watching* the other gardens take *shape*. The more I *looked at* the gardens, the *brighter the colours and shapes* of the shrubs and trees became, I was entirely *tuned into all the noise and sounds* of running water, and the *scent* of the roses was *intoxicating*. As I *touched every pebble I felt* amazingly *light and excited* in my body. Yes, I would do it all over again, I'm *hooked* now and the show is *fixed firmly* in my memory . . . the medal *tasted sweet*.'

When you want to get a message across so that people feel motivated and inspired by what you are saying:

1. **Draft a few introductory sentences for your speech.**

   Your first effort is likely to include some predicates and some neutral language that isn't sensory-specific.

2. **Rewrite the introductory paragraph using a stronger mix of predicates, making sure you cover at least visual, auditory, and kinaesthetic words.**

   By adding words reflecting taste and smell, so much the better.

3. **Write and develop the rest of your speech using what you have found out about VAK language so that the speech is engaging.**

Worksheet 6-8 gives you a flavour of how writing a predicate-laden introduction works.

Mel wants to encourage her colleagues to recycle more waste in the office. Worksheet 6-8 shows you how she revised her opening remarks to include more VAK predicates. (The predicates are italicised in both drafts, and notice how few predicates are included in the first draft where most of the vocabulary is neutral).

Worksheet 6-8	Mel's Articulating Your Passion Worksheet
First draft:	My subject today is about *recycling* in the office. The main reason I'm passionate about *recycling* is that I'm fearful that we are *destroying* the planet for future generations and I believe that we have a real responsibility to *look* after our planet. Recycling is very important so that we don't waste trees and *spend* precious fuel on waste collection lorries. There's a benefit to everyone too if we *clean up* our empty cans and bottles.
Rewrite with predicates:	Let's *look* today at *recycling* in the office. Cut the *talk* and *get going* to support the *move* to *recycling*. Once we *see* what's happening and *get a handle* on it, we can *let go of fears* and *stop destroying* the planet for future generations and *take* a real responsibility to *look* after it. *Cutting down* trees and *burning up* precious fuel on waste collection lorries must *stop*. *Picture* the benefits to everyone too if we *clean up* our empty cans after *eating and drinking*. It will even *smell fresher* round here. Does that *sound clear* so far?

Worksheet 6-9 offers you the chance to write your own message, and to strengthen it by using predicates.

Worksheet 6-9	My Articulating Your Passion Worksheet
First draft:	
Rewrite with predicates:	

Detecting Patterns

In *Neuro-linguistic Programming For Dummies*, we introduce you to the NLP concept of *eye accessing cues,* the idea that you move your eyes according to which representational system you're accessing. Paying attention to eye movement gives you clues as to whether a person is thinking in terms of images, sounds, or feelings and movement. (Remember that *kinaesthetic* refers to both emotional experiences and movement.)

Figure 6-1 is drawn as if you are looking at someone else's face and shows how you can see the person's eyes move in response to a question from you. (This is what you'd generally see for a right-handed person and may be reversed if the person is left-handed.) If you ask the person to recall a favourite friend, you can expect the person's eyes to move up and to his left showing that he is thinking visually and bringing to mind a picture of his friend. If the person's eyes move down and to his left, you can expect that the person is talking to himself about your question, having his own internal auditory dialogue.

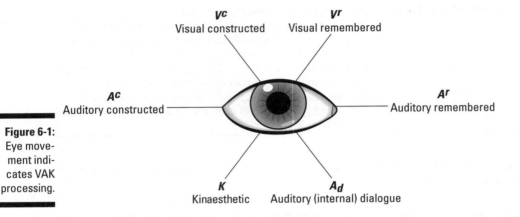

Figure 6-1:
Eye move-
ment indi-
cates VAK
processing.

You can keep up the detective work by examining which representational system some-one is using. Take in the person from head to toe, noticing how his eyes are moving, the tone and tempo of his voice, the style of breathing and general posture – by using the accessing cues.

Table 6-2 is a summary chart of accessing cues. The table lays out the different patterns associated with each representational system.

Paying attention to the accessing cues gives you more non-verbal information about people, adding to what you can detect from their spoken words.

Table 6-2	Summary of Accessing Cues		
VAK Representational System	*Eyes*	*Voice*	*Body and Breathing*
Visual	Looking up to the right and left.	Rapid, high, and clear.	Tense, upright posture. Shallow breathing in the top part of the chest.
Auditory	In the middle, looking side to side.	Looking down and to the left indicates the person is engaged in an internal dialogue.	Medium-paced and often rhythmic and varied in tone and pitch. Head tilts to the side in a 'telephone position'. Even breathing from mid-chest cavity.
Kinaesthetic	Looking down – usually to the right.	Often slow, soft, and deep, with frequent pauses.	Tendency to slumped posture. Deeper breathing from the abdomen.

Looking at your assistant Fenella, you notice that her eyes stay at mid-line, her voice has lots of variety and rhythm, and she tilts her head to the side, so you decide that she most likely has an auditory preference.

Use Worksheet 6-10 to track cues of the people you mix with frequently, focusing on people whose preferences it would be helpful to know. Don't be put off if you are finding it hard to place people in one category or another. Simply use the cues as a way of paying much closer attention to your friends and family. At the same time you're sharpening your listening skills even more finely than before.

Worksheet 6-10		My Watching People Worksheet		
Name	*Eyes*	*Voice*	*Body and Breathing*	*VAK Preferences*

After gathering data about your friends and family, consider how you can interact differently with them. If you realise that one person has a marked preference for a particular representational system, try communicating with him using that style of language.

People with a Visual preference need to see the pictures. Use drawings, colours, and shapes to relate to them. Having an Auditory preference means people need to talk things through until they can hear the message, so you need to listen attentively. People with a Kinaesthetic preference need to check in with their feelings and may have a preference for physical activity. In each case, practise using the favourite words and phrases you listed in Worksheet 6-4 'The News Quiz Skillbuilder'.

In Worksheet 6-11 make a communication plan of how you can adapt your way of interacting with key people in your everyday life based on the information you collected in worksheet 6-10. Choose a mixture of people who have different VAK preferences.

For example, for your auditory assistant Fenella, you may decide that above all she likes talking things through and making lots of notes. Now you plan to give Fenella more time to have a chat at the start of the day, letting her go away with her notes. No wonder she doesn't like following maps!

Worksheet 6-11	My Communication Planner
Name	*Communication Ideas*

Chapter 7

Developing Rapport

· ·

In This Chapter

▶ Sorting out with whom you want rapport

▶ Building rapport quickly

▶ Adapting your pace to get in tune with other people

▶ Closing down conversations politely

▶ Seeing another point of view

· ·

*Y*ou know what it's like when you have rapport with someone – the conversation flows easily and you know by just looking at one another that you're both on the same wavelength. Without any trouble you pick up the connection where you last left off. You enjoy the feeling that all is well. Now, contrast this feeling of rapport with what it's like when you find yourself struggling to communicate with someone, when the exchange is laboured and every interaction is hard work. How tough is that?

Gaining rapport with people is a fundamental life skill, the foundation for getting what you want. Think about rapport as a dance between two or more people who need to connect as partners for a period of time – whether that's for minutes, hours, or a whole lifetime. There needs to be a strong flow of energy joining you together. In this chapter, we look at the key people with whom you need to gain rapport, and how you can build rapport quickly, proactively, and with integrity.

Rapport is a core pillar of NLP, together with the other three pillars of sensory acuity, outcome thinking, and behavioural flexibility.

Looking at Your Key People

A *relationship map* is a visual representation of the key people you connect with. Start by drawing a circle and putting your name in the centre, then draw branches from the centre to represent key groups of people in your life – family, friends, work colleagues, and people you mix with for different activities. You may want to set up subgroups within each group depending on where you are focusing your attention right now.

At some time or another, you need rapport with all of the individuals on your map if you are to communicate effectively with them. Notice which people or groups you interact with easily and which ones you are struggling with. Highlight any relationships you'd like to work on in building greater rapport.

An example of a simple key-relationship map is shown in Worksheet 7-1.

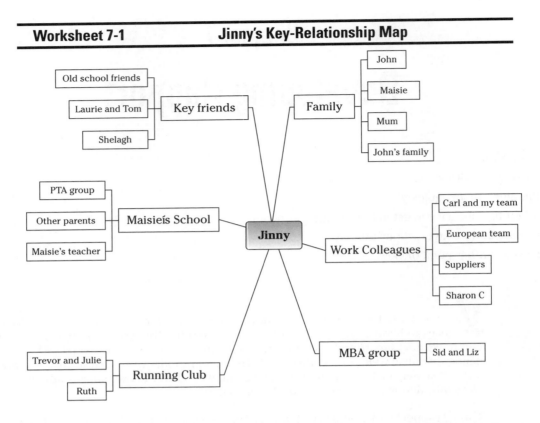

Worksheet 7-1 — **Jinny's Key-Relationship Map**

Now develop your own key-relationship map in Worksheet 7-2. You may choose to do one purely for your social life, or for your work, or you may like to link this key-relationship map to your Wheel of Life from Chapter 3, making sure you map people from all areas of your life. One of the benefits of mapping out your network visually is that you can see at a glance where you are putting all your time and energy.

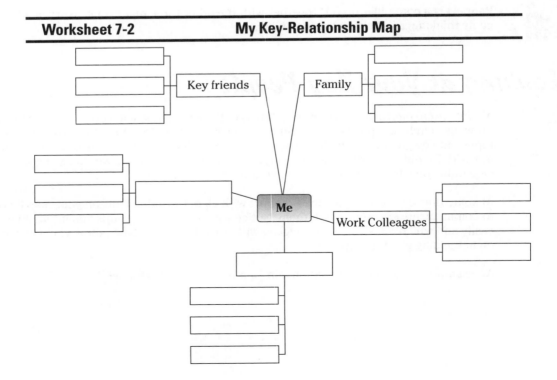

Worksheet 7-2 — **My Key-Relationship Map**

Matching and Mirroring

Have you noticed that when people get on well together they tend to move in unison? As one person leans forward, so does the other; they make similar gestures at the same speed and rhythm. This dance of rapport in which people naturally move in step with each other is called *matching and mirroring*, each person a reflection of the other. When you deliberately match and mirror another person, you have the chance to build rapport with that person quickly. Matching and mirroring is a useful skill when you're meeting and starting to get to know someone for the first time.

Matching is not at all the same as copying every detail of someone's voice and gestures. If you found yourself mimicking someone, you would certainly not be developing rapport; the person is more likely to feel she's being mocked.

Choose one or two essential characteristics of that person. For example, if she has a distinctive and repetitive movement such as scratching her head or taking a sharp intake of breath before she speaks, try making a movement with your hands, such as a soft tap, at the same time and in rhythm with her. This more subtle, indirect form of matching is called *cross-over mirroring*.

First hone your observation skills. Try this experiment to spot matching and mirroring in action between people who most likely have never heard of NLP: Go to a busy café, bar, or restaurant and select a couple of people who are sitting or standing together and look as if they have created rapport with each other. Look at the following four aspects of their non-verbal behaviour and how they naturally match and mirror each other in different ways. (You'll need to do this carefully so they don't think you're a private detective or just weird!)

- ✔ **Voices:** Listen to the quality of sound (tonality) and speed of speech. Is it loud or soft, fast or slow?

- ✔ **Breathing:** Watch the rate at which they breathe. Is it quiet or noisy, fast or slow? Pay attention to neck, shoulders, and torso and look for the fine movements indicating where they are breathing from. (If you're a man, beware of focusing on a woman's chest to watch her breathing – your attention may be misconstrued! Focus on the shoulders instead.)

- ✔ **Movement and energy levels:** Do they seem to have similar levels of 'bounciness' or 'stillness'? Would you describe them as fast-moving and high-energy or lower-energy people?

- ✔ **Body language:** Observe their eye contact and their postures and gestures. What similarities do you notice in their mannerisms? Do they have any distinctive gestures?

Be aware of each of these four categories and which of these you find easier and harder to identify. Then, in future, you can refine your observation skills with people that you want to match.

Next time you go up to the service counter in a shop or coffee bar, practise establishing rapport with the sales assistant by matching these four criteria.

Worksheet 7-3 shows Liz's matching and mirroring record after observing some of her new team recruits at work.

Worksheet 7-3	Liz's Matching and Mirroring Observations			
Name	**Voice**	**Breathing**	**Movement and Energy**	**Postures and Gestures**
Anna	Melodic, loud, and very fast.	Breathes from upper chest and sounds very breathy.	Fast and light movements – dances around very energetically.	Creases up face around eyes tensely when concentrating on a conversation.
James	Starts a sentence strongly and then voice trails off.	Breathes deeply from abdomen.	Slow moving. Sits steadily without moving much.	Slight face twitch when nervous. Dangles his arms and fidgets, especially when talking to a group.
Kevin	Gruff, clipped speech. Barks instructions.	Lot of tension in his breathing. Inhales noisily.	Likes to be up on his feet in meetings and on the phone.	Face goes red easily. Points with finger when talking to the clients.

Identify key people from your earlier Worksheet 7-2 with whom you'd like to have greater rapport. For each person take every opportunity to notice how they sound, look, use their bodies, and their energy levels. Capture your observations in Worksheet 7-4.

Worksheet 7-4	My Matching and Mirroring Observations			
Name	**Voice**	**Breathing**	**Movement and Energy**	**Postures and Gestures**

Practising your powers of observation allows you to gauge the normal behaviour of those people you spend time with and helps you notice quickly when something has changed. It also means that if you need rapport instantly you can match or mirror an aspect of their mannerisms.

Train yourself to notice how others breathe and be aware of your own breathing at the same time. Breathing affects your whole body physiology, which in turn affects your emotional state. Your emotional state determines your ultimate performance in matching and mirroring.

Pacing and Leading

Pacing is a technique that reminds you to listen attentively to what's going on for another person by patiently acknowledging that person. Only then can you *lead* someone else in the direction you'd like to take her and get your message across. Think of pacing as if you were trying to jump on a moving train – you need to run alongside it and gather speed before making the jump (but please don't even attempt it!).

Have you ever seen a toddler lying on the floor having a tantrum, banging and yelling and demonstrating the power of her lungs for all to witness? Or experienced a moody teenager or grumpy grown-up who is fixed on her own needs and oblivious to yours? Being able to pace, pace, and pace for even longer than you want to enables you to finally lead that person.

Mastering the NLP skill of pacing and leading takes you to a deeper level of listening as a way of building bridges between people who come from different communication directions, each with their unique styles and agendas.

Madeline serves as the Finance Director on the board of a multinational manufacturing company and is justifiably proud of her appointment, breaking through the notorious 'glass ceiling' as the first and only female member on that executive board. At her first few board meetings she had many bright ideas for change. However, she quickly became aware that her 'light bulb' moments were not being listened to when she first offered them. Instead, later in the meeting, when another member of the board offered the very same idea that she had come up with earlier, it was heralded as a brilliant solution. Madeline found this behaviour increasingly frustrating, wondering if her appointment was as the token female and whether she was hitting a wall of prejudice. She could have waded in and complained 'unfair, unfair' to her colleagues. Instead, by working with her coach, Madeline realised that she had no evidence of gender prejudice, she merely had a different style of working and that this particular group needed time to consider options before making a decision. Madeline is naturally a quick and decisive thinker, analysing a problem and coming up with a clear solution very fast. While this ability generally favours her, it doesn't work with this particular group of people. She realises she needs to pace her colleagues' style of debate and decision-making. So when she sees the breakthrough idea, she deliberately holds back on voicing her great suggestion until the group is ready to listen. By giving the men more processing time to think and debate several ideas, she chooses her ideal moment to place her ideas on the table. In this way Madeline leads her colleagues to some innovative programmes that are listened to and then acted upon.

Like Madeline in this example, you've probably had times when you've either fallen out with someone or received really negative feedback about how you connected with an individual or group. Most likely, you didn't pace and lead the other person very competently. The following exercise gives you a chance to learn from a bad experience and move on in order to improve your pacing and leading skills, and so get better at rapport.

1. Think back to a time when you lost rapport with someone unintentionally. Consider what that situation was like for you. How did you feel or act as a result of not pacing and leading that person.

2. What other problems did it cause for you? Maybe you wasted lots of energy going over and over in your head what went wrong or maybe an important relationship got damaged?

3. How specifically did you fail to pace and lead the other person? Think about her style and needs here. How was your style and need different from hers?

4. If you were going into a similar situation again, what would you like that to look like and feel like? Write down what rapport might sound like.

5. How can you pace this other person in the future? Do you need to slow or quicken up your pace? Would it help to be armed with more facts or cut the details and go straight to the bigger picture?

6. Do any other ideas occur to you? For example, now you know more about this situation, is there anywhere else that you can pace and lead people even better?

Lisa and her sister Angela spent a year finding it very difficult to be in each other's company due to an earlier misunderstanding where neither of them had practised pacing and leading. Take a look at Lisa's pacing and leading experience in Worksheet 7-5 before recording your own example in Worksheet 7-6.

Worksheet 7-5	Lisa's Pacing and Leading Experience
Incident you're examining and the name of person/group involved.	*My sister Angela – we fell out when I broke up with my boyfriend, Richard, and she insisted on inviting him to her flat-warming party.*
What was that like for you?	*I felt cross and frustrated that I couldn't get through to her.*
What other problems did the incident cause for you?	*It made things difficult for my parents and I dreaded any big family gatherings too. Relatives felt very uncomfortable if they wanted to invite Angela and me to their homes. We both missed out on lots of fun that we could have had for several months.*
How did you fail to pace and lead?	*I was so fixed on my own view that I didn't really listen to her point of view for long enough. I went into 'transmit' mode, telling her exactly what I thought and not giving her enough space or time to give her side of the story.*
If you were going into that situation again, how would you like it to be?	*I'd like to see a two-way dialogue between two adults who care deeply about each other.*
How can you pace this other person in the future?	*I'll be calmer when I feel a sense of frustration and give her plenty of space to air her views. I will go in with an open mind and the intention of listening to everything she wants to say until she has finished. I'll ask permission to give my side of the story before I give it.*
Do any other ideas occur to you as a result of this exercise?	*I can practise on my sister and then it would help me to get on better with my new boyfriend, Ben, as well. I can think of various friends who I don't pace well enough. This is all about being a better listener. I have a tendency to be headstrong.*

In Worksheet 7-6 you step back to the past when someone had a completely different agenda and style to you, to a time when you know full well that you struggled to get rapport and you did not manage to pace and lead the other person. Perhaps you even fell out, big time. The situation can be a really tough one that still upsets you or a simple misunderstanding and miscommunication that you would prefer to avoid in future and so get on the right track faster. You may like to choose a member of your family, a work colleague, or perhaps someone you met through your sports club, charity, or community activity. The exercise works with an individual as well as with a group of people.

Worksheet 7-6	**My Pacing and Leading Experience**
Incident you're examining and the name of person/group involved.	
What was that like for you?	
What other problems did the incident cause for you?	
How did you fail to pace and lead?	
If you were going into that situation again, how would you like it to be?	
How can you pace this other person in the future?	
Do any other ideas occur to you as a result of this exercise?	

Breaking Rapport

Rapport's all very well, yet what about the times when you have such great rapport that you chat all morning and get nothing done at all? At other times you're busy and it's not convenient to talk, so you need to break rapport. Or maybe you're so talented at building rapport that you attract all kinds of people who want to connect with you, and you don't want to connect with them!

In this section, we look at deliberately breaking rapport while being respectful to the other person. The methods here work well face to face or remotely.

Here's a party game approach to matching and mismatching. You just need a friendly playmate.

1. **Find a partner and sit facing each other.**

2. **Start up a conversation about something harmless that you can agree on.**

3. **Match and mirror the other person's body language.**

4. **Now as you carry on the conversation, begin to change your gestures and the tone of your voice to be very different from hers.**

For example, make your voice very loud or soft. Stand up when she's seated. But at the same time, continue to agree with what she's saying.

You immediately see how difficult being in agreement with someone is when the tone of your voice and your gestures do not match. So there you have it.

Bob is a master at elegantly disconnecting from people he doesn't want to spend time with. Yet once he got caught out by inviting some people from his sports club over for a drink, only to discover they had arrived with the intention of doing business, planning to sell Bob a quick revenue-earning wheeze that had no interest at all for him. Just as they were getting into their sales talk, Bob stood up and said with a smile. 'I can see that these things really appeal to some people and definitely not to others. I'm one of the latter.' Taking Bob's lead, the guys closed their sales presentation and agreed to have a beer instead.

To start disconnecting with people you want to spend less time with, note the person who slips through the gaps and wastes your time. Are you being chatted up by a person who doesn't interest you at all, or is a company representative trying to sell you goods or services and you find it hard to say 'no thank you' and move on? Perhaps you find it very hard to say 'no' to the requests of someone at work? Become aware of anything that person does or says that tugs at you to stay connected. Are any of your actions actually attracting these people to you? Maybe you're feeling sorry for them and willing to listen when nobody else will? Are you being too kind or pleasant for your own good?

Think what you can say and do that allows the person to depart gracefully with a clear message, without inflicting a personal attack on her identity. This is definitely the time to mismatch another person's voice and gestures rather than match and stay connected. For example, can you acknowledge that you think it's admirable that she's working hard to earn her living/find a date even though you don't fancy doing what she wants to do? Aim to be honest rather than making untruthful and lame excuses. Remember that you don't need to give full justification or detailed explanations of your own views and get drawn into a lengthy debate.

Get into the habit of stating your own needs clearly. Practise phrases and sentences that allow you to disconnect from people quickly, such as:

✔ 'Thank you for your interest. I'm saving all my spare cash so I won't be buying for the foreseeable future.'

✔ 'I need to preserve family time, so I won't be able to accept your invitation.'

✔ 'I have a deadline to meet, so I'll call you when I'm free.'

You may also like to:

✔ Set an expectation at the start of a meeting or call as to how much time you have so it's easy to conclude with a polite, 'Well, that's all we have time for today.'

✔ Give an advance warning when time is running out – 'OK, so we need be completing in five minutes – how would you like to use this time?'

✔ Politely look at your watch and look sad as you say: 'Gosh, why is it that time flies when we are having fun?'

✔ Change your tone of voice: 'Thank you. It's been great to talk/see you.'

✔ Make a physical move, stand up or move towards a door, mismatching the other person slowly at first and then gaining pace.

✔ Get someone else to arrive or telephone to break the connection.

Body language and tone of voice can convey much more than the words themselves. On average, 93 per cent of your communication is non-verbal. Make sure that your body language gives the same message of polite disinterest to reinforce your words.

Think about 'breaking rapport' like switching off a light or unplugging an electrical appliance when not in use, knowing that you can reconnect whenever you need to.

As a friendly nurse in a busy rural medical practice, Sarah has a loyal following of people in the community who always choose to make their appointments on the days that she's working. Her 15-minute appointments easily stretch to 30 minutes and she feels she's always running late and in catch-up mode. Her problem? She's great at building rapport with people, yet hates to break it. She invites patients to 'just pop back and see me next week' even when no real clinical justification exists for the follow-up appointment.

Sometimes you can more easily see what other people should be doing rather than what you need to do yourself. Imagine that you're Sarah's manager, coach, or friend and come up with ways Sarah can break rapport with her patients while still being professional and respectful to them. Think about how Sarah can use the physical space, manage her time, or ask other people to help her. What changes can she make in what she says, does, and how she looks at her patients? Worksheet 7-7 starts with three ideas to kick-start your thinking.

Keep going until you've finished racking your brain. Then leave the exercise for a while, maybe overnight, and come back to it fresh with one or two more ideas.

Worksheet 7-7	**Ways Sarah Can Break Rapport in Face-to-Face Situations**
Say 'We have fifteen minutes today' at the beginning of the appointment.	
Break eye contact and focus on making notes on the computer screen when she needs to complete the session.	
Ask the practice manager if she can arrange a patient charity coffee morning as a separate social occasion when patients and staff can chat.	

One of the most decisive ways of breaking rapport (mismatching someone) is by turning your back on the person. So be very careful of mistakenly doing this. It could be a way of ruining the most promising date you've ever had.

When you've finished Worksheet 7-7, consider for a moment what you can take from Sarah's situation and apply it to your own. Which of the ideas in Worksheet 7-7 might work for you at times when you're busy? Do you, for example, have a friend or client who takes up too much of your time, cutting into your leisure time?

Develop the skill of gently disconnecting; going slowly at first and then ramping it up. When you're too abrupt, you can lose friends and reduce your ability to influence with integrity. Body language can be a subtle way of doing this. If you were sitting forward with interest, gradually move back in your chair or place your glasses on your head. Stretch or stand up. Similarly with your voice, quicken the speed or raise the volume above that of the other person if she's speaking fairly quietly, or gradually go silent if she's noisy and animated.

You can block annoying intrusions on your time, space, and energy in a number of ways while being respectful to your fellows. Worksheet 7-8 helps you to track how you are most vulnerable to annoying callers – both strangers and people you know – and the ways in which you can disconnect from them.

Worksheet 7-8	My Elegant Disconnect
Who is the person most likely to catch me out; the one I don't want to spend time with at the moment?	
Is there anything that I do and say that attracts this person to me?	
What specifically does this person persist in that I find it hardest to disconnect from?	
What are some useful phrases I can say in this situation?	
How can I use my body language and voice tonality to convey the right disconnect signals?	

Stepping into the Other Person's Shoes

In our younger days when we worked together at Hewlett-Packard, we were immersed in a culture that Bill Hewlett and Dave Packard established 50 years ago that advised (in Dave's words) to: 'Think first of the other fellow. This is *the* foundation – the first requisite – for getting along with others. And it is the one truly difficult accomplishment you must make. Gaining this, the rest will be a breeze.'

Imagine for a moment that you need to negotiate a contract or arrangement with another person. Or, perhaps your partner has an idea for decorating a room and you have quite a different picture of what you want. In such a case, you find yourself working with someone who has quite a different approach to you. There are many times in everyday situations where adopting an alternative perspective is useful. However, if you can consider only two positions, you are faced with a dilemma – to take your view or the other person's? To open up even greater choices and options, the NLP approach is to explore the situation from many different perceptual positions – maybe three, four, or more positions. When you do so, you start to separate your perspective from an emotional attachment to any one position and are able to observe a situation much more objectively.

In the following mental rehearsal exercise think of someone who you'd like greater rapport with. This person will not be here with you physically, you just imagine her. If necessary go back to Worksheet 7-2 to remind yourself of your important relationships. Or perhaps someone else has proved important to you since you started reading this chapter. Capture your observations in Worksheet 7-9.

Begin the exercise by laying out three pieces of paper on the floor to form a triangular shape, or position three chairs for you to sit on. The paper or chairs represent the three different perceptual positions for you to step into in the following sequence. It's important that you physically move your body to a different space as you adopt each position.

When you are asked to 'break state' in this exercise, you can do this by moving physically – shaking your body gently or by thinking of something quite different, like where you went on your last holiday or what colour shirt you last ironed!

1. **In the first position, simply be yourself and look (in your imagination) at the person in the second position with whom you'd like greater rapport.**

   Notice what you're thinking and experiencing as you imagine looking at that person who is looking at you. For example, you may be feeling nervous, excited, or curious as to what is going on for the person you are looking at.

2. **Capture your thoughts in Worksheet 7-9. Then shake out of that (NLP calls this** *breaking state***) and step or sit into the second position.**

3. **In the second position, imagine being the other person and look (in your imagination) back at yourself from this perspective.**

   Notice what you are thinking and experiencing as you imagine being the other person who is looking at you. For example, as the other person you may also be feeling nervous, excited, or curious as to what is going on for the you in the first position that you are looking at.

4. **Capture your thoughts in the worksheet. Shake out of that and step or sit into the third position.**

5. **In the third position, imagine being an impartial observer.**

   From this perspective look (in your imagination) back at yourself and the other person and notice what you are thinking and experiencing as you imagine what may be going on for these two people.

   For example, as the observer, you may gain insights about the things that both people have in common and come up with ideas as to how they can bring their differences closer together.

6. **Go back to the first position.** Taking with you the insights you've gained from stepping through the different positions, ask yourself: 'How is this different now?'

7. **Plan action.** The most important stage is to take action. Ask yourself: 'What is the first practical step that I need to take?' This is so important that you have Worksheet 7-10 to record your key insights and make a commitment to the next step.

Worksheet 7-9	Stepping into the Other Person's Shoes
Position	**Observations from this position. What am I experiencing, thinking, and feeling?**
First position	
Second position	
Third position	
First position (for second time)	

Use Worksheet 7-10 to record your most important insights and how you're going to put those insights to use.

Worksheet 7-10	My Key Insights and Action Steps
What key insights have I gained from stepping through the different positions?	
How are things different now?	
What ideas have I gained?	
What has changed for me?	
What is the first step?	

Chapter 8

Influencing with Metaprograms

· ·

In This Chapter

▶ Identifying metaprograms

▶ Looking at workable combinations

▶ Deepening rapport by matching metaprograms

· ·

*N*ight and day, you're bombarded with messages demanding your attention – the detail in the view from your window, the roaring of tyres on the tarmac, background noises in your office, the rustling of your clothes. You cope with this deluge of information by filtering out a lot of the messages you're receiving. In NLP terms, one of these filters is *metaprograms*.

Your metaprograms affect your behaviour in that they're one of the means that help you decide what you pay attention to and how you behave in response to the information you receive through your senses. For example, one of the metaprograms we introduce in this chapter is the *primary interest filter metaprogram* that directs whether you pay attention to people, places, things, activities, or information. If you have a preference for people and are walking down the street with someone who has a high need for information, you might comment on a person's coat, the way he walks, or whatever strikes you about him. The person with you, however, may walk over to windows to study the products being advertised and comment on the information that he sees.

Everyone is different. Most of you play more than one role in your daily lives. Likewise you have different metaprograms for each role you play. As a parent, you find yourself running a set of metaprograms that are different from those you run as a lover, which are different again from those you're operating as a boss, or a colleague.

To interact and communicate successfully with people, whatever the context, you need to establish rapport, be on the same wavelength. In this chapter we show you how metaprograms can help you to get across what you're communicating in a way the other person can readily interpret and can then respond to.

Metaprograms operate on a sliding scale, and you may be farther along the scale according to your circumstances. Keep in mind that you, as well as the people you're communicating with, operate under different metaprograms to different degrees in different situations. Get into the habit of asking questions and listening closely to discover the other person's metaprograms in a given setting.

Listening for Metaprograms and Discovering Filters

In this section we give you a general overview of the NLP metaprograms and suggest the type of questions you can ask to discover other peoples' metaprograms. We don't go in for long-winded discussions about the metaprograms because you get to know far more about them by practising with the worksheets.

Start the ball rolling by listening for your own metaprograms and making a few notes. The great thing is, because you know how you tick and have experience of your feelings, you can safely use your feelings to support your ideas.

You can become even more skilled in using metaprograms by thinking beyond the examples in the exercises and working out where you can make the best use of what you're uncovering. For example: in your office, at home with your partner, your parents, your adorable teenagers; or even your four-footed friends, unless you're one of those people who's owned by a dog or a cat with absolutely no personality!

Are you one of those people who's into gadgets but has to make a real effort when talking to people? Or when asked about your holiday, can you tell someone about the architecture down to the finest detail but not remember the ambience of a restaurant at which you had dinner? The way you experience your world depends on your *metaprograms*, which are one of several filters you use to sift incoming information and also outgoing information, such as describing an experience, giving a presentation, or writing about something. The 'gadget person' is likely to have a metaprogram that filters more for things than people, and the person who talked about the architecture may notice the lie of the land because he has a metaprogram that notices places more than people. Some people can focus on the minutest detail of a task but can't see the big picture because they have a sieve that lets in the plankton but keeps out anything bigger.

You probably already have an idea of how your metaprograms work, but in this section we give you an overview. We take four metaprograms (shown in the following table) and show you in detail how you can learn to recognise someone else's tendencies and then use those tendencies to improve your communication skills with that person.

The Direction Filter	Toward to Away
Chunk Size Filter	Global to Specific
The Reason Filter (also known as the Modal operator)	Options to Procedures
Primary Interest Filter	People, Place, Things, Activity, Information

The direction filter: Going 'toward' or 'away from'

The *direction filter* is the metaprogram that drives people towards pleasure or away from pain. People are motivated by the 'carrot', representing pleasure and reward, known as *toward* in NLP jargon, or the 'stick', representing pain and punishment, known as *away from*.

A person showing *toward* tendencies is likely to be focused on goals and on what he wants. Someone fairly high on the 'toward' scale tends to rush into things, oblivious to the problems that may arise. A person with *away from* tendencies puts energy into avoiding situations that he considers to be risky and may be thought to be quite safe by someone else.

A person with high 'toward' tendencies can easily drive a person with 'away from' tendencies crazy with his enthusiasm. Having said that, an 'away from' person may well have the same effect on the 'toward' person because he can seem reluctant to take action!

In the world of work, people with 'toward' and people with 'away from' directional filters each have value. But woe betide the company putting a high 'toward' tendencies person into quality control or health and safety – although a person with 'toward' tendencies is likely to be great at managing and driving change. An 'away from' person can be a real boon when you want to know what the pitfalls in a project are likely to be. However, he may need to be pushed to give you answers if you're in a rush and he hasn't finished assessing all the possible problem areas. Many of the words people use give an indication of their filters, and Table 8-1 shows some of the terms associated with directional filters.

Table 8-1	Terms Indicating a Directional Filter
Toward Terms	*Away from Terms*
Let's go for it	Watch out for
I want, I wanted	I don't want
Easy	Stressless
The value of, value	The cost of, costs
Advantages	The down side
Safe	Risky
Accomplish, get things moving	Put off until
Solutions	Problems
Satisfaction	Unsatisfactory, unfulfilling, lacking
Afford	Can't afford, lack funds

To discover a person's directional filter (the things that trigger him to take action), the question to ask is, 'What do you want from X?' or 'What will having X do for you?' – where X can be a relationship, a job, a new PC, or something more imaginative. Finding out what motivates people is useful, especially if you're trying to get an outcome such as getting a bank manager to lend you some money or your kids to do some tidying.

You may need to ask at least three versions of a question to discover a person's 'toward' or 'away from' tendencies, as the tendencies are liable to stay hidden if you only ask one question.

In the following conversation Jill asks Harry several questions in an effort to decide which directional filter he favours. The **bold** terms indicate Harry's directional filters. Jill's interpretations of Harry's directional filters are in brackets.

Jill: Why did you become a travel rep?

Harry: Because **I wanted** to see the world. *(Toward)*

Jill: You could book your own package holidays and not have any strings attached.

Harry: But then I'd have to **pay for myself**, and I wouldn't be able to afford to travel. Besides, it would **take longer** that way and **I want** to have fun while I'm young. *(Away with some Toward)*

Jill: But you wouldn't have all the hassle of dealing with those people.

Harry: **I love meeting new people** and I **get a lot of satisfaction** sorting out their problems. *(Toward)*

In this conversation, Harry initially gave a 'toward' answer by saying, 'I wanted'. Had he said, 'I don't want to stay in one place', he would have revealed 'away from' tendencies. By digging a little, Jill was able to detect some 'away from' tendencies when Harry hinted at a shortage of money: 'wouldn't be able to afford to travel'.

Many of the words people use give an indication of their values; 'fun' and 'satisfaction' in Harry's conversation with Jill are examples. (Chapter 5 talks about how you filter your thinking.) Values (for more on values refer to Chapter 5) is another deep-seated filter you can use to improve your communication. Look at the way Harry assesses himself in Worksheet 8-1. Some of the words he uses are from other conversations that he has had with his colleagues and clients.

Worksheet 8-1	Harry's Toward and Away from Tendencies
Context:	Work
Toward words I have heard myself use:	I want; Fun; Help; Satisfaction; I'll sort it out; I won't give up; Love
Away words I have heard myself use:	Won't be able to afford; I won't have time; Problems; Time pressures
Where I am on the scale:	Toward ✗ Away
My observations:	I think I am more cautious at work because I have to take responsibility for my clients. I've just realised why I am broke. It's because I tend to have fun spending and am exhibiting a high 'toward' inclination to spending. I am more cautious when I spend on behalf of the company than on my own trips. Need to change my strategy!!

You need to understand your own ways of thinking, before you can begin to understand another person's ways of thinking. As author Stephen R. Covey says, 'The single most important principle in the field of interpersonal relations is this: Seek first to understand, then to be understood. Most people listen, not with the intent to understand, but with the intent to reply.'

With Stephen R. Covey's wisdom in mind, use Worksheet 8-2 to start assessing your own tendencies for the carrot (*toward*) or the stick (*away from*). You can then begin to build a pattern of your own make-up as you work through the other metaprograms.

Worksheet 8-2	My Toward and Away from Tendencies
Context:	
Toward words I have heard myself use:	
Away words I have heard myself use:	
Where I am on the scale:	Toward ⊢⊢⊢⊢⊢⊢⊢⊢⊢⊢⊢⊢⊢⊢⊢⊢⊢⊢ Away
My observations:	

Reaching the stage of recognising your own tendencies is great, but when recognising tendencies gets really useful is when you can pick up what a person is saying and adjust your language and behaviour to get the results you want. In Worksheet 8-3 please think of a person with whom you may not be communicating as well you as would like and work out where the likely mismatch is happening. Then you can work out what you need to change in what you're saying and doing. You get the feel that the exercise is just for you when you fill in the name of the person you're talking about in the gap.

Worksheet 8-3	Recognising a Person's Toward and Away from Tendencies
Person and Context:	
Toward words I have heard this person use:	
Away words I have heard this person use:	
Where I think this person is on the scale:	Toward ⊢⊢⊢⊢⊢⊢⊢⊢⊢⊢⊢⊢⊢⊢⊢⊢⊢⊢ Away
My observations and what I can do differently:	

Chunk size filter: Looking at the size of the chunk you see

Chunk size refers to the size of the information about an object or situation that you receive or transmit. When you see pictures of a beautiful blue orb floating in space, you see a very 'chunked up' version of the earth. As you drill down, you get more detailed data made up of people, cars, flora, and fauna, and if you go even farther down, you get to the level of fleas on dogs, bacteria in people, and so on.

This metaprogram is about people having *global filters* and *specific* filters. 'Global' people see the big picture, the grand vision, or the global overview, and find doing the detail stuff a burden. 'Specific' people are people who enjoy getting down to the nitty-gritty but have problems seeing the big picture. 'Global' and 'detail' aren't an 'either or' preference, rather that someone is farther along one side or the other of a continuum.

A global person isn't fazed by interruptions. He *can* 'see the wood for the trees' and move on from where he was interrupted or straight onto a related topic. A specific person doesn't see the main issues, and dislikes interruptions, which break his train of thought. He is so engrossed in detail and swallowed up by the trees that you may have to restart your conversation from scratch.

Tim is John's manager and really likes John. However, after working together for a while, Tim had begun to dread their weekly progress meetings because they always seemed to take twice as long as his other meetings. Tim found himself getting irritated with John repeating himself. But when Tim found out that John couldn't cope with interruptions because he lost the trail, metaphorically speaking, Tim simply asked, 'What happened after X?' – X being the point at which John had been interrupted.

A person who is able to focus on the details of a project finds jobs such as accounting, maintenance, and manufacturing easier than does a person with global tendencies. Next time you're flying, finding out that your pilot has high 'detail' tendencies may well be a comfort: you're assured that he isn't bored with carrying out the flight check, and alarming you by going, 'Done, Done, Done, never mind, we know the rest must be good'. It could be even worse for you if the pilot had 'toward' as well as global tendencies. Well, at least you wouldn't be sitting on the runway for long!

When you want to find where someone is on the 'global' to 'detail' continuum, the question to ask is, 'When you undertake a new project, do you need to know the big picture or do you need to know the details of what you plan to do?' As well as listening for the words listed in Table 8-2, notice the structure of the response. A person who is more 'global' may move his arms in an arc to 'paint' the big picture and say something like, 'I need to know in general terms so I have an idea of where we're headed to start with.' A person with more 'specific' tendencies relates a story straight through from beginning to end. For example, John's response to the question might be, 'Well, I need to know the detail steps because then I know I'm on track. I learnt this really important lesson when we moved office. I just couldn't keep track of what was happening because Tim was in charge and he didn't seem to know what he was doing. He was always flitting from one thing to another and my files went missing and I just lost my way and it took me a long time to get organised and arrange things in the right order when they did turn up.'

Tim's response might be. 'Tsk, big picture, of course. I tried to do it John's way but I just got bogged down by the detail.'

Working with people who are at opposite ends of the global and specific scale from you can cause a great deal of discord. A way of bridging the gap is to ask a 'global' person questions, the answers to which will give you the detailed steps. For example, a question for a person with a grand plan for running workshops might be, 'Who is your audience?' To help a 'specific' person who is finding getting the big picture difficult, try taking him out to the completion of the project. In the case of the office move, Tim could have said to John, 'Just imagine having an office all to yourself with all your own filing cabinets and the peace of not sharing it with Janice and her phone', helping to relieve John's anxiety about the move.

Table 8-2	Terms Indicating Chunk-Size Filters
Global Terms	**Specific Terms**
Overview	Precise
Global perspective	Stages
Big picture	Steps, step by step, detailed plan
We'll fill in the gaps later	What is the breakdown of the plan
Vague	Exact
Holistic view	Itemised picture
Broad brush strokes	Fine-tune, fill in the gaps

Assess your tendencies for global to specific filters in Worksheet 8-4.

Worksheet 8-4	My Global to Specific Tendencies
Context:	
Global words I have heard myself use:	
Specific words I have heard myself use:	
Where I am on the scale:	Global Specific
My Observations:	

Oh! And by the way, if you work for someone who micromanages, and who gets stressed because he prefers to do everything himself rather than delegating, chances are he is probably somewhere in the middle of the global to specific scale. Because he can see both sides of the scale, he tries to do it all himself. Show your micromanager you understand the big picture, then give him the details of how you'll carry out the project. Then if you've worked out that he prefers the carrot (*toward*), explain how it'll be better for you to run your own project, as he'll have more time to plan. With the stick (*away from*), point out the damage that stress is doing to him.

Practice makes perfect, so we are offering you Worksheet 8-5. Think of someone with whom you work or even just got talking to in the supermarket queue. Listen specifically for the words that give you an indication of his global to specific tendencies. The trick here is to listen for the words and not get caught up in the content of his conversation.

Worksheet 8-5	Recognising a Person's Global and Specific Tendencies
Person and Context:	
Global words I have heard the person use:	
Specific words I have heard the person use:	
Where I think the person is on the scale:	Global Specific
My observations and what I will do differently:	

The reason filter: Opting for procedure

The *reason filter* metaprogram is made up of 'options' at one end of the continuum and 'procedures' at the other end. If you ask a person high on the 'options' side to park in a car park with lots of empty spaces, he'll try every space before he settles for one! An 'options' person acts from choice, but a person more on the 'procedures' end feels he's obliged to do things and operates from a sense of duty. A 'procedures' person would simply park in the first available space. A person with 'procedures' tendencies is good at following rules whereas a person with 'options' tendencies is likely to be good at re-inventing the wheel because he'll try things all ways, to discover if he's tested all the options.

Please tick the statements you agree with in the following list.

- ❑ I love the challenge of sorting out a problem.
- ❑ I like creating a series of processes to solve a problem.
- ❑ I find it hard to then follow a process I created.
- ❑ I want to move onto the next problem.
- ❑ I always find ways of 'fixing what ain't broke'.

Got a lot of ticks? You probably go in the direction of the *'options'* end of the reason scale.

If, however, you find life challenging if nothing follows a pattern, change is disconcerting, following processes is enjoyable, and you don't mind repetition, you can be described as having a *'procedures'* bent.

If you want to know where someone is on the *options* or *procedures* scale, you ask the question, 'Why did you choose to X?', where X is working in his current job; buying the car he drives; living where he does; going into business with his business partner; or living with his life partner, if you're feeling really nosy. A person with 'options' tendencies will give you a list of reasons and his values for making a particular choice, perhaps something like the following:

> Well, I wasn't very **happy** with my last car. It wasn't very **reliable**. Because **I'm travelling more** with the new job, I decided to bite the bullet and invest in a better car. Besides, it's got **lots of knobs and buttons** and **really goes** when I want a bit of **fun** but it's economical when I need to drive any distance.

In this example *values* are indicated by words like 'happy', 'reliable', and 'fun', while the *reasons* are that he's travelling more so needed a better car and that the car has lots of knobs and buttons and can go fast.

A 'procedures' person tells a story by including the steps of how he reached his decision, perhaps like the following:

> You know I wasn't very happy with my last car. Remember the project you and I worked on in Düsseldorf and you had to drive me home because the starter motor went? It's been the same with niggling problems and when Jack came for dinner last month and he said they were having a lot of trouble recruiting an IT project manager at work – you remember Jack don't you? He was at my leaving barbecue and he asked if I'd step in as an interim. The interviews went well and I'm starting in a fortnight so I decided to to bite the bullet and invest in a new car and wasn't sure whether I wanted a Japanese or European car so have been studying all the car magazines to see which fits my list of criteria.

Table 8-3 shows some of the words you can listen for to decide whether a person has options or procedures tendencies.

Table 8-3	Terms Indicating Reason Filters
Options Terms	*Procedures Terms*
Possibility	Just so
Choice	Ordered
Can do	Have to follow the rules
Who says	Regulations say
Try this, if that doesn't work, try that	When all else fails, read the manual
Value words such as *value, fun,* and *limitless independence*	Ranking words such as *first, second,* and *last*

Worksheet 8-6 helps you to work out – you guessed it – your tendencies on the options-to-procedures scale. Working out where you are on the scale may not happen overnight, but if you set yourself a day when you think you want to focus on a set of metaprograms, you can start noticing the words you use. The funny thing is that by writing down the words in your workbook, you begin to notice other words and phrases as your unconscious mind starts playing along with you.

Worksheet 8-6	My Options to Procedures Tendencies
Context:	
Options words I have heard myself use:	
Procedures words I have heard myself use:	
Where I am on the scale:	Options Procedures
My Observations:	

One of the ways someone can be like you is that you both use similar metaprograms. The challenge is in understanding and learning to deal with the metaprograms that aren't natural to you. Often, you may have difficulty dealing with someone you can't understand but if you can stretch yourself to understand and utilise someone else's metaprograms, you may find you have greater influence and may get on really well with people who you may otherwise have ignored. Worksheet 8-7 can help with this.

Worksheet 8-7	Recognising a Person's Options and Procedures Tendencies
Person and Context:	
Options words I have heard the person use:	
Procedures words I have heard the person use:	
Where I think the person is on the scale:	Options ├┴┴┴┴┴┴┴┴┴┴┴┴┴┴┴┴┴┴┴┴┤ Procedures
My Observations and what I will do differently:	

The primary interest filter: Placing your focus here

The *primary interest filter* metaprogram is made up of what people feel most interested in and drawn to. You've probably come across folk who are passionate about their hobby, apparently putting their hobby first and people second. This type of person often finds a 'people' person far too familiar, too touchy-feely. Other people have people as their primary interest filter, and they focus on the 'who' rather than 'where' or 'what'.

You can discover a person's 'primary interest filter' by asking him to tell you about his favourite holiday, restaurant, or pastime, for example. His primary interest filter comes through in how he answers:

✔ **People filter:** A person with this filter talks about people. In answering this question, he tells you about the *who* of the experience. A person operating a people filter functions well in jobs requiring him to interact with other people

✔ **Place filter:** A person with place as his primary filter tends to focus on locations and finds his environment very important to his wellbeing. With a place filter, you hear all about the '*where*'.

✔ **Information filter:** Folks with this filter get high on the *why*. This is the person who can answer virtually any question you can ask.

✔ **Activity filter:** You probably know one or two 'doers', like the person who never sits down and leaves you exhausted just watching him rushing past like a hurricane. This type of person tells you '*how*' he is spending his time and what he's doing. He can do a lot of damage if he's allowed to get bored in a job by storming ahead with things.

✔ **Things filter:** This type of person buys gadgets and gizmos because his primary focus is having and showing off the latest products and toys. A person with a things filter can give you all the *'what'* about his gadgets, cars, and gizmos. He is a person who lives to accumulate possessions, just like some of those celebs you read about in the glossy magazines.

Table 8-4 lists some of the words people with the various primary interest filters tend to use.

Table 8-4		Terms Indicating Primary Interest Filters		
People Terms	**Place Terms**	**Information Terms**	**Activity Terms**	**Things Terms**
They	Location	Data	I can't sit still	Target
Feel	Distance	Knowledge	I have to be doing something	Books
Us, ours, my	Near	Why	Time is of the essence	Clothes
Team	Home	I'd love to know	Must be off	Company
Family	Cosy room	Process	Let's go for it	Gadget

In Worksheet 8-8, we ask you to pick one of your favourite subjects and write a short paragraph, changing the words for each primary interest filter to make the topic more interesting for a person with that filter. The more you practise switching between the different preferences, the easier it will become for you to move across the primary interest filters until one day, you say to yourself, 'By George! I've got it' because you realise that not only are you moving across the primary interest filters automatically but you're also doing it in response to an unconscious recognition of what the other person is saying.

Worksheet 8-8	Modifying Language to Match Primary Interest Filters
Subject:	
Primary interest filter: People	
Primary interest filter: Place	
Primary interest filter: Information	

Primary interest filter: Activity	
Primary interest filter: Things	

Winning Combinations

In the preceding section 'Listening for Metaprograms and Discovering Filters', we deal with single metaprograms. However, in reality, people are a pretty complex bunch and don't run just one metaprogram in isolation. For example, doctors and nurses are trained to follow procedures, but in an emergency their options tendencies come to the fore, in order for them to deal with the emergency. Or, you may be looking for a creative accountant who can find ways of keeping your money out of the tax-man's hands while still following the correct procedures and staying within the law, so that you avoid the tax-man and the police.

You can flex your metaprogram muscles by looking at combinations of metaprograms that can be useful to people in particular professions. For example, a marketing manager may need to:

✔ Have the ability to see the big picture (global).

✔ Put in place marketing targets in order for the company to achieve its goals (procedure).

✔ See how the marketing department fits into the overall company structure (global).

✔ Be able to implement and monitor the procedures necessary to make the marketing succeed, so as to create an action plan (activity).

✔ Have a 'toward' tendency in order to meet the marketing goals for the organisation.

✔ Be a 'people' person to understand how to lead his staff (people) but also to have an awareness of the steps needed to produce the results (procedures, information).

Take the example of a teacher at school. Ideally a teacher can present a big picture view of the subject or lesson in order to reach his students who have a 'global' preference. A teacher needs to not only understand the details of the subject he's teaching, but also to have the ability to explain it. Designing a lesson requires that a teacher has the ability to follow a pattern (procedure) but he also needs to have the flexibility to adapt his teaching to reach students who aren't able to understand the lesson. Depending on the subject, the primary interest filters are different (geography – places, psychology – people). The point of this example is to recognise that if you do have certain preferences, you need to be aware of other tendencies and have the knowledge to adapt these when needed. In the case of the teacher, he'd have to keep in mind that his role is to educate and keep a focus on this goal (toward) rather than think about what he isn't meant to teach! The primary interest filters that are likely to be common to good teachers are activity (how to keep the students involved) and information (being able to digest vast amounts of data in order to stay abreast of the changes in their field).

Putting Metaprograms to Use

Recognising and matching a person's metaprograms helps you build on your rapport with that person.

Keep in mind that copying a person's mannerisms and language is a delicate business that needs to be done with the utmost respect!

Scripting for results

The adage is, 'People like people like themselves'. When someone is similar to you in the language he uses, you don't need to try to translate and rapport happens more quickly.

If you want to deepen rapport with people who aren't like you, listen for the expressions they use that indicate their metaprograms and use the same expressions back. If you have the luxury of time to prepare, you can use the process in the next section to design and rehearse a script that you can use on the phone or face to face.

For the moment, simply pick out as many words and phrases that a person uses and practise incorporating them in responses that make sense.

Working out what you want to get across in your message is useful. You can then say or write it in a way that the recipient can't fail to respond to. And what's more irresistible than being able to communicate well with the person you're interacting with?

Until you're experienced enough to know how to use metaprograms off the top of your head, you can always prepare a script. For you to do this effectively, you need to to keep the following points in mind.

- ✔ **Know what to listen out for.** The section 'Listening for Metaprograms and Discovering Filters' earlier in the chapter gives you examples of the expressions people with different metaprograms use. You can start building a list of the words used by people who you want to influence.

- ✔ **Think of the message you want to get across.** Building the metaprogram patterns into a script for asking your boss for a pay rise is very different to asking someone out on a date.

- ✔ **Rehearse your script by saying it out loud, preferably in private.** That way, what you say doesn't sound alien when you come to use it in reality and you sound sincere.

This is what Tom, our manager, had to do when he wanted his girlfriend to say, 'YES!' And before you decide he's a controlling, conniving, calculating bloke, we say in his defence that he and Sue have been happily married for five years. Sue did turn him down at least half-a-dozen times because she was scared of being tied down and this was his last ditch effort to convince her he really wanted to marry her.

Worksheet 8-9	Tom's Script to Get Sue to Marry Him!	
Desired outcome: *Sue agrees to marry me*		
Sue's Metaprograms	*Indicative Behaviour*	*Words and Phrases to Use*
Detail	Sue is an accountant. She can find missing pieces in even the most detailed instructions. She's brilliant at checking contracts. Her time-keeping is impeccable. When we go out for dinner, she wants to know exactly what's in each dish.	I LOVE YOU. Just think of all the planning you'll have to do in organising all the detail of the wedding. Remember how upset Uncle Peter was at my brother's wedding when my mother hadn't ordered enough posies and he got left out? Of course if you think planning all those details is too much for you, we can always get my mother to do it.
Options with some procedures	She is always saying she needs to keep her options open. She always has to have a taste of everything. She's very good at keeping track of her spending because she has a very efficient computer system that she uses religiously.	When we do get married, think of all the things we'll be able to do. A whole new world of opportunities will open up.
Quite high away from	I know she frets about financial security and wants some freedom to explore other avenues of work.	We can rent out one of our properties and you can set yourself up as a landlord. We can move in together and we won't have the driving back and forth between houses.
Place primary interest filter	She is always rabbiting on about how beautiful Scotland is, what fantastic buildings there are in Vienna, how she wants to see the world, and what she's going to do when the company's offices move to bigger premises.	When we get married, wouldn't Belize be nice for our honeymoon? It's so green, and lush, and warm, and has lots of flora and fauna to see.

Worksheet 8-10 gives you the opportunity to conduct a similar exercise to Tom's to get something you really want. Think about a person who is proving difficult and refusing to see your point of view. Try to work out how to get your message through. (You can leave out the 'I LOVE YOU', especially if you're in a work situation!)

Worksheet 8-10 My Script to Achieve My Desired Outcome

Desired outcome:

The Person's Metaprograms	Indicative Behaviour and Words	Words and Phrases to Use

When you want to build rapport, try *matching*. If you've got yourself tied up in knots and can't work out whether the person's 'global' or 'detail', 'toward' or 'away from', or whichever combination, just bring to mind some of the person's favourite expressions and repeat them back to him – in the right context, of course.

Part III
Honing Your NLP Toolkit

The 5th Wave   By Rich Tennant

"Let's see if we can identify some of the stress triggers in your life. You mentioned something about a large wolf that periodically shows up and attempts to blow your house down..."

In this part . . .

Here we help you to manage your emotional state, even in situations that are out of your control, and we enable you to change the way you perceive difficult situations from the past. Working with your beliefs and values you get a stronger sense of your personal drivers, which can propel your own development to align with a stronger sense of purpose.

Also in this part you find out how the core NLP concepts make a real difference as you take them on board – tools such as anchoring, logical levels, submodalities, modeling, and timelines. All of these concepts help you to shift annoying habits and make your goals exceptionally compelling.

Chapter 9

Managing Your Emotions

In This Chapter

▶ Examining anchors

▶ Switching your emotional states

▶ Overcoming challenges

▶ Capitalising on the good times

▶ Escaping negative thoughts and criticism

▶ Keeping track of triggers

▶ Turning criticism into feedback

*W*alking down the street you catch a whiff of perfume and in a flash you are transported to another time or place. Or, you spot someone who instantly reminds you of a dear friend or an annoying colleague. Or maybe your heart leaps at the sound of that special voice on your phone or answering machine.

Sight, hearing, smell, taste, and touch – your five senses – have the ability to trigger memories and change your emotional state. In theory, your human intellectual ability for complex, rational thought has made you smarter than the animal kingdom. Nevertheless, as a perfectly wonderful human being you have a natural tendency to respond to stimuli just like Pavlov's dogs in the early behavioural experiments. There are times when you are ruled by your emotions – such as love, hate, rage, and fear. When this happens your breathing and heart rate speed up and threaten to spiral out of control.

So imagine a world in which you can instantly change how you think, feel, and react to situations simply by clicking your fingers. This is the controlled world that you create for yourself once you master the use of NLP anchoring techniques. In this chapter we take you through the practical steps of controlling and managing your emotions.

Appreciating the Abilities of Anchors

An *anchor* is a trigger that links to an action or emotional state. The process of anchoring works by associating one experience with a particular state, thereby producing that state in you.

For you to function at your best you need to be able to create a state of excellence for yourself, and NLP shows you how. The NLP process of anchoring teaches you that you can deliberately fire off an anchor when you are under pressure to change your emotional state. In all areas of your life it's handy to have mental toughness, by which we mean the resilience to cope with anything that life chooses to throw at you. Anchors allow you to do this instantly. Mastering anchors puts you firmly in the 'at cause' position rather than the 'at effect' position that we talk about in Chapter 2.

Luckily, you have naturally created *anchors* holding you firmly in place, just as a boat has an anchor that stops it floating out to sea. These are your senses, which have an effect on your emotional state. Some of your senses bring out the good feelings and others less good. For example, in Kate's office above her desk sits a beautiful photograph of the sea, taken by a close friend. The sight of that photograph puts Kate into a good mood, allowing her to think clearly and enjoy her work. It's a welcoming sight when she comes back to her office.

There's a moment in the film *The Parent Trap* (1961) when Hayley Mills buries her face in her grandfather Charles's jacket and says: 'I'm making a memory. Years from now, when I'm all grown up, I'll remember my grandfather and how he always smelled of peppermint and pipe tobacco.' You may not find it so easy to conjure up a smell at will, yet often a distinctive smell acts as a powerful anchor transporting you back to a previous experience. Are you curious about how your favourite perfumes and other aromas affect your state, and which ones make you feel good? A trip to your favourite coffee shop or a spray of perfume may make all the difference to your sense of well-being before the next job interview.

What you notice as you master anchoring is that it makes fantastic use of your good memories for those times when you need to hold your emotions in check when you are under pressure. You get ongoing value from the good times.

Other senses can have a negative effect. When Richard sees his income tax forms drop on his door mat, he groans when he smells the brown envelope and hides the forms away in a drawer until his accountant chases him for them to be completed.

Anchors trigger habits. (Advertisers know this and so design jingles and brand images that stay memorable and prompt you to buy their product when you're next indulging in a bit of retail therapy.) This is why if you want to change the habit, then you need to change the anchor. If every time you have a nice cup of tea, you reach for the biscuit tin, you may find you want to break that chain reaction. However, if every time you enjoy a hot drink, you feel relaxed and want to dance around the kitchen, that drink is likely to be a positive anchor you want to keep, especially if there's space to go wild and have fun burning off the calories!

Use Worksheet 9-1 to make quick notes of the everyday things around you that have the effect of making you immediately feel good or bad. Notice the sights, sounds, smells, sensations, and tastes that act as anchors to good and bad emotional states. In this way you observe more closely the subtle changes in your emotional state from anxious and tense to happy and relaxed. Capture your initial thoughts, paying attention to all your senses. Make a note of things such as objects, people, activities, and places that affect you and identify those worth keeping and those you'd like to let go of. You may have many things that make you feel good in the short term which are not so healthy for you in the long term.

Most of your feel-bad anchors are probably worth ditching, but be aware that some of them may have a useful purpose in prompting an important good habit, such as completing your tax form. Someone we know leaves an unpleasant photograph of some blackened lungs on her pin board at work to remind her of the damaging effect of smoking. She has a strong 'away from' metaprogram (Chapter 8 has more on metaprograms) that motivates her to stay healthy.

Worksheet 9-1	My Everyday Anchors

Feel-good anchors:

_____

_____

_____

_____

_____

Feel-bad anchors:

_____

_____

_____

_____

_____

Which of these do I want to keep?

_____

_____

_____

_____

_____

Setting Anchors

In this section, we show you how to go about setting an anchor to change your emotional state – based on an earlier memory of being in that emotional state.

Creating your circle of excellence

The *circle of excellence technique* is the classic NLP anchoring technique to summon up your confidence in a crisis or for giving your best performance in public. You can use your circle of excellence, for example, when you're about to give a talk, go into a tough negotiation, or boost your performance for a race or sporting event. The circle of excellence simply allows you to use a trigger – that of stepping forward into an imaginary circle, usually accompanied by a hand gesture – to boost a positive state of mind when under pressure.

Work through the following steps to create your own circle of excellence.

It helps to do this exercise with a coach or buddy who will talk you through the actions. Your buddy can then write down your thoughts on the worksheet for you.

Begin by standing up and drawing an imaginary circle on the floor in front of you. Make it wide enough to step into.

1. **Staying outside the circle, identify the state of mind you want to anchor and tell your buddy what that is in your own words.**

   For example, you may want to be in a state of 'confidence'. If you were to describe that more fully in your own words it may be 'clear-headed' or 'in control of the situation'.

2. **Step into the circle and remember a time when you were in that particular state. Relive that experience vividly as if you were there. Notice the sights, sounds, smells, and your feelings.**

   This recalled experience is likely to be in a completely different context to the one that is problematic for you now, and that's fine.

3. **When you have the experience in your mind at its strongest, hold that thought, then anchor it with a distinctive hand movement that you don't normally use during the course of a day.**

   For example, you could pinch your thumb and index finger together in a circle, or grip your little fingers together.

4. **Step out of the circle and repeat Step 2 and Step 3 recalling a second experience when you were in the same best state. Step out of the circle.**

5. **Think of a time in the future when this state will be useful to you.**

6. **Step into the circle imagining the success of the future event and firing off the distinctive hand anchor that you created at the same time.**

   Notice how much easier this event can be for you and the intensity of the future experience. (NLP calls this *future pacing*.)

You can repeat the circle of excellence process if you want the anchor to become stronger.

Worksheet 9-2 offers an example of the set of positive hand anchors Teresa is creating for herself.

Worksheet 9-2	Teresa's Positive Memories and Hand Anchors	
Emotional State I Want to Create	*Memory that Triggers the State – Including the Sights, Sounds, and Feelings*	*My Hand Anchor*
Energetic	I am on a skiing trip to Chamonix and can feel the cold air on my face as I set off for a day up the mountain. The sky is blue and I feel on top of the world.	Placing one hand firmly on the other as if I've just pushed my ski glove on and I'm ready to go.
Authoritative	I'm explaining how the graphics software works to the team. I can see them nodding their heads and really feel I know what I'm talking about.	My left thumb pressed firmly into my right palm.

Setting your own anchors

Worksheet 9-3 gives you the blank space to record your own distinctive anchors. You can do a couple now and come back to this exercise as your pool of anchors widens.

As you practise your skills at anchoring positive states, start to build a collection of them so that you can trigger your positive memories when you need to. Try changing your state at will by firing off your personal hand anchors.

Practise developing your circle of excellence ahead of the time when you'll need it so that you can summon up the positive state at will. Keep reinforcing your skills. You can access the hand anchor so discreetly that no one else is aware of what you're doing.

Worksheet 9-3	My Positive Memories and Hand Anchors	
Emotional State I Want to Create	*Memory that Triggers the State – Including the Sights, Sounds, and Feelings*	*My Hand Anchor*

Debbie was planning her wedding day with the same immaculate attention to detail that she applies in her job as a personal assistant in a law firm. As the wedding day approached she found herself getting more and more nervous about it to the point where it was spoiling her enjoyment of the build-up to the day of her dreams. 'What is all this fear about?' she wondered. Once she began breaking down all her worries with Kate, her NLP coach, Debbie realised that her greatest fear was that one of her young bridesmaids would misbehave with all the excitement of the occasion and spoil the ceremony. It had got to the point where she panicked each time she met with her young bridesmaids for the dress fittings. Her fear was becoming infectious and the bridesmaids were starting to feel afraid of their responsibilities on the 'big day'. When practising the NLP circle of excellence technique with Kate, Debbie anchored a calm and confident state and held that with a discreet hand movement. When she noticed she was getting worried, she fired off her new anchor by the simple hand movement. Then she found she was relaxed once more and began to have fun with the little ones involved in her big day. By the way, Debbie also found that anchoring came in handy at work when a few lawyers were under pressure with difficult legal actions and starting to squabble amongst themselves.

Some people find anchoring amazingly powerful the first time they experience it, while others need more practice. As you develop your personal anchors, these three pointers can help you:

✔ **Set the hand anchors at the peak intensity.** The time to set an anchor is when you recall a memory at its most intense, as if you are right there in the experience again, and choosing your best moment to do this.

✔ **Make the hand anchors distinctive.** Make sure that the hand movement you create is sufficiently different from the way you normally hold or use your hands; also make your hand movement something you can do discreetly.

✔ **Make the hand anchors unique.** See how you can make the anchors your own, rather than copying someone else's.

If you find that hand triggers aren't powerful enough for you, instead you can experiment with capturing an image or sound associated with your positive mental state. Make the image or sound something that you can easily summon up in your memory without needing to actually see a picture or hear a sound, as that would be a bit tricky to access just when you need it.

Facing Up to Challenges

Think about the times when you found it most challenging to manage your emotions. Do you feel silly for weeping uncontrollably at weddings, funerals, or at the movies? Or do you find yourself sweating profusely before an important date you've been looking forward to all week?

In Worksheet 9-4 you can see a list of situations in which people typically find it hard to manage their emotions. Highlight any that are relevant to you. The worksheet gives you space to fill in the details of your own examples and record the best emotional state you'd like to hold.

Imagine that you're taking part in a debating competition and need to think quickly on your feet. You might say that the desired emotional state that you want to anchor is 'clear-headed'.

After you complete the worksheet make a note of any specific states that you need to anchor for yourself and if necessary go back to the circle of excellence technique to anchor the desired emotional state.

Worksheet 9-4	My Personal Challenges	
Challenging Situations	*My Example*	*Emotional State I Want*
Taking part in a competition		
Playing a sport or doing exercise		

Challenging Situations	My Example	Emotional State I Want
Getting through a conflict situation		
Going to an emotional occasion (such as wedding or funeral)		
Attending an important meeting		
Making a complaint		
Attending a job interview		
Negotiating the best deal		
Other difficult times when I feel the pressure:		

Capturing the Positives

By now you will have a greater awareness of the experiences that trigger your emotions and realise that accessing the memory rather than the actual experience is enough to trigger the emotion. For example, Rowena in Worksheet 9-5 can summon up an image in her head of the spring tulips in the park to make her feel good; she doesn't have to have the tulips in bloom all year round.

Worksheet 9-5	Rowena's Positive Triggers
Anchor Category	Anchor Experience
Visual – sights	The tulips in the park. Photo of me in Geneva. My in-tray when it's clear.
Auditory – sounds	Signature tune of Newsnight. John Lennon singing Imagine.
Olfactory – smells	Mark's Hugo Boss after shave. Freshly baked bread at the local deli.
Gustatory – tastes	A glass of dry white wine. Slice of Brie on a cracker.

(continued)

Worksheet 9-5 (continued)

Anchor Category	Anchor Experience
Kinaesthetic – feelings and movement	The feel of my velvet skirt when I dance the tango.
	Walking in the woods on the crunchy leaves in autumn.
	Cold air on my face when I'm skiing.

Continue to build your personal record of your positive triggers as these help you to anchor good states when you are under pressure. Use Worksheet 9-6 to start you off.

Get into the habit of carrying a small notebook around with you to capture the emotional highs just as you would capture images with your camera. Think of this notebook as your photo album, recording your ideas for the future.

Now begin to build your own library of experiences that you want to anchor. Put a sticky note on this page to remind you to come back and revisit your triggers when you feel stressed so that you can change state quickly just by accessing the memory.

Worksheet 9-6	My Positive Triggers
Anchor Category	Anchor Experience
Visual – sights	
Auditory – sounds	
Olfactory – smells	
Gustatory – tastes	
Kinaesthetic – feelings and movement	

Breaking the Chains that Bind

Ship anchors with heavy, rusted chains that fix a boat in place are incredibly hard to shift. Similarly, you may have some tenacious chains that you'd like to break free from.

NLP makes it surprisingly easy to shift heavy anchors, allowing you to lighten up on any problems you're carrying around with you.

Do you find yourself remembering the times when things went wrong more than the times when things went well? Perhaps you find yourself agonising about mistakes, embarrassing moments, and painful situations long after the event has past?

After five years of living happily with him, one day Jagdesh's boyfriend met her on the front doorstep of their house, and with his car on the drive loaded up with his possessions. He announced that he didn't love Jagdesh any more and was leaving her for a mutual friend. Jagdesh was shocked. For some months after he'd gone, every time she returned home from work she found herself in tears when she reached the front door. The mere sight of the front door reminded her of the unhappy departure of her loved one. With the help of a friend who was an NLP practitioner, Jagdesh dissolved the unhappy trigger, which she defined as sadness by using the collapsing anchors technique. Jagdesh replaced her sadness with a more resourceful calm state that allowed her to think carefully about the next steps in her life where she needed to take important decisions about selling the house and moving away.

One of the difficulties with being bound by negative memories is that it can hold you back in fear that the same thing may happen again. An actress who has had some bad reviews may be able to think only of the bad reviews every time she steps on stage. Imagine the effect on her acting!

Collapsing the anchors is a tool that allows you to overcome the memory of an unhappy or unpleasant experience and override the experience with a powerful and positive memory. This works by setting two physical anchors on your body (usually on each knee) and letting go of the one you want to release while holding the one you want to keep:

1. **Begin by defining the two contrasting emotional states: the first is the one that gives you a problem and is associated with a negative state, while the second is positive.**

   In Jagdesh's case, she defines the problem emotion as _sadness_ and the positive state as _calm_.

   Get clear about the words you are using for defining your states.

2. **Set a negative anchor by recalling your problem state for yourself, and as you do so hold it down firmly with the flat of your hand just above one knee.**

   You already have an experience that anchors the problem in place so there's no need to dwell on it too much – the mere thought of the experience can set off your unhappy state.

   In Jagdesh's case, the trigger is the sight of her front door, which reminds her of her boyfriend leaving.

3. **Now set the positive anchor (such as _calm_) by remembering a pleasant and positive memory. As you recall that much better experience, anchor it to the same place on the other knee.**

4. **Now think of a time coming up for which you want to be in a positive state, yet the problem memory might get in the way. As you imagine that situation, fire both the postive and negative anchors off at the same time by pressing firmly on both knees. Gradually let go of the problem anchor on the one knee while holding firm with the positive one on the other.**

   What happens is that you radically change the power of the negative anchor and are left with the positive anchor going forward.

You can do this exercise on your own. However this is an NLP technique that is familiar to NLP coaches and practitioners and you can get a better result by asking one to help you. You can also explain the steps to a friend who you feel comfortable with to touch your knees! When you work with someone else, that person can follow the step-by-step process, leaving you free to concentrate on your experience. An alternative approach to using the knees is to set the anchors on the knuckles of one of your hands.

Checking the Triggers for a Week

As you go about your daily business you collect experiences that you naturally anchor for yourself in good and bad ways. Worksheet 9-7 has a seven-day planner to monitor your habits over one week. The way to make the best of this planner is with a daily check-in point at the end of the day. Think back over the events of the day and jot down for yourself the highlights of the day. Observe what triggered the feel-good moments for you. Was it the pleasant conversation at the café or the sight of an impressive building? Then contrast these with the low points, if there were any, and notice what triggered any negative habits for you. Were you feeling cross after an argument at home, or because your laptop crashed, and you then had a chocolate bar to cheer yourself up?

Remember the saying 'the devil is in the detail'? It's by noticing the details of your everyday life experiences that you pick up on the habits that serve you well and those that don't. Check in with what good things you'd like to have more of tomorrow and the negatives that you would like to have less of. Once you know what triggers a negative state for yourself, use your circle of excellence techniques to instantly change your emotional state so that you can change the habits that you want to break.

Worksheet 9-7		**My Daily Highs and Lows**	
Day	*Highs*	*Lows*	*Lessons and Changes to Make*
1			
2			
3			
4			
5			

Day	Highs	Lows	Lessons and Changes to Make
6			
7			

Dealing with Criticism

There are times in your life when you have to face harsh criticism and as you get more and more successful the criticism gets more frequent. Perhaps the memory of a difficult conversation still awakens unpleasant emotions in you. Maybe there's a time when you've put in lots of work only to be picked to pieces. Can you feel the knot in your stomach, hear the critical voice in your head, or see someone's cross face and feel the response that it triggers?

Think about the areas where you feel most sensitive to criticism. Is it your work, your appearance, or a pet project that's dear to your heart?

The key to working through criticism is to realise that it's not about the essential 'you' but about the role you have in a particular situation. Learn from the experience of being criticised and move swiftly on – there's no point in wasting your energy dwelling on negatives.

Jenny works for a large company that has a formal appraisal system for all the staff. She once worked for a boss who can only be described as a bully, an unpleasant character who placed unrealistic demands on his employees. Eventually the boss was fired and Jenny moved to a different organisation. However, every year when Jenny's performance appraisal came up, she was still hearing her old boss's voice in her head saying: 'You're not the kind of person we want round here. You're not good enough.' The effect was to make Jenny feel anxious about giving and receiving appraisals. By working with her NLP coach, Jenny was able to let go of the past negatives and discover new ways of dealing with criticism. Today Jenny is an exemplary manager who pays a lot of attention to nurturing and mentoring young people in her organisation and is committed to giving very clear and honest feedback even with those who are not performing at their best.

NLP leaders Steve and Connirae Andreas first developed a procedure for handling criticism through modelling people who operated successfully in turning criticism into feedback. The following exercise is a way to shift your thinking by turning criticism into feedback and moving on. It works by taking the key NLP skills of *dissociation* and adopting three different *perceptual positions* to respond effectively to criticism. This is also a good technique for dealing with fears (refer to Chapter 4) and many other issues.

Dissociation is the NLP term for separating your feelings from an experience. Through dissociation, you can view a situation impartially in your mind's eye by seeing yourself stepping out of it and not becoming emotionally involved. The *perceptual positions* used in NLP are *first position* (being yourself), *second position* (imagining the situation from another person's point of view), and *third position* (observing both first and second positions from the viewpoint of an impartial observer).

Take the following exercise slowly, working through it step by step and then capturing your thoughts in Worksheet 9-8.

1. **Get into a great state.**

   Recall a time when you were on top of the world and nothing could topple you from that pinnacle. Really get into that experience, noticing how you felt, what you saw and heard. You need to hold this state throughout the exercise, so hold it with a hand movement that you can recall if you find yourself becoming less resourceful.

   Your circle of excellence anchoring technique from 'Creating your circle of excellence' earlier in this chapter can help you here.

2. **Picture yourself taking the criticism at a distance as if you are watching the action on a movie screen.**

   Listen to the other version of you 'out there' with the 'critic' – the person who gives you the criticism and with whom you have difficulty in interacting. Imagine that you are holding the role of 'the movie director' viewing the action as if on a screen. Figure 9-1 gives you a visual of this situation.

3. **Now as soon as the criticism begins to unfold, watch yet another version of yourself step out of the you 'out there'.**

   This second version of the you 'out there' is going to take the role of the *observer* of the two players (observing the *you 'out there'* and your *critic*). So you now have two versions of you 'out there' on the screen – the you being criticised and the you observing and evaluating this taking place.

4. **Behaving as if you're the movie director watching all three actors, see if you can make an impartial movie in your head of the criticism.**

   Invite the *observer* in your movie to ask each party – the *critic* and the *you 'out there'* – for the story from their points of view. The *observer* then asks each party to give clear and specific feedback about what went wrong. Invite *you 'out there'* and the *critic* to remain respectful towards each other.

5. **Remember to hold your great state and stay fully dissociated from the action.**

   If you get any strong emotions about the critic or the event, step back and concentrate on your state. You can take the action as slowly as you like, one shot at a time.

6. **Still in your movie director role, evaluate the two stories and ask yourself how they match up.**

   If your own personal memory of the event is very different from the critic's one, ask for more information. Often criticism is vague or a personal attack. If you hear such statements as, 'You are useless', ask for specific evidence and examples of what you did that was wrong. Decide how you want to respond.

7. **From your safe movie director position, give an impartial response to the critic.**

   Respond first to the criticism that you agree with and then to the points that you disagree with, explaining why.

8. **Bring everything you have learnt together.**

   If you discovered something new about yourself from exploring the criticism, then take those points on board. Think of an occasion in the future when you can make use of this feedback.

9. Remove the screen, step into the film, and combine the learning from the two versions of you 'out there' giving yourself time to bring together all you have seen, heard, and experienced.

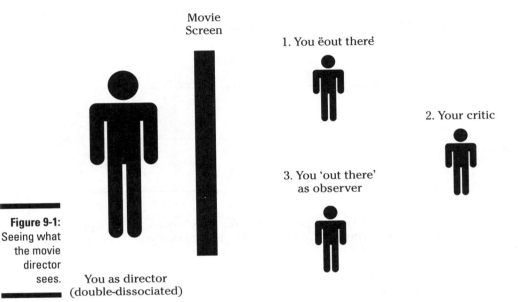

Movie
Screen

1. You 'out there'

2. Your critic

3. You 'out there'
as observer

You as director
(double-dissociated)

Figure 9-1:
Seeing what
the movie
director
sees.

Worksheet 9-8 lets you capture key points from the exercise so that you can record the benefits from it. Make a note of the best emotional state you can be in to take criticism wisely. For example, you may want to be in a state of curiosity, to be calm, and listening openly. Next take the different roles in turn and capture any ideas you gained from the different points of view of all the parties involved in the exercise. When you do this, try to experience what it feels like to be the other person, such as the critic, and understand what might be going on for her. Finally, think about how you can use this information to your advantage if a similar situation comes up in the future. Make a note of anything you can do differently next time.

Worksheet 9-8   **My Dissociating from Criticism and Taking
the Learning Forward Worksheet**

Describe a great state for you to be in when reviewing criticism in your own words here:

_____

Record what you found out about yourself from the different positions of:

Movie director:

_____

You 'out there':

_____

Critic:

_____

(continued)

Worksheet 9-8 (continued)

Observer (the second you 'out there'):

_____

Choose three points from the criticism that are most useful for you to take forward:

1.

_____

2.

_____

3.

Remember the NLP presupposition 'There's no failure – only feedback'? This presupposition can be very helpful when you're faced with criticism that you find unpleasant. (To jog your memory about NLP presuppositions, nip back to Chapter 2.)

NLP shows you how to model excellence – finding people who do something exceptionally well, working out what they do and how, and then reproducing the magic. When you manage your emotions well, your emotional state is infectious. Think of the old saying, 'Smile and the world smiles with you; cry and you cry alone.' However, you do need to acknowledge your negative states or what therapists refer to as the 'shadow side of yourself' because if you don't you can become what one of our NLP colleagues wonderfully calls a 'bliss ninny' who denies her tiredness and burns herself out. Yet, when you find the bright side of the toughest situations you find that people want to be with you and support you. Keep on practising your positive states, drop the negative anchors, and guess what? You'll have so much fun.

As you come to the end of this chapter, take the time to reflect on what you have discovered that is most valuable for you – your personal golden nuggets. Grab a piece of paper and make a note of them now, while you remember.

Chapter 10

Taking Charge of Your Experiences

. . . .

In This Chapter

▶ Rethinking your memories

▶ Seeing, hearing, and sensing your memories

▶ Re-creating your memories

▶ Changing beliefs and inventing resources

▶ Reducing the pain of the bad times

. . . .

Think back to the last time you walked through your favourite department store. Picture the occasion. Do you see the colours of the goods on display, are you smelling the bottles of aftershave, lovingly feeling the scarves and ties, touching the dangly earrings *or*, those fetishists among you, shock! horror!, sniffing the leather goods? Or are you winding up the sales staff by playing with *all* the chimes hanging from the pergola? Serves the store owners right for tempting you to part with your money!

In this chapter you discover how your memories are programmed and how you can begin to change them. The ability to change your memories can help you do more of what you want and less of what is getting in your way.

Recording Your Memory

This section is all about getting you to become aware that your memories have certain qualities to them. By bringing these qualities to your conscious awareness, you can enhance the good memories and dim or eradicate effects of the painful ones. In order for you to do this, you need to recall memories more consciously.

Take a moment to stop and think about something or someone that makes you feel good. Perhaps a book, a place, a person, or a pet. As you remember, you find that you've conjured up a picture, heard sounds, or experienced some feelings. Or you may have a combination of picture, sounds, and feelings. Notice some the characteristics of the picture – is it still or moving, how big is it? What are the qualities of the sounds you hear – are they in your head or outside, do the sounds have a pitch or rhythm? What are the feelings like? Where are the feelings located in your body, and do those feelings have a colour or texture?

Like the property programmes you see on television, Worksheet 10-1 is the 'before' exercise allowing you to recognise what you notice about the qualities of the picture, sounds, and feelings of your memories. Worksheets 10-2, 10-3, and 10-4 give you a breakdown of each modality for you to bring the different submodalities to your conscious awareness and appreciate qualities of the memory that you missed or of which you were unaware.

Chapter 6 discusses how you record your experiences predominantly in pictures, your VAK: sights (V: visual), sounds (A: auditory), and feelings (K: kinaesthetic – movement, feeling, or touching). These VAK mental images are called *representational systems* or *modalities*. You work with these qualities of your memories in more detail in 'Getting Acquainted with Submodalities' later in this chapter.

Everything you experience is as a result of information that you take in through your senses: *visual* (what you see), *auditory* (what you hear), *kinaesthetic* (touch, movement, and feelings), *olfactory* (smell), and *gustatory* (taste). These experiences are known as *modalities*. Each modality has a level of fine-tuning known as *submodalities*. For example, a picture can be bright or dull, and black and white or colour. A sound can be loud or soft, and so on. Worksheets 10-2, 10-3, and 10-4 give you a breakdown of the visual, auditory, and kinaesthetic submodalities.

Pick a memory that doesn't remind you of anything too ecstatic or too horrible; basically, nothing very emotional. Pick something along the lines of dinner with friends, a seaside trip, or whatever pops into your head. Your memory can be happy or 'niggly', or just something you found mildly upsetting.

Hold on to this memory because you'll be using it for Worksheets 10-1, 10-2, 10-3, and 10-4.

In Worksheet 10-1, describe the memory. You can delete 'happy' or 'niggly', depending on how you classify your memory. Classes of memories have similar submodalities. For example, 'happy' memories have more or less the same characteristics, which are different from 'niggly', 'sad', or 'indifferent' memories.

Once you get into the swing of working with your submodalities, you're able to give them classifications of your own which are different from 'happy' or 'niggly'. Use Worksheet 10-1 to describe the VAK qualities of your memory in as much detail as possible.

Worksheet 10-1	My Memory Snapshot
My memory is happy/niggly:	
Short description of my memory:	
What I notice in my memory – how I record the sights, sounds, and feelings:	
Visual *What I see*:	
Auditory *What I hear:*	
Kinaesthetic *What I feel*:	

Getting Acquainted with Submodalities

You will have your own way of using submodalities to group your experiences together. The way you list your experiences helps you check whether they are good, bad, happy, pleasant, sad, gruelling, exciting, and so on.

Because submodalities are the basic building blocks of your experiences, they are crucial tools in managing your mind and your emotions. Start keeping notes on how you can use submodalities to enhance the good areas in your life or change what isn't working. The exercises in this chapter give you a framework that you can adapt and develop to suit your specific circumstances.

Worksheets 10-2, 10-3, and 10-4 give a breakdown of the VAK submodalities most likely to come within your experience.

The purpose of working through Worksheets 10-2, 10-3, and 10-4 is to help you recognise that there's more than just, 'Oh! I see pictures', 'I know I have conversations in my head', or 'I have very strong feelings'. These worksheets enable you to begin to recognise that pictures, sounds, and feelings can have many more distinctive qualities. Table 10-5 consolidates the information and puts the three sets of submodalities into one easy-to-use format. Please feel free to copy this and use as many times as you want.

Terry was being coached to help him overcome the anxiety he felt whenever he set off on long journeys. During the coaching session he discovered that his memories of his holiday in Italy and his holiday in Hawaii were *both* slightly off-centre and to his right, approximately three feet in front, in panorama, and with vivid colours. The sounds of the sea breaking and birdsong were over to his left, a little below the level of his ear, and were rhythmic. The generalisation Terry can make, even if he doesn't do further research into how he stores his memories, is that his memories relating to his different holidays are stored in a particular location and have very similar qualities.

When filling out Worksheets 10-2, 10-3, and 10-4, use the column 'My Observation' for making more detailed notes such as, 'Sounds just like Grandad' instead of just saying, 'Heard a sound'. If some submodalities are missing from your memory, that's okay; just note this by marking an X in the box corresponding to the particular submodality. The quality of a submodality, such as dimness or loudness, is just that – a quality, with no value judgment; simply a way of showing you that you record some memories one way and others in other ways. You can use this knowledge as a yardstick as you progress through this chapter and you discover how to change the submodalities of a picture, sound, or feeling so you can change the emotions that the memory brings up.

Now, going back to the memory you chose in Worksheet 10-1, look at Worksheet 10-2 and note the visual qualities of the memory, some of which you may not even have been aware of when you filled out Worksheet 10-1.

Worksheet 10-2	My Visual Submodalities	
Submodality	*Description*	*My Observations*
Location	Point to where the image is located. To make this easy, imagine standing in front of a big clock face. Your image may be at 2 or 9 o'clock, for example.	
Brightness	Is it bright or dim?	
Detail	Is there much detail in the foreground or the background?	
Size	Is the picture small or big?	
Distance	Is the picture close or far?	
Framed or panoramic	Is there a border around the picture or is it as if you're standing on a hilltop looking around you?	
Colour/black and white	Is the picture in colour or black and white?	
Movement	Is it a movie or a still picture?	
Associated/ Dissociated	Are you looking out of your own eyes or are you observing the picture as if on the television?	

Do the same thing again in Worksheet 10-3 by writing down the additional auditory qualities of the memory you chose in Worksheet 10-1.

Worksheet 10-3	My Auditory Submodalities	
Submodality	*Description*	*My Observations*
Location	Is the sound inside or outside your head?	
Pitch	Is the sound high- or low-pitched?	
Volume	Is it loud or soft?	
Duration	Is it short, quick, broken notes or continuous?	
Tempo	Is it fast or slow?	

Submodality	Description	My Observations
Mono/stereo	Is the sound coming from one direction or from all around?	
Rhythm	Does the sound have a beat?	

You guessed it! Now in Worksheet 10-4 you need to make a note of the additional kinaesthetic qualities of the memory you chose in Worksheet 10-1.

Worksheet 10-4	My Kinaesthetic Submodalities	
Submodality	**Description**	**My Observations**
Quality	Is the sensation tingling, warm, relaxed, tense?	
Intensity	How strong is the feeling?	
Duration	Is the feeling continuous?	
Location	Where is the sensation in your body?	
Still or moving	Is the feeling in one place or does it move around your body?	
Size	What is the size of the feeling?	
Temperature	Is the feeling hot or cold?	

Noticing the way you catalogue your memories is a useful way of getting acquainted with submodalities – the aim of Worksheet 10-5. (You may choose to go to town and list *all* the subtleties of *all* your memories on additional sheets of paper.) In Worksheet 10-5 you may find yourself holding all your happy memories in roughly the same place and that they have similar characteristics, which are very different from where you hold memories that are unhappy or unpleasant. Likewise, perhaps you have the same way of holding people you like in your memory, which is very different from how you hold the memory of people you heartily dislike or positively detest.

Worksheet 10-5		All Together Now			
Visual		Auditory		Kinaesthetic	
Submodality	Description	Submodality	Description	Submodality	Description

Associating and Dissociating

If you find tears welling up in your eyes because you can 'feel someone's pain', then finding out how to dissociate can help you to keep your emotions under control. This is a good tool to help stay resourceful and not get too caught up in emotions.

Having the ability to *associate* into or *dissociate* out of a memory gives you the control to feel things more strongly or to diminish the intensity of a feeling in response to the memory of a situation. Remember when you got home last evening? Hold that picture and now look down and see yourself standing outside your front door. Put in the key, turn it, and step across the threshold. If you felt yourself relive all this, you were *associated* into the memory. Now pretend you're standing on the street across from your house, look down, and see the pavement. Now look up and 'watch' yourself walk up to your front door, put in the key, turn it, and step across the threshold. If you saw yourself watching yourself, you were *dissociated* from the memory.

Sometimes when you find yourself submerging in a feeling, dissociate yourself by moving out of the picture and into the position of an observer. If you need to really feel an emotion, step into the picture and look out and around you as if you were a participant in the memory.

Now pick another couple of memories. These need to be memories to which you have given different meanings in your list of memories. Also the memories need to have different contexts – for example, visiting your grandparents or going for a job interview. Your memories can be of people – friends, acquaintances, or even your deadly enemies. Record the VAK submodalities of each memory in Worksheet 10-6, noticing the similarities and differences for each memory. If you choose friends and acquaintances, they may well have similar characteristics; but make a note of any subtle differences or similarities between them.

Worksheet 10-6	Noticing How I List My Memories	
Visual	*Auditory*	*Kinaesthetic*
Memory 1:		
Memory 2:		
Memory 3:		

Mending Memory Lane

Using one of the memories from Worksheet 10-6 – or coming up with another memory, but avoiding one that is traumatic or upsetting – you are going to play at changing the memory. In the process, you will discover just how much control you have over how you hold your experiences and also how you can change the effect the experiences have on you.

In this section, you find out how to change each VAK submodality of your memory and examine the effect the change has on the whole. For example, you may notice that by moving the picture to a different location, the sounds you hear get softer or the feeling disappears.

Worksheets 10-2, 10-3, 10-4 are your record of your submodalities, so keep the worksheets in a safe place. If you get the collywobbles when changing your chosen memory (which can happen because submodalities are so powerful), you can refer to the worksheets to quickly put your memory back to how it was until you are steady enough to carry on with the exercise.

Worksheet 10-7 lists the submodalities of John's memory of splashing about in an open-air swimming pool with his friends.

Worksheet 10-7	John's List of His Submodalities
Submodality	*Description*
Visual: Location	The picture is of the time being at two o'clock on a clock face, approximately 20 degrees above eye level.
Visual: Brightness	The picture is very bright.
Visual: Colour/Black and White	It is in vivid colour.
Visual: Associated/Dissociated	I am associated into the picture.
Visual: Still or moving	There is a lot of movement in the picture.
Auditory: Volume	The only sound I hear is all of us laughing, splashing, and screaming and it's very loud.
Kinaesthetic: Temperature	The sun feels very warm on my skin and I feel a warm glow in my heart.

Changing submodalities can feel odd, so find yourself a quiet place to work on your own or with a trusted friend who can talk you through the list of submodalities and also help you, calmly, to go back to more familiar submodalities. Remember, changing submodalities is only permanent if you choose to keep the change. So if you feel uncomfortable with the new configuration of submodalities, you can change them back. You can start with any of the VAK submodalities or you can choose to work with them in the order that you find in this chapter.

Change each visual submodality one at a time while noticing the impact, if any, the change has on the memory. For example, you can move the picture to a different place on the clock face, or move it closer or farther away. You can make the picture dimmer or brighter. Make a note of the changes you experience. Repeat the process for the auditory and then the kinaesthetic submodalities. For example, vary the loudness of sounds or make one of the voices sound like Homer Simpson to discover how changing the voice changes how you feel about the message. You might choose to move the location of a feeling in your body or, if your memory has a colour, to change the colour.

John shifted the visual location of his memory and made a record of the results, writing them down in Worksheet 10-8.

Worksheet 10-8	John's Results of Shifting His Submodalities
The shift that had the strongest impact:	I moved the location of the picture farther to my left.
The changes I noticed:	The sounds of our playing suddenly went almost silent and the feeling in my heart became subdued. Changing each of the other submodalities in turn had very little effect on the quality of the memory.

Record in as much detail as you can the qualities of the memory you chose in Worksheets 10-2, 10-3, and 10-4. Then use Worksheet 10-9 to note the changes you experience when you alter each submodality. Change each submodality and record the way your memory is affected – are feelings more intense or flat? You might change a tingling sensation to one of being stroked or dissociate from a picture and observe it in full panorama. You can decide to move a sound that you observe as coming from your left to coming from your right.

Worksheet 10-9	Effects of Changing My Submodalities
Submodality	*Effect of Changing My Submodalities*
Visual:	
Visual:	
Visual:	
Visual:	
Auditory:	
Auditory:	
Auditory:	
Auditory:	
Kinaesthetic:	
Kinaesthetic:	
Kinaesthetic:	
Kinaesthetic:	

If you're going 'Aargh!' because you find that, for example, by changing a visual sub-modality like location it not only changes the way you feel about an event or a person but also changes the auditory and kinaesthetic submodalities, stay calm. Or, do the opposite – get very excited and rejoice because you have found the driver or critical submodality.

The *driver* or *critical submodality* is the one that, when you change that submodality, changes other submodalities. For example, if you allow yourself to feel put down and angry in response to criticism from one of your parents, it may be because the meaning you give to the criticism is, 'He doesn't trust me'. Changing a driver submodality may change not just the picture, sounds, and feelings but make you realise that your parent is doing the criticising out of fear. Suddenly the meaning you give the criticism is, 'He is doing this to protect me'.

Such changes can happen across all the VAK modalities. Take the situation where you change the location of a feeling in your body. This may in turn impact on the picture you hold of an event, the sounds you hear relating to the event, and ultimately the meaning you put on that event.

Cleaning Up Your Experiences

In the earlier sections in this chapter we show you how to manage your submodalities and thus change the associations of your memories. Instead of letting the memory of an experience hold you back, you can tone the memory down by putting it into black and white, moving it to another location so that you practically have to crane your neck to look at the memory, turn down the sounds, and move the feelings outside your body.

You can use the same techniques to change a belief that limits what you want to achieve in life and to create the resources you need in order to succeed.

Changing a limiting belief

Changing a limiting belief may be *the* most important exercise that you ever do because limiting beliefs are treacherous, often growing from a faintest suspicion that arises from observing the way people are behaving, or from taking on the criticisms other people offer. You can have a belief about other people that might limit your inter-action with them – for example, 'young people are ill-mannered'.

Limiting beliefs can also look like:

- ✔ I am a slow reader.
- ✔ I can't read maps.
- ✔ I'll never stand on my head like that skinny yoga teacher.
- ✔ Motorway driving is scary.
- ✔ I am too ordinary to have X, or achieve X or do X, where X is something that many other people can have, achieve, or are doing fairly easily.
- ✔ People from my background are always poor.
- ✔ I can't spell.

After repeating the belief just a few times, the faintest suspicion becomes a full-blown limiting belief and suddenly you're limited unnecessarily because you have allowed someone else's opinion to cloud your judgment.

Research has shown that people process pictures more quickly than sounds and feelings. So if you want to experience change quickly, please play with the visual submodalities.

'But I don't do pictures', you may find yourself saying.

'Oh yes you do!'

'No I don't!'

'Oh, yes you do!'

'Where?'

'No. Not behind you – in your head.'

This little pantomime is just a bit of fun and the reason is to assure you that you do make pictures, even though you may be more aware of feelings and sounds. Such as not giving your big toe a thought, until just now. However, now that your big toe is mentioned, your thoughts go straight to your feet and you are immediately aware of your big toe!

Now's your chance to go for it and break out of the cage where you've got yourself trapped. The process is simple, just take the following steps. You are asked to pay attention to pictures, but if you're more comfortable using the auditory and kinaesthetic submodalities, feel free to use those instead.

1. **Think of a limiting belief you have and make a note of the picture that comes to mind.**

2. **Think of a belief that you no longer find true.**

   This can go along the lines of, 'I used to believe in Santa'. Look at the picture presented by the belief that is no longer true.

3. **Think of a belief that, for you, is an absolute certainty.**

   Need help? Think of the stars when you're sitting in a brightly lit metropolis. Even though you can't see them close to, you know the stars exist and you know the sun will rise in the morning. The exception is for parents of teenagers on holiday who are pretty certain that the *son won't rise in the morning!* Then picture your son – or no, *the* sun – rising, or picture whatever belief you choose for Step 3.

4. **Think of a belief you would rather have than the limiting belief you picture in Step 1.**

   This may be the opposite of your limiting belief, stated in the positive. 'I can be fit, healthy, and weigh 140 pounds again.' And then notice the picture that accompanies your new belief.

5. **Change the submodalities of the limiting belief from Step 1 into those of the belief that is no longer true for you in Step 2.**

6. **Change the submodalities of the belief you would rather have from Step 4 into those of the belief of which you are absolutely certain from Step 3.**

Voilà! Simple! Just notice the difference and enjoy. You now have an empowering belief in place of the limiting belief. You can use Worksheet 10-10 to record changing your limiting belief.

Worksheet 10-10	Changing My Limiting Belief
	The Submodalities
My limiting belief is:	
The belief I would rather have is:	
The belief that is no longer true for me is:	
The belief of which I am absolutely certain is:	
My limiting belief now looks like:	
The new empowering belief now looks like:	

Creating the resources you need

Often, recognising that the resources you need are right under your nose is difficult, especially when you find yourself behaving in a way that holds you back or experiencing emotions such as boredom or a lack of confidence, or feelings of hate, depression, or fear. Remember that you don't behave like this all the time nor do you experience these emotions all the time. That means you have other ways of behaving and feeling emotions. You can focus on the more positive times when you felt energised, excited, loving, confident, or fearless. So if you're fed up of being in a negative frame of mind, step into the memory of the time you felt how you would rather feel or did something you feel good about.

If creating the resources you need seems impossible for you to do on your own, ask your guardian angel for help, or a real-life friend, or call on a figure from the annals of history, or a celebrity from the world of television or film. You can choose different people to help you with different problems. One of Romilla's favourites has to be MacGyver; a TV character who never gives up, can cobble together implements and weapons from scraps of string, pieces of rubber, and ball bearings, and always saves the day despite insurmountable odds. If the person is unavailable or imaginary, you can hold a make-believe conversation with your helper, (a good move to allow you to dissociate yourself from your problem to give yourself breathing space), and have him offer you a solution. Or you can imagine the helper standing in front of you so you can physically move into his body in order to look at your problem from his eyes. You'll probably be amazed!

Dermot saw himself as one of life's victims. He believed wholeheartedly in Murphy's law, adding his own special 'PS' – if it can go wrong, it will, *especially for me*. Feeling the way he did, Dermot booked himself on a course of coaching and insisted on asking for extra sessions because his situation was much worse than anyone else's, and with his luck things wouldn't work out as well for him as for the other participants! Dermot's experienced coach had Dermot think of situations and people so as to build himself a set of resources that he could draw on and use to pull himself out when he felt he was descending into his mindset of victimisation. You can see an example of Dermot's resource set in Worksheet 10-11.

Worksheet 10-11	Dermot's Resource Set
Problem:	I get really tense when I think of working with Timothy because I really don't like him and I know he doesn't like me.
Resource:	Anita, my singing teacher. I really like her and she makes me feel really calm.

By holding the feelings of calm that Dermot felt when he thought about Anita, he was able to take a lot of the emotion out of his dealings with Timothy. Things still aren't brilliant, but Dermot is able to work with Timothy more effectively.

Use Worksheet 10-12 to think of a problem you're experiencing. Then think of a resource you can use to ease the symptoms of the problem or even remove the problem altogether.

Worksheet 10-12	My Resource Set
Problem:	
Resource:	

Overcoming Tough Emotional Times

It may seem trite to say, 'time heals', so okay, you're sceptical, but if you're going through a tough time, try holding the 'time heals' thought and think of a time in the future when your problem is solved. When you're caught in the drama of a tough situation, thinking straight is often hard because of the pictures, sounds, and feelings buzzing all around you. But, by imagining a scenario in which your problem has been resolved, you have the luxury of designing a satisfactory solution as well as giving your unconscious mind the idea of what the submodalities will be like when you have an answer.

In Worksheet 10-13 you can practise discovering the submodalities of your imagined solution to your problem. This may not give you an immediate resolution but it can help you become more resourceful about how you are feeling right now. Once you stop spurting your energy in all directions and start focusing in a calm and collected way, you can move mountains.

Whenever you start fretting, just bring the submodalities from the future into the here and now and you will feel better.

The more vivid you can make your future submodalities, the more your submodalities will impact on your wellbeing.

Worksheet 10-13	Changing the Submodalities of My Problem
My problem at the moment is:	
The submodalities when I think of my problem are:	
The submodalities in the future when my problem no longer exists are:	

No one can tell you how to organise your submodalities. Now that you know how to change your submodalities you can choose to change them so they affect the way you want to feel and in changing how you feel, live your life the way you want. So if you don't like what you see, hear, or feel, simply change your submodalities!

Chapter 11

Aligning Yourself with Your Purpose

*B*ringing about change is easy when you know how. Begin by thinking about all those things you keep putting off: What your options are and what you need to do to give yourself a kick-start. Yes, we're sure you have a few dreams and practical tasks to work on.

In this chapter you have a chance to check out one of the most valuable frameworks NLP has to offer, the Logical Levels model (also called Neurological Levels in the NLP world), created by leading NLP trainer Robert Dilts. We'll say up front that the logical levels model is Kate's favourite tool from NLP – the trusted tool Kate turns to when she or her client are stuck in a rut. The reason? The logical levels model allows you to get a handle on what is happening in your internal and external worlds, and shows you how to achieve the well-formed outcomes that you began to consider in Chapter 3.

Looking at the Logical Levels

Applying the logical levels model helps you bring about vision and purpose in your life as well as helping you enjoy a general state of flow and wellbeing. (How powerful is that?) The logical levels are:

✔ Your sense of purpose

✔ Your identity

✔ Your beliefs and values

✔ Your capabilities

✔ How you behave

✔ The environment in which you operate

You work top down as well as bottom up through the levels. The exercises allow you to think constructively about who you are and why certain things are more important to you. You build on what you discover about the different parts of yourself and the values work you do in Chapter 5.

As you work through the logical levels, don't forget to acknowledge how wonderful you already are: the skills and talents you have and the positive intents lying behind your behaviour.

Imagine that you're an investigative journalist armed with a set of questions for finding out everything there is to know about a person or situation – the who, what, when, where, how, and why questions. The logical levels model is a way of breaking down your personal experience into six different categories that connect you to key questions. Here are the categories and the questions. Figure 11-1 gives you a visual reminder of how you can apply the logical levels.

- **Environment** refers to external opportunities or constraints and answers the questions *where* and *when* and *with whom*.

- **Behaviour** is made up of specific actions within the environment and answers the question *what*.

- **Capabilities and Skills** are about the knowledge, the 'how-to's' that guide and give direction to behaviour. Here, you answer the question *how*.

- **Beliefs and Values** provide the reinforcement (motivation and permission) to support or deny your capabilities. This level answers the question *why*.

- **Identity** factors determine your sense of self and answer the question *who*.

- **Purpose** goes beyond self-consciousness to relate to the bigger picture about mission to ask *what for* or *for whom*.

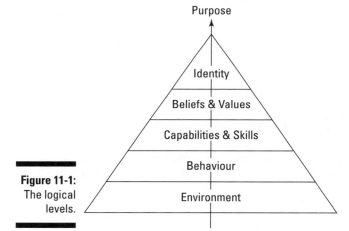

Figure 11-1:
The logical levels.

Going for Easy Change

In this section we show you how you can painlessly apply the logical levels model to yourself, a client, or a group situation.

When leading a busy life, it's natural for some parts of your life to get out of balance at times. Fine, as long as you're aware of what is happening. Perhaps you're putting lots of energy into building great friendships with people and your bank balance is suffering. Or, you're working very hard and not taking time out to look after your home or yourself. The logical levels model can help you readjust the balance easily.

Balancing key areas

Worksheet 11-1 lists key areas about aspects of a balanced life. As you look at this list, think of one area where you're stuck or you feel you have room for improvement. Circle the one area that you're ready to focus on.

Worksheet 11-1	Keys to a Balanced Life
Family	
Fun	
Health	
Job	
Learning	
Living space	
Money	
Romance	
Social network	
Spiritual life	
Add your own:	

Next, you use the logical levels to help you visualise and achieve your goal. We give you an example of how to do this using Freda as the model.

Freda works for her local water authority and has recently been promoted to a senior strategic role. She's well educated and bright and does a great job at keeping the authority's finances in order. She's meticulous and competitive at work. So guess what? Freda's personal finances are in a mess. All Freda's spare cash goes on socialising with friends, and shopping for designer clothes and handbags. When Freda came for coaching, she was becoming more and more frustrated that she was still living at home with her parents in the house she was born in 30 years ago. Freda's debts were mounting and she needed to take decisive action. By working with the logical levels model, she quickly came up with a practical plan to pay off her debts and buy her own home. Worksheet 11-2 shows what she said about where she wants to be a year from now.

Worksheet 11-2	Freda's Balanced Life Worksheet
Key area:	Money.
Environment: Where, when, and with whom am I?	It's 10 October 2009 and I am moving into my own flat. My friends and family are helping me.
Behaviour: What am I doing?	I'm just unpacking my books and clothes. I've saved the deposit, taken out a mortgage, and bought my first flat. I have sold lots of unnecessary clothes and stopped buying recklessly. I also have a part-time job teaching evening classes in bookkeeping at the local college.

(continued)

Worksheet 11-2 *(continued)*

Capabilities: How am I bringing my skills and talents to enable me to make changes in the area I'm focusing on? And what new skills might I need?	I'm very practical and resilient. I know how to manage money and make savings, based on my experience at work, and I am applying my knowledge to my personal finances. I'm developing my skills as a lecturer so that I can get higher-paid assignments in the future.
Beliefs and Values: What do I believe to be true here, what's important to me? (Remember that your beliefs and values are key drivers to motivate you to action.)	It's important that I am in control of my money as this gives me the independence to have more fun in the long term. I believe that by the age of 30 I should have my own place to live. It's important that I have privacy and can do my own thing in my own space.
Identity: Who am I in this context? What roles do I play that are relevant to this situation? How do I describe myself?	I'm a financially responsible adult. I call myself 'Freda the Financial Whizz' to remind me how good it feels to be in control of my finances.
Purpose: What meaning do I draw from my experience in this specific situation and how does it relate to other areas of my life?	Now all my friends are asking me for help on budgeting and saving wisely. I feel that I can get on with my life more confidently and make a difference for others as well.

Now, use Worksheet 11-3 to record your answers to questions about what you would like to be different a year from now in the key area you circled in Worksheet 11-1. The questions refer to the six categories listed in 'Looking at the Logical Levels' and you may want to check out the pyramid image of the logical levels in Figure 11-1 as well.

Although we ask you to imagine the future as a year from now, write your answers on your worksheet in the present tense as if you have carried out the change you wanted to make. That way you engage your unconscious mind to help you make your goals happen for you. The unconscious mind doesn't distinguish between imagination and reality.

Worksheet 11-3   My Balanced Life Worksheet

Key area:	
Environment: Where, when, and with whom am I?	
Behaviour: What am I doing?	

Capabilities: How am I bringing my skills and talents to enable me to make changes in the area I'm focusing on? And what new skills might I need?	
Beliefs and Values: What do I believe to be true here, what's important to me? (Remember that your beliefs and values are key drivers to motivate you to action.)	
Identity: Who am I in this context? What roles do I play that are relevant to this situation? How do I describe myself?	
Purpose: What meaning do I draw from my experience in this specific situation and how does it relate to other areas of my life?	

Strengthening your NLP muscles

One of the reasons NLP techniques provide such robust learning is that many of the exercises engage your body – movement and breathing. While doing the exercises, you can stand or sit in different places as you do them and find out how different the exercises feel.

Often when working with groups of people and business teams, we put pieces of paper on the floor or chairs to show the six logical levels. People then remember the experience more powerfully than hearing about the logical levels in an abstract way.

Here's an exercise to try out with your team at work.

1. **Take six pieces of paper and on each one write the name of one of the logical levels (if you need to recap, see 'Looking at the Logical Levels' or Figure 11-1).**

2. **On the floor of your meeting room place the pieces of paper in a line spaced out like individual stepping stones. If you have lots of space, so much the better.**

3. **Have each member of the team take turns in stepping from level to level and saying what he or she thinks about the team's current status and future goals, through two rounds of questions:**

   - **Round One:** Working from Environment up to Purpose, ask what this team is like today at each level.

   - **Round Two:** Working from Purpose down to Environment, ask how this team would like to be in two years' time.

The questions to ask at each logical level are similar to the questioning in the earlier section 'Balancing key areas' – they're simply adapted for the work context:

- **Environment:** Where, when, and with whom are we working?
- **Behaviour:** What are we doing?
- **Capabilities:** How can we bring our skills and talents to support us?
- **Beliefs and Values:** What do we believe to be true here, what's important to us as a team? Why is that the case?
- **Identity:** Who are we? What part do we play in the organisation?
- **Purpose:** How do we fit with the bigger organisational perspective? Why are we here?

Jan was appointed as Customer Services Supervisor for a medical products manufacturing company. The job was a challenging promotion for her. She'd never managed people before and had to change her identity from being a fun-loving member of the team to leading the team at a time when customer service had a poor reputation in the company, and many complaints from outside. When Jan discovered the logical levels model, she decided to introduce it at her monthly team meeting and surprised her new team by inviting them to explore how they wanted to work together by placing the pieces of paper on the floor. From the exercise, the team aired their concerns, promised to work together with honesty and respect, and aligned themselves firmly with the medical products made by the company. The team members realised that they were part of an important service that saved lives. Psychologically the employees bought into being part of an important team in a worthwhile business and went on to win quality awards demonstrating the team's motivation.

You can be creative and adapt the logical levels exercises by looking at them on paper, talking them through, and walking them through. The more senses you bring into play – by adding colours, sounds, tastes, and smells – the better. Think about different situations where the logical levels can help you. For example, if you're planning a trip away with friends, getting everyone to explore the logical levels up front will help you make sure each member of the group has a good time in his or her own way.

Focusing on Your Identity, Values, and Beliefs

As you work with the logical levels model, you find that you get the fastest impact when addressing the questions at the higher logical levels – from the Beliefs and Values level, up through Identity, to your sense of Purpose. You can help yourself by exploring the higher questions with an impartial friend, mentor, or coach who is likely to be open-minded about your course of action.

Take one of your more challenging situations in which you're struggling to make decisions or get started, and use the Identity and Values exploration to plan some more empowering Beliefs to respond to the situation.

If you're struggling to think of a situation, here are some examples: Changing jobs, moving home, building or breaking up a partnership, making a cultural change in a business, and undertaking major decisions concerning children and education.

Exploring your identity

You play many roles in your life which together make up a rich tapestry that is the reflection of your unique essence. This essence makes you special and different to anyone else. Some of the time you slip easily between roles; for example, as hairdresser and parent, or manager and homemaker. Yet at other times the different roles bring tension. In order to integrate all these different parts of you into one whole, consider a positive name or label that you can give that encompasses all these roles. Maybe you consider yourself to be a wise woman, a kind warrior, an explorer, a courageous diva, or an exotic tiger. Find a name for your identity that describes all of you at your very best.

Frank is debating whether he wants to make a lifestyle change and emigrate to Australia from the UK with his children and Australian wife. Many conflicting questions are running around his head and he told Kate how confused he feels. Frank has recently taken up a new job that he loves and is happily settled living in an English country village – getting involved with running the local cricket and football teams with his young son. His parents live nearby and all seemed fine until his wife suddenly announced that she was very homesick and wanted to go back to live in Melbourne close to her family. Living in Australia was a subject they had never discussed before they had a family. Frank feels that he'd be letting his parents and employer down if he moved, and his wife if he didn't move. Frank used Worksheet 11-4 to explore how he thinks of himself and his role.

Worksheet 11-4	Frank's Identity-naming Worksheet
My names for the different roles I play in my life:	Hero husband Doting dad Magical son Warrior software developer Cricket supremo
What is a role that includes all the other roles?	Intrepid explorer
What is the view of the situation from each of the different roles?	I'll be a hero husband if I find a way to give my wife what she wants. My son dotes on me as much as I dote on him and he's at a good age to move. The sticking point is how guilty I feel about leaving my parents in the UK. How can I still be a magical son living so far away? As the Warrior software developer there are ways I can work in Australia — if not for this company, then for another one. And I can certainly enjoy being the cricket supremo out there. As an overall intrepid explorer, it's good to travel and move on.

Does the title of this book say that it's a 'workbook?' Then the opposite is true too: *Neuro-linguistic Programming Workbook For Dummies* is a 'playbook' to help you break through challenges quickly. So you've been procrastinating because the problems seemed tough. That's OK. No time like the present. Jump into Worksheet 11-5, naming your own identities in relation to a challenge you're addressing.

Worksheet 11-5	My Identity-naming Worksheet
My names for the different roles I play in my life:	
What is a role that includes all of the other roles?	
What is the view of the situation from each of the different roles?	

Lining up your values

In their purest, deepest form, *values* are your emotional drivers, the things that are most important to you, that you're passionate about having in your life. Core values are your bedrock even though different things will be important to you in different situations. When we talk about beliefs, we don't mean religious beliefs but those things you hold to be true – the rules you make for yourself that help you get to decisions quickly.

Frank used Worksheet 11-6 to ensure that any action he takes fully honours his values. If he didn't align his values, he'd soon find himself under stress.

Worksheet 11-6	Frank's Values Alignment
My Top Life Values	*Impact of My Values in This Situation*
Family	I'll be honouring my wife and son, I'm not sure yet how to honour my parents as well.
Honesty	I'm going to be honest with everyone about my plans as they develop and share my feelings.
Risk taking	It is risky to move and I like the buzz that gives me.
Peace	The UK doesn't feel a peaceful place to live compared to Australia.
Responsibility	Whatever I do, I will take care of my dependents and honour my job commitments.
Health	I think we'll have a healthier outdoor lifestyle in Australia. My parents can visit Australia and avoid the UK winters.

From exploring his Identity and Values, Frank arrives at new possibilities and opens up choices for himself.

Using Worksheet 11-7, think about your values and how they affect your situation.

Worksheet 11-7	My Values Alignment
My Top Life Values	*Impact of My Values in This Situation*

Making your beliefs more powerful

When you hear yourself saying 'I can't' do something or 'I'll never be able to . . .' you may be restricting your choices due to fears for the future or a view of yourself that isn't necessarily accurate. Beliefs are assumptions that you make which may or may not be true. Check whether the beliefs you hold serve you or whether they're outdated. You may hold a limiting belief about yourself that's worth putting to the test, and the way to test it is by asking yourself to think about another possibility. You can quickly switch limiting beliefs to empowering ones by taking a positive and opposite view. Empowering beliefs involve an element of choice, such as: 'I can choose to take control of my finances/become the fittest I've ever been/find the job of my dreams.'

Worksheet 11-8 shows Frank's limiting belief and some of the more empowering and liberating beliefs he can choose to adopt as he explores his options.

Worksheet 11-8	Frank's Empowering Beliefs
My most limiting belief:	I can't be a good husband and good son at the same time if I move to Australia.
My empowering beliefs:	I can find ways around difficult situations. I've made major changes before and they have worked out. I can work out plans that take things step by step. We don't have to rush at this. I keep my commitments. After I make a move to Australia, others in the family may well want to follow. We live in a global world where communication is getting better all the time.
My new most empowering belief:	I can be a good husband while being a good son, wherever I live.

Using Worksheet 11-9 write down how you can turn your limiting belief into an empowering belief.

Worksheet 11-9	My Empowering Beliefs
My most limiting belief:	
My empowering beliefs:	
My new most empowering belief:	

Valuing the Job of Your Dreams

You may find that the job you're doing today was great for you a year, five years, or ten years ago, but is no longer exciting or satisfying. You're not alone. In our career coaching work we come across people every day who want to change jobs and have no idea what they want, other than to escape from what they're doing.

Do any of the following statements apply to you?

✔ There are times when I'm bored at work.

✔ I feel stifled.

✔ I'm not using all my talents to the full.

✔ This job used to be great and now I'm not so sure.

✔ I wish I could quit and do something different.

If you answered 'yes' to any of these statements, read on to consider how you can develop your career in a more positive and rewarding direction. And if you answered no, then read on anyway because things can change overnight and you never know when you may need a 'plan B' for your working life.

In this section we help you do the necessary groundwork in shifting away from the wrong kind of work – to the work that fits with who you are today.

A truly satisfying job takes into account your core values – the fundamental ideals most important to you. Worksheet 11-10 helps you decide what your core working values are.

Here are some things that people typically value about their work. Notice what resonates for you as you look at the list.

✔ Competition

✔ Courage

✔ Fun

✔ Freedom

✔ Honesty and integrity

✔ Innovation

✔ Intellectual satisfaction

✔ Learning/personal growth

✔ Recognition

✔ Responsibility

✔ Security

✔ Service to others

✔ Teamworking/collaboration

✔ Trust

Money is a 'means' value rather than a 'core' value: money may buy you freedom and choices but it's not an end in itself. View money as a resource that can get you independence or knowledge. Money by itself and purely for its own sake quickly proves to be a disappointing guide to live by.

Worksheet 11-10 gives you the opportunity to discover the top three times when you were happiest in your work. You may find that all three instances were at different times in one job or each time may be from a separate job. You then create a list of no more than ten key points to describe what you were doing (your behaviours) and what skills you were using, asking yourself:

✔ What was important about this?

✔ And what did that give me?

These questions will help you drill down to your core values, which in turn form your personal selection criteria for the next job opportunity that comes up for you. As you think about what's important to you, you can also substitute the question of what's most satisfying or valuable for you. Go through each item in your list of key points in turn. For example, if one job that you really enjoyed was stacking the shelves in the supermarket, you may have found a sense of freedom and fun in that. Another job where you were a personal assistant may have satisfied your love of learning and you may have enjoyed the responsibility.

Worksheet 11-10		Discovering Dream Job Qualities		
Times When I Was Happiest at Work	**What Was I Doing? (Behaviour)**	**What Skills Was I Using?**	**What Was Important about This Experience?**	**And What Did That Give Me?**
Job experience 1:				
Job experience 2:				
Job experience 3:				

When you come to an understanding of your core work values, record them in Worksheet 11-11. Make a copy of the worksheet and carry it around with you as a reminder whenever you're talking to people about job roles or going for interviews.

Don't be tempted by jobs that sound good but don't fit your set of values. You may get offered shiny opportunities that don't match your core values. Be wary; if your values aren't met, you haven't found the job of your dreams.

Worksheet 11-11	My Core Work Values
My personal core values checklist for my dream job:	
1.	
2.	
3.	
4.	
5.	

Flowing Through the Levels for a Purposeful Life

Think of an occasion when you were so wrapped up in what you were doing you just didn't notice how time had flown by. Maybe you were engrossed in a hobby, a piece of work, or a sporting activity. You were alert, absorbed, and operating effortlessly – just like a child playing on the beach or with a favourite toy. Athletes talk about this state of flow as being 'in the zone' – operating at peak performance. In his book, *The Psychology of Optimal Experience*, Mihaly Csikszentmihalyi coined the phrase *the flow channel*: the space you occupy when your capabilities and interests are aligned – that space between being bored because an activity is too easy and stressed because the activity is too difficult.

Perhaps you have a sense that life could be more relaxed or easy so that it flows for you but are not sure how. Worksheets 12 to 15 help you discover how to go with the flow.

The logical levels can help you understand the flow of your feelings, thoughts, and actions so that your life finally has a sense of purpose and you're motivated and inspired. In the NLP world, the word *congruence* describes that sense of power you have when you're acting in accordance with what feels right at all the levels.

Imagine you're writing about how you live your life for a popular lifestyle magazine. Tell your story as frankly as you can. (And don't worry about grammar, we promise our editors won't look.)

Starting at Environment, the bottom level of the logical levels (see 'Looking at the Logical Levels' or Figure 11-1), capture information from your personal life in Draft 1 of your imaginary lifestyle magazine article. Think about adjustments that you would like to make to your life story so that you feel truly aligned to your sense of purpose, then rewrite your life story from the top logical level, Purpose, to realign yourself. Capture this version in Draft 2.

Make your life story real for you by writing in the present tense.

Worksheet 11-12	Jeremy's Life Story, Draft 1
Environment:	I live in a small village just outside a large town in the North of England with my wife, Denise, and our three sons. My job in sales with a print company suits me well and we've got a nice house. My workmates are a good bunch of people and I like going out with them one night a week to see how the business is going and bond with the team. The weekends are family time — I'll cook a good meal on Saturday night and play football with the lads on Sunday.
Behaviour:	I have an easy-going nature and like to have fun in my family life. Work can get a bit tense when we're finishing off large projects so I'm the one who keeps a sense of humour and keeps the team going to a deadline.

(continued)

	Worksheet 11-12 *(continued)*
Capabilities:	My first job was with a firm of accountants — it was too inward-looking for me. I'm good with people and also with figures. I have to confess I haven't grasped all the technology of the latest print machines although I can see they are very sophisticated and flexible.
Beliefs and Values:	Family life is important to me, and I worry about the future for my kids. I was brought up in a mining family and am so relieved that life is healthier and more secure for us. Although I enjoy the rewards of my work — house, car, and holidays, I also think community life and looking out for my neighbours is important. I've always believed in working hard and being honest and straightforward in all my dealings with people. I also believe that what goes round comes round.
Identity:	I'm a sales manager and a family man. Sometimes I feel a bit of an impostor — what right do I have to drive around in a comfortable car when my dad and my grandfather mined underground for all those years. I've tried to give my children a better quality of life than I had and to be a good role model for them.
Purpose:	I'm not someone with a burning ambition to change the planet but I do think I have a responsibility for how we treat the world and leaving it in good shape for future generations. I'd like to be remembered as a decent citizen who gave back to the community.

Jeremy then imagined a more purposeful life for himself and wrote Draft 2, in Worksheet 11-13, starting at the top logical level and working down.

Worksheet 11-13	Jeremy's Life Story, Draft 2
Purpose:	I've always felt an affinity with the great outdoors here in this part of the world and want to do my bit to see the countryside preserved and improved for future generations to enjoy. That's something I instil into my children and workmates.
Identity:	I'm an enlightened family-friendly manager at work, a responsible husband and father, as well as a strong contributor to the local community.

Beliefs and Values:	I believe it's possible to be honest and give back to others in life as well as taking the rewards when they are deserved. I value security and freedom, strong relationships with people, and businesses that create valuable products and services for customers, treating all fairly. I think we have a duty not to waste materials and I'm encouraging my customers to use environmentally friendly printing paper.
Capabilities:	At work I'm embracing new ways of doing things with the latest technology so I can sell the benefits of our latest print machines and use e-mail when I'm out of the office. I think it's important to keep on learning and I take a keen interest in my team and their skills development. I think good managers train their people to constantly grow and take on bigger challenges.
Behaviour:	As I get more mature, I get calmer, wiser, and more content in my work and my home life. People come to me as a trusted pair of hands. I rarely lose my temper and I know how to get my point across with respect. I get a great buzz out of working with younger people and also my football coaching on Sundays with the boys and their friends.
Environment:	I prefer to spend time with like-minded people who have a 'can-do' attitude to work together. I have created a flexible working pattern so that I can drop the boys off at school on two days a week to give Denise a break and work from home at least one day a week. This helps me to save my energy if I've been driving a lot in any one week to customer appointments. It also means that Denise and I can get to one dance class together every week.

Now it's your turn to write your life story, and you can be as imaginative as you want. Use Worksheet 11-14 for your first, bottom-up version.

Worksheet 11-14	**My Life Story, Draft 1**
Environment:	

(continued)

Worksheet 11-14 *(continued)*

Behaviour:	
Capabilities:	
Beliefs and Values:	
Identity:	
Purpose:	

In Worksheet 11-15, while writing your second draft, top down, develop your life story as powerfully as you can, showing how proud you are of the life you're living.

Worksheet 11-15	My Life Story, Draft 2
Purpose:	
Identity:	
Beliefs and Values:	
Capabilities:	
Behaviour:	
Environment:	

After writing the two versions of your life story, go back to one account and polish up your life story until you have a version that is truly inspirational. Then write another version of your life story saying what your life is like in two, five, or ten years from now.

Chapter 12

Changing Strategies for Success

. . . .

In This Chapter

▶ Understanding strategies

▶ Checking out your strategies

▶ Breaking down strategies

▶ Modelling other people's strategies

▶ Changing troublesome strategies

. . . .

Have you ever noticed how some people have the knack of doing everything well, while other people are quite inept – everything they touch is a disaster. Take cooking, for example. Why is it that one person can produce delicious meals while another person can't boil an egg? (By the way, one of your authors is incapable of cooking a soft-boiled egg, but we'll leave you to guess which one of us it might be!) Please forgive the pun, but doing things well boils down to strategies. Sticking with the example of the successful cook, getting great results can be broken down into steps (which can have further steps within them):

1. **Having the belief, 'I am a great cook'.**

2. **Setting the intention: The meal is going to taste wonderful.**

3. **Planning the menu.**

4. **Making sure you have all the right ingredients.**

5. **Following the recipe.**

So, your softly boiled egg turned out solid? You got distracted during the cooking process, or you forgot to set the timer, or . . . there's always a reason. Even boiling an egg requires a strategy, and maybe even strategies within strategies.

In this chapter, we show you how to make things work for you. For example, having the right strategy for getting something done immediately instead of procrastinating, or becoming a model motorist instead of experiencing road rage. We talk about developing new strategies, analysing or modifying present strategies, and adopting other people's strategies. Best of all, understanding how a strategy works is your recipe for success.

Describing Strategies

A *strategy* is a pattern of behaviour that can be copied and reproduced. Strategies in themselves aren't bad or good, but rather are deemed effective or ineffective upon checking their results. Another word for strategy is *habit*. Patterns of behaviour are initiated by a trigger, taking you through a series of steps, and ending when a condition is satisfied. For example, your routine for getting dressed in the morning may be initiated by the alarm clock going off. Your series of steps includes brushing your teeth, taking a shower, examining your appearance in the mirror, and saying, 'my goodness you are irresistible'. The 'getting dressed' strategy ends when you're satisfied with how you look. You then move into the 'eat breakfast' or 'get to work' strategy.

Judy was at a prestigious networking event where she caught herself watching a well-dressed, good-looking man, called Archie Archer. Archie certainly seemed to have the X factor; he was the centre of attention in an animated and lively group. However, after about 40 minutes or so, Judy saw Archie standing quite alone and looking dejected. She soon discovered why after engaging him in conversation. Archie was funny and interesting until he suddenly said, with real feeling, 'Gosh you really are so much cleverer than you look'. Ouch!

Archie suffers from the 'foot-firmly-in-mouth' syndrome. Does this mean that there's no hope for Archie? Well, no. The foot-firmly-in-mouth syndrome is actually a strategy that Archie has inadvertently perfected over time. If Archie can recognise that he has a problem, that his behaviour is often offensive, and is willing to change his behaviour, he will have no trouble changing his strategy from 'engage-mouth-before-brain' to 'engage-brain-before-mouth'.

Archie may eventually get the message that speaking without thinking isn't an effective strategy for winning friends and influencing people – after discovering that people move off when they see him approaching (strategy evaluated as ineffective). On the other hand, some generous-spirited folk may actually find Archie's frankness quite endearing (the same strategy evaluated as effective). The people evaluating Archie's 'foot-in-mouth' strategy as ineffective activated their 'avoid Archie' trigger. The others who evaluated Archie's strategy as effective ran their 'choose to accept Archie' strategy. If Archie understood how strategies worked, he would be in a position to alter his strategy and get a different response from the people around him.

A strategy is a set pattern that can be copied. If you come across someone who has a strategy that you would like to build into your life, study the strategy and adapt it to suit you (we show you how to do this in 'Discovering Someone's Strategy' later in this chapter). For example, Tom a six-footer, has a tried and tested strategy for high jumping, which he now finds a doddle. Vertically challenged Sandra would love to copy Tom's strategy and reach his dizzy heights but may have to settle for lower jumps or wear spring-loaded shoes.

Evaluating Your Strategies

Do you find yourself rapping yourself over the knuckles for your bad habits but seldom giving yourself credit for things that you do well? Think about your good and bad habits and how they affect your particular strategy. Throughout this chapter we give you ideas for changing your habits and strategies, but just for now here are some points to help you sort out your thoughts about whether your strategy is working for you.

> ✔ **Describe the strategy you're evaluating.** You can check out any strategy, such as how you decide which outfit to wear; how you make sure you're putting diesel, not petrol, in your car; or how you react to a comment. For example, if you think someone is being overly critical of you, you may lash out at even the most innocent remark.

✔ **Decide whether you think your strategy is effective or ineffective and why you think so.** How effective or ineffective your strategy is depends on the outcome you want. Take choosing an outfit. If you leave choosing what to wear until the last minute and it makes you late and your goal is to be smartly dressed and on time, then you may consider your strategy as ineffective because the first part of your strategy fulfilled one desire (being smart) but not the second (being on time). If your goal is for your outfit to be just perfect, then you may think of your strategy as being successful.

✔ **Identify other people who are evaluating your strategy and whether they believe it's effective or ineffective.** Often one person judges another person's behaviour by his own. You know that he thinks what you're doing is good when he's praising you and bad when you're being criticised.

If you perceive the feedback you receive as being critical and believe that criticism is justified, then you can choose to adapt your strategy. As with the example of choosing the outfit, if someone important to you said,'You look really terrific', you'd accept it as a compliment. If however you were told, 'Great outfit, shame you missed the grand opening', next time you may well plan to have your outfit ready and sorted the night before and focus on arriving on time.

✔ **Consider the result you get from using the strategy and whether that result works for you.**

If your strategy isn't working, identify the secondary gain you're getting through using the strategy (Chapter 3 tells you about and gives examples of 'secondary gains'). In the case of having the perfect outfit but being late, your secondary gain may be that making an entrance is your crowning achievement!

✔ **Identify your process.** Break down your strategy into steps to identify where you can build in a change. In reacting to an overly critical person, you may adopt a strategy of letting the person act in his usual critical fashion but at the same time choosing to think of someone who makes you feel good about yourself, or silently thank your critic for giving you the opportunity to discover how to manage your thinking.

If your strategy isn't working, find someone who is getting the results you would like to have. You can then copy that person's strategies – a topic we detail in 'Discovering Someone's Strategy' later in the chapter.

ANECDOTE

Joanna liked to claim that she excelled at being a mediocre accountant. On the other side of the coin, when she heard the sound of dance music, she felt her soul soaring. During an NLP coaching session, when she was in a light trance, she remembered a school disco and being chastised for her dancing, which at the time was considered lewd by the standards of her strict girls' school. A teacher humiliated Joanna in front of the rest of the girls and their guests. As Joanna talked the memory through with her coach, Joanna realised that it was then that she'd decided, unconsciously, never to put herself in a position where she could be ridiculed and to avoid conflict at all costs. Now Joanna has joined a dance class and is proving to be the star pupil. Because she is happier, she is getting on better at work, although she acknowledges that she will never be more than an average accountant. Joanna is exploring other avenues for leading a more fulfilling life, perhaps as a part-time dance teacher.

Worksheet 12-1 shows how Joanna assessed her perceived mediocrity, her desire to put other people's needs before her own, and her unwillingness to stand up for herself.

Worksheet 12-1	Joanna's Assessment of Her Strategy
Describe the strategy:	I'll do anything to avoid conflict. For example, I let my family tell me what to do, and I also know I'm overdue for a pay rise but can't face confronting that miserable boss of mine.
Decide whether you think your strategy is effective or ineffective and why you think so:	I don't like the way I give way, and as I get older, suppress my sense of fun and adventure, and always am the good girl everyone wants me to be. I don't think it helps me because I am actually quite unhappy and frustrated. I comfort eat, so that's bad, and am being judged as not good enough by my family.
Identify other people who are evaluating your strategy and whether they believe it's effective or ineffective:	I think, unconsciously, Dad actually sees it as good because I do what he wants. I think my boss likes me being a doormat, as he doesn't have to waste time and energy on me.
Consider the result you get from using the strategy and whether that result works for you:	I earn a good wage and life is on an even keel. I live at home and although that isn't much fun, there is security and safety.
If the result isn't what you want, decide what your secondary gains are:	There is less agro and Dad doesn't turn on Mum for raising a stupid girl. Besides I am quite scared of going off and finding work away from home or the people with whom I work because I don't know what to expect.
Identify your process:	I want to do something different but always agree with Dad when he starts to shout.
If your strategy isn't working, find someone who is getting the results you would like to have:	Sarah, my dance teacher, is pretty much her own woman and is good at knowing what she wants and how to get it. I've noticed that Sarah never shows anger and is always calm when she is getting her message across. She stands with her weight evenly distributed and makes eye contact and repeats what she wants to say in several different ways.

Joanna's strategy for conforming and avoiding conflict has been going on since the incident at her girls' school and is actually very unhelpful. A way of changing her strategy may be by changing her time line (Chapter 13 shows you how).

Joanna decided to make a few changes to the strategies she had for dealing with her father whom she saw as the biggest obstacle in her life. She realised she had an 'allow myself to feel bad' strategy when her father started to shout. Joanna started using sub-modalities (lots more on 'submodalities' in Chapter 10) to help keep her emotions under control by reminding herself of times when her father had been very loving and supportive towards her. Joanna decided to put in place a strategy for holding her ground when she and her father had disagreements. She adopted Sarah's stance and body language and way of speaking in a calm and collected manner. One very important step she took was to work out her goals using the well-formed outcome process we outline in Chapter 3. Working with her coach, Joanna had come to realise that her present strategy of letting other people tell her how to run her life was ineffective. Now she adopted a strategy for working out what it was she wanted from her life.

Samuel Johnson said, 'It is a most mortifying reflection for a man to consider what he has done, compared to what he might have done.' Johnson's quote certainly applied to Joanna's situation when she continually allowed others to run her life. After changing her strategies, Joanna started to live her life on a new level, experiencing self-fulfilment and success.

Worksheet 12-2 gives you an opportunity to examine one of your strategies, decide whether the results you're getting are what you want, and then assess your strategy as effective (gives you the result you want) or ineffective (doesn't give you your desired result), and how you can fine-tune your strategy to achieve your goal more efficiently; keeping in mind that a strategy is another word for a habit.

Worksheet 12-2	My Assessment of a Strategy
Describe the strategy:	
Decide whether you think your strategy is effective or ineffective and why you think so:	
Identify other people who are evaluating your strategy and whether they believe it's effective or ineffective:	
Consider the result you get from using the strategy and whether that result works for you:	
If the result isn't what you want, decide what your secondary gains are:	
Identify your process:	

(continued)

Worksheet 12-2 (continued)

If your strategy isn't working, find someone who is getting the results you would like to have:	

Deconstructing Strategies

Recognising how a strategy is broken down lies in working out the steps involved and carrying them out exactly. Knowing which steps to take is especially useful when you want to 'reverse engineer' a strategy – to use an expression from the TV sci-fi series *Stargate* (for finding out how an alien device works). Applying the technique of reverse engineering to strategies means that once you have mastered the steps, you can pretty much do what you want with a strategy – from changing your own strategy to adopting someone else's, and using the strategy in whichever area of your life you choose. Follow these steps to discover how a strategy works:

1. **Start by asking, 'How do I know when to run the strategy?'**

The answer gives you the trigger that fires off your strategy.

2. **Repeatedly ask 'What happens then?' or 'What do I do next?'**

The answers to these questions give you the steps within the strategy.

3. **Ask 'How do I know when to stop?'**

This gives you the information that ends a strategy.

After discovering the structure of a strategy, you can modify the strategy however and whenever you see fit.

Looking closely at how you're failing at something can give you valuable insights into how to tweak the steps for success.

Figure 12-1 illustrates how a strategy involving leading a healthy lifestyle can be broken down. The strategy is built up from different steps to help you to reach your goal.

If your health strategy is being sabotaged by your inability to get enough exercise, study someone who exercises regularly and try adopting his recipe for success.

Please use the space in Worksheet 12-3 for drawing a diagram of your chosen strategy. Remember to indicate the steps you're taking to achieve your goal.

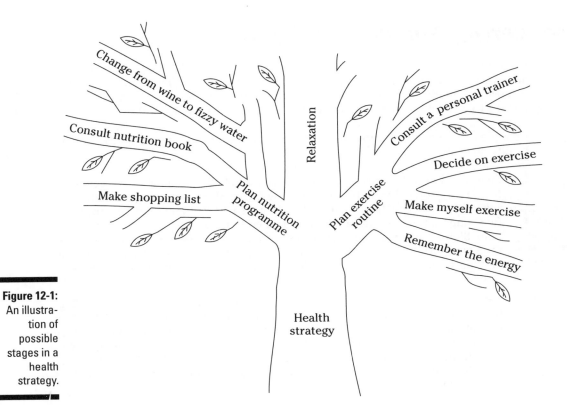

Figure 12-1:
An illustration of possible stages in a health strategy.

Worksheet 12-3   **My Strategy Illustration**

Discovering Someone's Strategy

If a particular strategy just isn't working for you, look around for someone who is operating in a similar situation as yourself and has an apparently effective strategy that you can usefully model. Copying an aspect of someone else's behaviour may well be the answer to your difficulties and help you to run your life more smoothly.

Here are a couple of scenarios illustrating how modelling another person's strategy brings success.

- ✔ Simon had been in sales for some time but was failing to meet his targets – his strategy on cold calling just wasn't working. He was running an 'I'll be rejected' strategy, which then pushed him into his 'procrastination' strategy. Realising that his job was at stake he turned to a successful sales colleague for help. Simon's colleague explained his strategy and the steps he took to maintain targets. Once Simon's overall 'failing to meet targets' strategy was broken down, and his strategy for cold calling was re-engineered, he began to achieve his targets.

- ✔ Ben, new to teaching maths, thoroughly enjoyed his job in a sixth form college. Ben's conventional 'chalk and talk' method worked well for all the students, except one particularly bright student. Ben realised he needed a different teaching strategy for that student and an experienced colleague suggested giving the student the opportunity to 'learn by doing'. After a short time this method of teaching proved very effective and Ben, by adapting his teaching style to the student, had progressed in his learning as well.

Reading the eyes

A way of uncovering a person's underlying behaviour, his strategy, is by asking him questions and watching his eye movements. The answers give you the structure of the strategies that the person is using consciously and the eye movements give you the unconscious clues.

You can refer to the Cheat Sheet at the front of the workbook to remind yourself of how a person's eye movements indicate their preferences: Visual (V), Auditory (A), Kinaesthetic (K), or Auditory dialogue (Ad).

Strategy for detecting if someone is 'normally organised'

In NLP-speak, right-handed people are called *normally organised*. If you know whether someone is normally organised you can use that knowledge to build rapport with him. Take care: you may sometimes encounter exceptions to this rule.

Always check whether a person is right-handed or left-handed. When in doubt, calibrate! How? The following scripts of imaginary conversations between Kate and Samantha, and later between Kate and Tom – Samantha and Tom are people Kate has just met – show you how you can *calibrate*, that is, gauge whether a person is left- or right-handed.

Kate: 'Do you have the time?'

Samantha, looking at her left hand: 'Oh! Sorry I don't wear a watch.'

Kate, innocently: 'Oh! You're left-handed.'

Samantha, looking puzzled: 'No I'm actually right-handed.'

Kate, disarmingly: 'Tsk, I always get my left and right muxed ip or even mixed up.'

Or

Tom, looking at the watch on his right hand: 'It's ten past nine.'

Kate, innocently: 'Oh! You're left-handed.'

Tom: 'Yes, I am.'

In both cases, Kate got her answer!

Doing a spot of calibrating doesn't hurt because, as they say in the north of England, 'Nowt so queer as folk', and it could well be that the watch was on the wrong hand.

Building rapport is a core pillar of NLP so we suggest you steer away from being flippant and saying things like, 'So you're not normally organised' or 'You're a south paw' – putting your foot in it won't win you friends! (For lots more on building rapport, refer to Chapter 7.)

In the diagram on the Cheat Sheet, you see how a right-handed person moves his eyes. Remember that a left-handed person may move his eyes in the opposite direction. In Worksheet 12-4 we suggest a few questions to ask in order to read a person's eye movements. We also give you space to think up questions of your very own.

Worksheet 12-4	Questions for Calibration		
Our Suggestions for Questions to Ask	*Likely Eye Movements for a Right-Handed Person*	*Questions You May Want to Ask*	*Anticipated Eye Movement*
So what was your journey here like?	Eyes move upwards to top left (visual) – remembering pictures of the trip, or horizontally left (auditory) – remembering the traffic noise or conversation, or to the bottom right – remembering how the car seat felt (kinesthetic).		
I was wondering what that irate warden would sound like if he was a contented kitten?	Eyes move horizontally to the right (auditory construct), imagining the irate warden as a contented kitten.		
Would you agree that knowing what we know now, it's illogical to think we're at the centre of the Universe?	Eyes may go to the bottom left as he works out the logic of the statement.		

Surveying for a strategy

And now we get down to the nitty-gritty of how you can usefully apply what you've discovered about uncovering strategies. First, because people have different strategies for different situations – like planning meals, deciding what is going on their shopping list, dealing with anger, and so on, it is useful to bring a person's VAK thought processes into play. For example, when planning a picnic – how the person feels about picnicking (K), conversation about the picnic (A), how he visualises the picnic (V), and if he feels happy about the picnic (K). Second, if you want to find out when and how a person is involved in an activity, a simple question asked at the right time might be, 'When was the last you did X?', where X was planning a meal, making a grocery list, or getting angry. As the person being asked the question about X considers his answer, his eyes will reveal his thinking process. And lastly, before asking your questions, make sure you're in a situation that you're comfortable with, such as at work, in a meeting, in a café with your friends – and only ask questions that are appropriate for the situation.

Tom wants to sell a car to Jan. Wouldn't it be good for Tom to know Jan's purchasing strategy in order for Tom to get Jan to buy?

Tom is watching Jan's eyes and we pick up the conversation after the preliminaries are over during which Jan said that she might be interested in a used car and Tom has discovered that Jan is right-handed.

Worksheet 12-5 shows you how a simple question can reveal the way someone thinks by the way his eyes move. The idea is that Jan's response can be broken into sentences that tie in with distinct eye movements. Tom then matches his follow-up statement to call up the pictures, feelings, and conversation in the same sequence as Jan experienced.

Ethics are involved in wielding a powerful tool like NLP. We're working on the assumption that Tom is passionate about the cars he sells and totally convinced that the car Jan is interested in is the most suitable car for her lifestyle.

Worksheet 12-5	Tom's Discovery of Jan's Thought Processes			
Tom's Questions	*Jan's Answers*	*Jan's Eye Movements*	*Jan's Thoughts*	*Tom's Responses*
So when you bought your last car, what made you choose that specific car?	Well! I remember walking into the showroom and my eyes were drawn to the lovely red, sporty-looking car.	👀	Remembering herself in the showroom.	I watched you admiring that gun-metal beauty there. (V)
	I knew she'd be my little pocket rocket.	👀	Accessing feelings of excitement.	She might not fit in your pocket but she goes like a rocket and I'm sure you'll enjoy the feeling of being pushed into your seat when you give her some welly. (K)

Tom's Questions	Jan's Answers	Jan's Eye Movements	Jan's Thoughts	Tom's Responses
	I did think it was more than I could afford.		She has an argument with her logical mind: Oh! I know you're probably weighing up the pros and cons of going for a new car as opposed to a second-hand one.	(A$_d$)
	Then I thought, what the heck, you only live once.		She talks herself into buying the new car: I'm sure you'll ask yourself why you went for the cheaper option.	(A)
			But her heart wins as she talks herself into owning her dream car.	You know you'll feel better about running in your own car and you'll feel safer, knowing her history from scratch, even though we do check our used cars thoroughly (K).

Worksheet 12-6 gives you an opportunity to discover a person's thought processes for yourself.

- ✔ Think of someone on whom you would like to make an impact.
- ✔ Decide what isn't working, or could be better in your dealings with this person.
- ✔ Remember when you last met and, trusting your intuition, think of a series of harmless questions to ask. You can always hone your questions when you next meet up.
- ✔ Work out what you plan to do differently in the way you behave and the language you use.

Note: If you want to 'play' with a friend first to build up your confidence and get some practice, please do.

Make sure you rehearse the questions so that you can keep watching the person's eyes. If you just read the questions, you miss the eye movements. A trick is to draw arrows to indicate the movement of the eyes. This keeps things simple and won't alarm your subject. You can always make notes about what the eye movements mean later.

People can get self-conscious about someone staring at their eyes. There are a couple of approaches you can take to overcome shyness or resistance. Casually mention that if he sees you staring at him it's because you sometimes get lost in your thoughts. He can just ignore you and focus on answering the question or you can look at him in peripheral vision, by keeping your eyes focused on a spot just above his head.

Worksheet 12-6	Uncovering Thought Processes

Name of the person you're working with:

The context in which you're planning to work out your strategy:

Questions	Eye Movement	Thought Process: Visual (V), Auditory (A), Kinaesthetic (K)

Now use Worksheet 12-7 to note how you're going to adjust your behaviour and language to strengthen your impact on the person in the light of your assessment of this person's thought processes. You might think about changing your approach if you're struggling to communicate because his 'avoid communicating' strategy kicks in when you run your 'need to know something' strategy, which then starts with you saying, 'I need to ask you a question'. By the time he's worked out your new strategy, you'll have worked out when to hit him with the latest version of your communication strategy.

Worksheet 12-7	Adjusting My Behaviour and Language

_____

_____

_____

_____

_____

_____

_____

_____

_____

Creating New Patterns

Habits take 21 days to make or break, or so the experts say. When trying to set yourself up to make a change, it may be daunting to think of a block of *21 days!* So try this strategy for breaking the process up into one-day bite-sized chunks.

Say that you seriously need to cut down on the red wine and although you don't want to give it up completely, you want to enjoy just one glass of wine a day. You can write down your goal in your diary, blog, or wherever you choose to record the change. Make your one glass of red wine a day an enjoyable ritual by sitting down and savouring your glass of wine to the full, remembering to update your record of the number of days that you've stuck to your decision.

Supposing that now and then you have two glasses of wine a day, think about what's different about days you have one glass and days you have two, and then fine-tune your thought processes.

When Sue, one of Romilla's clients, wanted to give up eating bread, we put the following strategy in place:

✔ Sue designed a well-formed outcome (turn to Chapter 3 for the how-to's of well-formed outcomes), to find out exactly why she wanted to do without bread, and what she wanted in her life instead.

✔ Because her lead system was Auditory, Sue anchored her outcome to the chorus of a song sung by Helen Reddy. Every time Sue hankered after bread or wanted reminding of her goal, she would sing the first two lines of the chorus to herself: *One day at a time sweet Jesus, that's all I'm asking from you.* (You may favour one sense over the other five. This is called your Lead or Primary Representational System.)

Not being a masochist, Sue allowed herself bread on certain days and she made sure she enjoyed her treat to the full. If ever she felt tempted to nibble a slice of bread, instead of beating herself up, she simply burst into the Helen Reddy chorus to help her stick to her non-bread strategy. A year down the line, bread hardly features on Sue's nutritional landscape.

Deep Breathing: A Calming Strategy

Learning to take a break and do some deep breathing is an important NLP strategy for coping in stressful situations. Because you can do deep breathing so unobtrusively that it is almost silent, you can bring your deep breathing into play even while some cantankerous person is ranting and raving at you.

Please feel free to adapt this strategy for releasing tension and relaxing your body to suit your own needs.

1. **Learn to recognise your stressors (triggers that you respond to unfavourably).**

2. **Get to know how your body feels when it's tense.**

3. **Draw in your breath to the count of four into the part of your body where you're feeling tense.**

4. Hold your breath to the count of four.

5. Breathe out softly through open lips to the count of eight.

6. Hold for a count of four.

7. Feel your body relaxing.

If you find yourself hyperventilating and feeling panicky, breathing slowly and systematically into a paper bag will help you stop hyperventilating and get your breathing back to normal.

Why wait till you're stressed? Create a trigger – such as a star on your computer screen or on the dashboard of your car – to remind you to keep up your deep-breathing strategy.

Chapter 13

Working with Your Time Line

*Y*ou're sure to know someone who without fail arrives on the dot for an appointment – then you have another friend who because she is always late is routinely told that an appointment is half an hour earlier in order to get her there on time. So, how do *you* deal with time? Are you an 'on the dotter' or are you the more 'chill out, man' variety? These are the two basic approaches for dealing with time and both affect your thinking and behaviour, and your relationship with everyone around you. Essentially, you relate to time in one of two ways: You experience time as going *through* your body or you have a perception of time *outside* your body, so that how you manage time depends on whether you experience time as 'through time' or 'in time'.

This chapter shows you that working with your time line can be a very powerful way of clearing up the debris strewn across your path as you navigate your way through life. However, a word of caution: If you need to sort out really important emotional issues, such as a trauma or phobia, do find yourself a qualified NLP practitioner to help you with your problem – do not use the exercises in this chapter.

Discovering Your Personal Time Line

The way you hold your memories forms a time-based pattern. Your time line may be laid out in front of you, in a straight line or in the shape of a V, and you may be referring to some place in the past or in the future. Although the way you express time doesn't always say where you are on your time line, it does help you to recognise that there's a pattern to the way your memories are stored.

Do you use expressions like

> ✔ I've put the past behind me
>
> ✔ I'm so looking forward to
>
> ✔ There's no looking back

Listen out for the time-based expressions you use, and add more to your list by noticing what expressions other people are using.

Using Worksheet 13-1 record what you say and what you hear other people saying about time.

Worksheet 13-1	Noticing Time-Based Expressions
Name of Person	*Time-Based Expression*

Okay! So you're now aware of the words you use when talking about time. The words and phrases you use show you how you record your memories. You now to get to draw what your time line looks like to you.

Picturing your past and present

To help you get a picture of the way you hold your memories, do this short exercise:

1. **Think of an event from your past.**

2. **In your mind, point to this event.**

3. **Think of an event that you know is going to happen to you in the future.**

4. **Point to this event.**

5. **Point to where you see 'now'.**

6. **Join the points in your mind to get your time line.**

Ask yourself whether you're standing on the line or whether the line is running through you. If you have an 'in time' time line, you have to physically turn your body to look back at the past or towards the future because your time line runs through you. If your time line is laid out so that you can see all of it in front of you, and all you have to do is turn your head to the left or right to look towards your past or your future, then you have a 'through time' time line.

Figure 13-1 is a picture of what a straight 'in time' time line looks like. An 'in time' time line can also be in the shape of a V with the past on one side and the future on the other. The important point is that the line joining the past to the present runs through some part of the body.

Figure 13-2 shows a 'through time' time line. Notice that the person is standing well away from the time line, which is outside the body. Again, as with the 'in time' time line, this could form a V but would be laid out in front of the person, though not passing through her.

In Time

Figure 13-1:
Sample
'in time'
time line.

Past   Future

Present

Through Time

Past   Future

Present

The distance between where you are on your time line is less important than where you are in relation to the line between a past event and a future event. If the line goes through your body, you have an 'in time' time line; if the line is outside your body, you have a 'through time' time line.

From the information that you now have, use the space in Worksheet 13-2 to draw a picture of what your time line looks like. Include yourself in the picture. Please feel free to use every scrap of artistic flair you possess, and if your picture looks like a full-blown technicolour cartoon, so much the better.

Worksheet 13-2   **My Time Line**

If your time line runs through your body, you show mostly 'in time' tendencies. If your time line is outside your body, you show mostly 'through time' tendencies. Table 13-1 lists 'in time' or 'through time' characteristics for you – perhaps you're a combination of both.

Table 13-1	'In Time' and 'Through Time' Characteristics
'In Time' Characteristics	**'Through Time' Characteristics**
You're completely laid back about time.	You put a really high value on punctuality.
You have an aversion to diaries and electronic devices that aim to help you schedule your life.	You probably have a time planner surgically attached to you.
You can be very subjective, and you do what your heart tells you.	You keep your emotions in check and think with your head.
You take one day at a time.	You have your life planned out and you stick to it.
You love to keep your options open so you tend not to make up your mind until the *very last* minute.	You have a high need for closure.
You can drive the 'through time' people nuts!	You can drive the 'in time' people nuts!

Now use Worksheet 13-3 to note your 'in time' or 'through time' characteristics.

Worksheet 13-3	My Time Line Characteristics

My time line characteristics are mainly in time/through time (circle the one that applies to you)

My characteristics are:

Putting Your Time Line to Work for You

Just knowing about your time line isn't going to do you a lot of good – making your time line work for you is what matters. Climb on board because we are about to take you off into the skies in an imaginary hot-air balloon to experience flying over your time line. Once you get the hang of this type of flying, you can fly at will up and down your time line, and back and forth to your past or your future.

When you're up high above your time line observing events in your life way below, you see your whole time line, and the distance from the events separates you from your emotions that might otherwise hinder you. And learning from past events is a lot easier if you don't have to experience the pain all over again.

Worksheet 13-4 is a useful exercise for familiarising yourself with the technique of floating upwards and moving back and forth above your time line.

If you're an 'in time' person, the experience of distancing yourself from the events on the time line and feeling more detached allows you to understand why 'through time' people seem less emotional than you do – simply because 'through time' people are onlookers, observing the events unfolding on their time line.

Worksheet 13-4	Flying Practice

1. **Find a comfortable place to sit down and close your eyes.**

2. **Breathe in, and then breathe out slowly, and feel yourself beginning to relax.**

3. **Repeat the breathing exercise half-a-dozen times or so, until you feel totally relaxed.**

4. **Imagine yourself floating gently upwards and drifting up and over the building in which you're sitting and looking down over the rooftops, and floating higher and higher above the clouds and beyond.**

5. **You're in space and can see your time line way below you, like a ribbon. You can see yourself on the time line.**

6. **Now float back over your time line until you're directly over a recently experienced event.**

7. **You can hover there as long as you like.**

8. **Float forwards over 'now' and beyond until you're directly over an event that you know is going to happen in the future.**

9. **You can hover there as long as you like or move between your past and your future events.**

10. **When you're ready, float over your time line until you're directly over 'now' before gently floating back to the present and down into your own body.**

You can use this flying technique to address issues in the present that may have begun in your past and have implications for the future.

SEE-ing root causes

Your memories of a particular past event are frequently marshalled together into a collection called a *gestalt*, an organised whole. If the events in a collection occur at different times or in a different order, however, the collection isn't a gestalt. A gestalt (or collection) has one unified meaning, unlike the meaning you may give to an individual event.

A gestalt can be triggered by an emotional response to an event in your past. This Significant Emotional Event, SEE for short, is also called a *root cause*. When similar events give rise to similar emotional responses, you link the events into a chain and then you have a gestalt made up of all the events in a specific order and given a meaning depending on your frame of mind at a particular time.

By revisiting specific incidents in your time line, you can let go of a limiting decision or negative emotion that may be holding you back. (Chapter 5 explains limiting decisions.)

Janki used to dread telling her husband about any of her successes at work. She had got herself into the pattern of being excited and wanting to rush home and share her news with her husband, but then stopping herself because she dreaded hearing from him the litany of: 'But this isn't bringing down our overdraft'. This pattern of behaviour was affecting their relationship dramatically. Janki knew it was up to her to find a way of changing how she felt and reacted to her husband's comments. She decided to do some time-travelling and go back into her past to when she had made the decision to allow her husband's comments to make her feel bad. Janki realised that was the point at which she'd decided to shut her husband out of her work life. Although he's still quite a negative person, Janki is unaffected by his attitude. Janki used Worksheet 13-5 to discover the root cause of her problem.

Worksheet 13-5	Janki's Recognition of Her Root Cause
Event/occurrence I react to:	John saying, 'But this isn't bringing down our overdraft'. It's as if he views life only in terms of money.
Meaning I attach to the event/occurrence:	Because I feel my husband isn't listening to me, I've stopped sharing anything with him.
Root cause I want to change:	The first time I allowed his attitude to my successes at work to make me feel bad.
The result of removing the negative decision:	I feel pretty good about releasing the decision that limited me in telling him about work. Now I start my statement with, 'I want to tell you something and I want you to share in my success.' Things are changing.

A negative feeling can bring to mind a limiting decision you made in the past. For example, you're frustrated because you're 'not earning enough'. But this may be because early on in your career you equated earning a lot of money with being greedy.

Do you find yourself reacting badly to a negative comment that someone has made to you? Does your reaction stop you from doing things or progressing? Use Worksheet 13-6 to identify the root cause of your problem.

Worksheet 13-6	My Recognition of My Root Cause
Event/occurrence I react to:	
Meaning I attach to the event/occurrence:	
Root cause I want to change:	
The result of removing the negative decision:	

Watching the past unfold

Using the flying technique can help you uncover the root cause of your gestalt, your pattern of thinking and behaviour, and overcome negative emotions from the past that are holding you back in the present, and look at limiting decisions that are preventing you from enjoying life to the full. Take the following steps to look back at your past:

1. **Fly back over your time line to a time when your unconscious mind recorded the significant emotional event (SEE) that's affecting you.**

2. **Figure out what created the SEE and how you can learn from it.**

This is the key to the process. In your daily life, you draw upon a lot of experiences and wisdom from your past. When you give yourself time to look back at the past, you benefit from lessons you weren't equipped to learn when your SEE occurred.

3. **Float above your time line to about 15 minutes before the SEE occurred and notice that you feel no emotion about the SEE.**

You discovered what created the SEE and learned from it in Step 2, and you're now at a point when the event hasn't occurred yet.

Having learned from your SEE, you no longer need to hold onto the emotions attached to the event. You can release your emotions and now function productively. Taking the learning from an SEE breaks up the gestalt.

If you feel there are too many steps to remember in any of the exercises, record the instructions, in appropriate hypnotic language, and play them back to yourself. (Chapter 15 is great for checking out the use of hypnotic language.) Or you can have a friend read the instructions aloud as you do the exercise. In the context of time lines, working with someone else is always useful while you clear your negative emotions and limiting decisions. However, if you do choose to work by yourself, treat your unconscious mind as another person by asking questions like, 'Is it okay for you to release the negative emotion?' (To discover more about your unconscious mind, go to Chapter 4.)

Healing negative emotions

Negative emotions such as guilt, sadness, anger, and frustration have a time element attached to them. Maybe you feel guilty about something you've done in the past. For example, you snapped at someone because she told you for the umpteenth time, 'Don't be so stupid', or because your need to hear 'I love you' wasn't met yet again! At the time you snapped, you could only feel anger. But looking back at the event, you remember the look of stunned surprise and hurt and realise that instead of snapping, you should have asked yourself the reason for the other person's behaviour. Was it because of her background and upbringing; perhaps from childhood no one had ever said to her anything but 'Don't be so stupid' or ever told her that they loved her.

Worksheet 13-7 shows you how you can get rid of a negative emotion. For example, you may have a proclivity for road rage or you may choose to feel sorry for yourself and behave like one of life's victims. Use this process to free yourself and reclaim your life.

Worksheet 13-7	Letting Go of Negative Emotions

1. **Find yourself somewhere safe and quiet to relax to get you into the right frame of mind for the exercise.**

   Tell your unconscious mind that you would like to get to the root cause of whatever issue you want to resolve by learning from what happened, so you can get rid of the emotion and the hold that it has on you. Sometimes speaking your intention out loud can attract the attention of the unconscious mind more effectively than just thinking things in your own head.

2. **Ask yourself whether it's okay to take any learning you can and release any emotion.**

   In a lot of cases, you have the problem because you haven't learned lessons from your past experience. Negative situations can lead to you feeling bad, frustrated, and desperate to name other negative emotions. After learning your lessons, you now know what your pattern of behaviour needs to be, allowing you to release the emotion.

    Please be aware that the questions in the exercise are directed at your *unconscious mind*.

3. **Ask your unconscious mind, 'What is the root cause of this problem? Was it before, during, or after my birth?'**

    It's really important that you keep an open mind about when your unconscious mind decided the root cause occurred. Your unconscious mind absorbs a lot of information and makes a lot of decisions without your conscious mind being aware and you can be surprised at the responses you receive.

4. **When you decide what the root cause of your problem is, float way above your time line so that you can see your past and your future stretching below you.**

5. **Float back along your time line until you're above the root cause.**

   Really get to know what created your limiting decision or negative emotion by seeing what you saw, feeling what you felt, and hearing what you heard. The feelings won't be as intense because you're floating so far above the event, so you can learn from the event without getting caught up in the emotions.

6. **Ask your unconscious mind to learn what it needs to from the event in order for your unconscious mind to let go of the limiting decision or negative emotion easily and quickly.**

   This is the key to the process. In your day-to-day life, you draw upon a lot of experiences and wisdom from your past. When you give yourself time to examine the past, you can benefit from lessons you weren't equipped to learn when the event happened. You do this by watching what is happening

7. **Still way above your time line, float to 15 minutes before your SEE.**

8. **Face the present so that you can see the root cause in front of you and below you.**

   Notice that you feel no emotion about the SEE. You discovered what created the SEE and learned from it, and you're now at a point when the event hasn't occurred yet.

9. **Give yourself permission to let go of all the negative emotions associated with the event. Breathe out slowly to release the emotions associated with the SEE.**

   If you're working on a limiting decision, notice that it has disappeared along with any associated negative emotions. If you're working on releasing a negative emotion, notice that has gone as well.

10. **When you're ready, float back until you're above the present.**

Move only as fast as your unconscious mind can learn from all the events that made up your gestalt, and let go of all the associated emotions.

11. **Float back down into the room where you're sitting.**

To find out if you've been successful in letting go of your negative emotion, think of a time in the future when an event would have triggered the emotion and notice that the negative emotion has gone.

Overcoming a limiting decision

At some point in your life, your unconscious mind made a decision to protect you from an unhappy event you experienced by creating a limiting decision, of which your conscious mind is blissfully unaware. A limiting decision (which we address in depth in Chapter 5) acts as a barrier to you achieving a desired goal. For example, you may think you'd like to go abseiling but your unconscious mind has decided that you're not brave enough, are scared of heights, or abseiling is dangerous, and so for reasons your conscious mind can't pinpoint, you don't go.

Jarmila put a tremendous amount of effort into writing an essay, which she felt was her best work. Unfortunately her teacher, being of the old school, ruled with an iron hand, and instead of praising Jarmila for the excellence of her work, looked only for faults, such as focusing on a couple of minor spelling mistakes. Jarmila was absolutely gutted. Over the next year, Jarmila's teacher continued making what *she* thought were helpful criticisms. The result? Jarmila grew up thinking that English was her worst subject, which later affected her confidence at work and stopped her from progressing in her career. Jarmila was lucky enough to work for a manager who saw the value of professional development and employed a coach to help her with her career. During a coaching session, Jarmila remembered the event when her English teacher had criticised her work, and although most of the emotions around her 'poor English' had apparently been forgotten, she still had remnants of anger. After a trip back over her time line, Jarmila realised she had never got to the root cause of her lack of self-confidence – that first time the teacher had criticised her severely for the two spelling mistakes. The emotion disappeared completely when Jarmila realised the criticism had more to do with the teacher's lack of knowledge and understanding than Jarmila's ability to use English.

A limiting decision nearly always has a clutch of negative emotions attached to it. Please be aware of the difference between negative emotions in general and a specific emotion such as anger. Worksheet 13-7 takes you step by step through the process of letting go a negative emotion.

Tuning in through your time line

By revisiting specific incidents in your time line, you can let go of a limiting decision that is holding you back.

Figure 13-3 shows the positions you hover over as you float above your time line and learn the lessons from a significant emotional event (SEE) allowing you to get on with the here and now. The three positions on your time line are

✔ 1 is way above now, the time you're going through this exercise.

✔ 2 is above the place where your unconscious mind first experienced the SEE or root cause. This is the point where you take the lessons which, had you understood them consciously at the time of the SEE, would have prevented the formation of the gestalt and stopped you from staying trapped in repeating the unhelpful behaviours you have been doing until now.

✔ 3 is 15 minutes before the SEE occurred. At this point, the SEE hasn't occurred and as you turn to look forwards from 3 to the present, you realise that the negative emotions or the emotions related to your limiting decision don't exist as they were created at the same time as the SEE. The problems born at the time of the SEE built up from then on, and came into play each time you experienced an event that went into building your gestalt, your pattern of behaviour, relating to a specific negative emotion or limiting decision.

Figure 13-3:
The process
of clearing
a SEE.

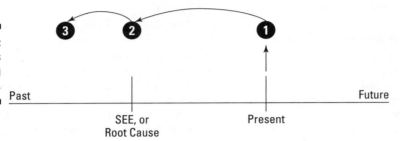

Past   Future

SEE, or   Present
Root Cause

Can you think of a limiting decision that is stopping you from living the way you want and that you want to work on? For example, having a health problem or a family concern that gets in the way of you living your life differently. Write down your thoughts in Worksheet 13-8 on overcoming your limiting decision.

Worksheet 13-8	Overcoming My Limiting Decision
The limiting decision with which I want to work is:	
Because it stops me from:	

Use Worksheet 13-9 to help you identify a negative emotion that you find yourself falling prey to on a regular basis. It could be something like self-doubt or any of the emotions mentioned in this chapter.

Worksheet 13-9	Overcoming a Negative Emotion Affecting Me
A negative emotion that I am prone to:	
Because it has the following negative effects on my life:	

Overcoming anxiety about a future event

Anxiety is simply a negative emotion about something that hasn't yet happened. If you feel anxious about a future event, such as giving a talk, holding a meeting, or going on a date, you're likely to have made a limiting decision that is making you anxious about the situation. You can clear the limiting decision by going back along your time line. If the event is a one-off, you can use the process described in Worksheet 13-10 to overcome your anxiety by floating forwards into the future above your time line.

The process in Worksheet 13-10 asks you to fly up and away until you're way above the present and can see your past and future stretching below you. This time you're invited to turn towards the future to face the event about which you're feeling anxious. You then fly into the future and hover over the event that is causing you anxiety, as shown in Figure 13-4. Once you've allowed your unconscious mind to learn what you need to do for a successful outcome, you float further into the future to where you know that you achieved your goal, and turning to look back to the present, see all the events aligning to give you the success you're aiming for.

Figure 13-4:
Time
travelling to
overcome
anxiety.

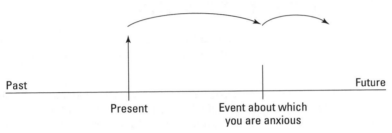

Past

Future

Present

Event about which
you are anxious

Worksheet 13-10   Overcoming Anxiety

1. **Find yourself a safe and quiet place to relax and think about the event that is making you feel anxious.**

2. **Set the stage for overcoming your anxiety by asking your unconscious if it is okay for you to let go of the anxiety.**

   Tell your unconscious that you function more effectively when you're in a calm state of mind rather than keyed up about the future.

3. **Float way above your time line so that you can see your time line stretching below you.**

4. **Still floating above your time line, move forwards into the future until you're above the event causing you anxiety.**

5. **Ask your unconscious mind to learn what it needs to from the event in order for you to let go of the anxiety easily and quickly.**

6. **When you feel ready to move on, float further into the future to just after having successfully completed the event that you were feeling anxious about and notice that your feelings have changed and the anxiety has gone.**

7. **When you're ready, float back to your present as slowly or as quickly as your unconscious mind needs for you to re-evaluate the event you were anxious about.**

   You can test your anxiety level by following your time line into the future, perhaps to another time where you have had to experience the event that you were anxious about, and realise that the anxiety no longer exists.

Use Worksheet 13-11 to help you to consider something you have to do that may be making you stressed by just thinking about it. Practise the process we describe in Worksheet 13-10 to help you put your mind at rest and overcome your anxiety.

Worksheet 13-11	Overcoming My Anxiety about a Future Event
I am anxious about:	
The lessons I learned from this exercise:	

Placing Goals in Your Time Line

Make your time line work for you by floating out over your time line to the future and dropping a wished-for goal into your time line for your unconscious mind to take care of and nurture.

Before placing your goal in your time line, you need to set your well-formed outcome, which helps you to establish a clear picture of what you're aiming to achieve. (We talk about well-formed outcomes in Chapter 3 'Planning Your Road Map'.) You can go back to Chapter 3 and use the well-formed outcome for a goal you chose in that chapter, or choose a new, completely different goal. Whatever you choose to do, make sure your goal is compelling: Seeing it, feeling it, and hearing it in all its richness. And if your goal is anything to do with culinary matters, you may even be able to smell and taste it!

Follow the steps in Worksheet 13-12 to drop your goal into your time line.

Worksheet 13-12	Setting a Goal in My Time Line

My goal is:

1. **Find yourself a safe and quiet place to relax.**

2. **Visualise your goal.**

   Give life to your goal, by making the picture bright, the sounds loud, and the feelings strong, but not so much that the brightness, sounds, and feelings become a distraction.

3. **Step into your visualisation and really savour what you will experience when you achieve your goal.**

4. **Step out of the picture, and as you step out turn the visualisation you created in Step 2 into a picture.**

   Compress your picture into whatever size you want and put a frame around it so that you can hang it on the wall.

5. **Holding onto your framed picture, float way above your time line so that you can see the past and your future stretching below you.**

6. **Still holding onto your picture, float along your time line to the future to the time you set for attaining your goal, using your well-formed outcome.**

7. **Give life to your goal by breathing into it – take a deep breath in through your nose and breathe all the energy into the picture. Repeat this four times.**

8. **Drop your framed picture into your time line.**

9. **As you watch the picture drop into your chosen spot, you can bless your goal or simply state your goal out loud.**

10. **When you feel ready, turn and face the present and notice how the events on your time line have been realigned to create your goal.**

11. **When you're ready, fly back to the present and float back down into the room where you're sitting.**

Once you've released your goal, really let it go. You may feel that you want to keep an eye on it to see if it is forming and growing, but leave it to your unconscious mind to point out to you what you need to do in order to achieve your goal.

Connecting Back

Have you ever spent time wrestling with a problem only to find that the solution lay in your past? Modelling excellence is a tried and tested NLP technique. But how often do you think of your own achievements as being worth modelling? We are now going to show you how you can draw on the lessons from your past experiences and use them to improve your present circumstances.

Katy was getting quite depressed about her 'perfect' job. She loved what she was doing but wasn't getting the promotion she really wanted. Because she didn't want to leave her job, she decided to reassess her position. Katy realised she needed to change the way she communicated with her boss, Karen, allowing Karen to see how good Katy was at her job and so gaining promotion. Katy decided to look back at her past to find situations which had been difficult but from which she'd taken away lessons that could be applied to her present problem. She came up with a number of past events that had taught her valuable lessons and settled on the three set out in Worksheet 13-13, because they were the ones most appropriate in her present situation of trying for promotion.

By examining her values around her work and putting together her well-formed outcome, Katy acknowledged that her goal was to stay in her current job. She used her planning skills to work out a strategy for influencing Karen. The first step of her strategy was to discover Karen's way of thinking, her metaprograms, and observe Karen's behaviour. Katy made out a case for her promotion to present to Karen, making sure she used the phrases best suited to Karen's metaprograms, as well as building in some hypnotic language patterns. Katy knew that building rapport was one of her strengths, which allowed her to be relaxed in her meeting with Karen. (See Chapter 8 for more about metaprograms, and Chapter 15 is useful for checking out hypnotic language patterns.) Worksheet 13-13 shows the resources Katy used from her past to achieve her aim of influencing Karen and gaining promotion.

Worksheet 13-13   **Katy's Resources from Her Past**

My current problem: *No matter what I say, Karen can't see the merit in my work.*

Past Event	What I Learned	My Resources
1 – I was having trouble with Sheilagh when she was trying to bully me	I decided to look at what I wanted from life and decided that because I loved my job, I would stay and fight for it. It's okay for people not to be friends and having a truce is enough. It's worth re-examining my values again even though I've done it before.	Knowing how to work out my values and how to find out what I really want in my life by using the well-formed outcome process.
2 – When Sandy and I weren't getting on at work	Sandy was feeling intimidated because I wasn't communicating in a way he understood. As he's quite introverted, I scared him.	Working out someone's psychological make-up using metaprograms. Knowing how to build up rapport with other people.
3 – Preparing for my peer review	I was really nervous until I'd set down what I wanted to say to appeal to a wide range of people. I learned how to overcome my anxiety and set a really brilliant outcome.	My ability to plan and use hypnotic language patterns as well as being able to create my time line the way that I want.

Use Worksheet 13-14 to draw on past experiences to help you achieve your goals in life. Think about a problem that you have at the moment. Then think of at least three events from the past you can draw on to help resolve your problem, and then write down your plan of action.

Worksheet 13-14   **My Resources from My Past**

My current problem:

Past Event	What I Learned	My Resources
1		
2		

Past Event	What I Learned	My Resources
3		

My plan of action to overcome my problem:

_____

_____

_____

_____

_____

_____

In Worksheet 13-15 we give you the chance to get physical! The advantage of 'walking your time line' over 'imaginary flying' is that it can heighten your emotions. So please only do this exercise when you know the emotions you're likely to experience are positive. The disadvantage of this exercise is that the amount of space you have to perform the exercise is likely to be limited, and for some of you walking may be distracting.

Worksheet 13-15   Walking My Time Line with My Resources

1. **Find yourself somewhere safe and quiet, and where you won't be disturbed.**

2. **Lay out a physical time line on the floor.**

   You can do this by putting down a piece of string or ribbon on the floor, or you can just use your imagination by visualising a piece of string or ribbon.

3. **Step onto your time line at 'now', looking towards your future.**

   You need to allow yourself enough space to take three steps back and one forward from 'now'.

4. **Take three steps back to the oldest of the three events.**

5. **Recall what happened, paying attention to the feeling of success or achievement you get when you think of that time. Think of the resources you discovered you had.**

6. **Holding onto the resources from Step 4, step forward to the second of the three events and repeat Step 5.**

7. **Holding onto both sets of resources from Steps 4 and 6, take a step forward to the third event, and repeat Step 5.**

8. **Holding onto all the resources from Steps 4, 6, and 7, take a step forward into 'now'.**

9. **Stop walking. Savour the moment knowing that you have the resources to overcome your present problem.**

10. **When you're ready, step forward into your future where your problem has been overcome, letting the events realign accordingly.**

Popping In and Out of Time

If you happen to be a laid-back 'in time' kind of person, wouldn't it be great to know what it feels likes to lead a well-ordered life? And if you're a driven 'through time' personality type, wouldn't you benefit from taking time out to appreciate your surroundings and count your blessings? (Refer to the earlier section 'Discovering Your Personal Time Line' about 'in time' and 'through time' people.) Even if your answer is NO!, trying on someone else's way of thinking and feeling gives you greater flexibility in the way you think and behave as well as allowing you to understand how other people tick. Changing and adapting your behaviour to suit different situations helps build rapport and leads to successful relationships.

If your time line is 'in time' and you want to experience being a 'through time' person by laying your time line out in front of you, all you have to do is mentally step off your time line and turn your body so you're looking at the time line stretching out in front of you. Similarly, as a 'through time' person if you want to experience what it feels like being 'in time', you can take an imaginary step onto your time line.

Cassy is a busy mum who works part-time as a lawyer. She was finding life frenetic and was trying to run her home with the same precision as she ran her office. With young kids, she found running a family and having a career anything but easy. Once Cassy learned about time lines and being able to switch from being 'through time' to being 'in time' she got into the habit of switching her time line to 'through time' when she arrived at the office, using turning the key to turn off her car as the trigger. When it was time to go home, she would turn the key in the ignition and switch her time line so she was 'in time'. Now Cassy not only gets greater satisfaction from her job but is enjoying more quality time with her family. To quote Cassy, 'So what if the house isn't spotless, at least we are all well and happy and we get on really well with our pet germs. We give them a home and they help us build an immunity.'

In Worksheet 13-16, you get to work out if and when you might want to switch your time line and decide on how you might want to trigger the change.

Switching time lines can make you disorientated, and you may feel a bit sick and dizzy, so make sure you're sitting down while doing this exercise!

Worksheet 13-16	Practising Being 'In Time' and 'Through Time'
I am in time/through time (present situation):	
I would like to be more in time/through time (desired situation):	
My trigger for switching my time line is going to be:	

Part IV
Riding the Communications Escalator

The 5th Wave   By Rich Tennant

"I've always been impressed with Larry's ability to control his audience."

In this part . . .

You're ready to weave some spells with your own style of magic communications dust. In this part you head down deep into the specifics of language by highlighting the detail of how a person thinks, using the Meta Model patterns. Then you travel high again into the artfully vague patterns of the Milton Model to entrance your audience. Finally, you take your storytelling talents to the next level to entertain others and get your message heard loud and clear.

Chapter 14

Adapting Language with the Meta Model

*T*he underlying principle behind the classic Meta Model is the presupposition: 'The map is not the territory' (covered in Chapter 2). What this means is that the models you make of the world in your thoughts and words aren't the whole world, simply your experience of it. Your models can serve you but also limit you, and you can identify these models in the way you speak.

The Meta Model was developed by the originators of NLP, John Grinder and Richard Bandler, when they listened to the *way* that clients spoke in therapy rather that *what* they talked about. Grinder and Bandler also recognised how exceptional therapists communicated with these clients to help them to overcome their personal problems and limitations.

The Model concentrates on the quality of your oral communication, how you speak, and what this indicates about how you're thinking. In this chapter you work with some of the specific linguistic categories of the Meta Model that are evidence of the broader communications patterns of deletion, generalisation, and distortion (refer to Chapter 5) and specific questions that you can use to achieve clearer communication in any situation.

Defining the Meta Model

The benefit of the Meta Model, with its language patterns and questions, is that it enables you to challenge assumptions the speaker demonstrates that may not be helpful, and get more detail about what he says in order to connect to the heart of his experience. This method is invaluable in all walks of life, not just in therapy. As parents, coaches, partners, workers, and members of a community, communicating your messages clearly is incredibly helpful.

The Meta Model is powerful because it takes you from general statements to specific ones – from vagueness to articulating your ideas in detail. As you go through this chapter, think of your goals in the light of the Meta Model, and ask yourself questions that get increasingly precise. Ask yourself: 'What specifically do I want?' and 'How specifically will I get it?'

The Meta Model addresses the three key processes of natural communication that you first encountered in Chapter 5 and read about in the NLP Communications Model – the ways in which you and those around you *delete*, *distort*, and *generalise* in everyday language. This chapter helps you to understand how these processes can be picked up in language. We break down these three main processes into further categories. By asking key questions you can expand the level of detail and therefore, the clarity of what is being said. It turns you into a language detective revealing important facts to solve any mysterious messages!

In *Deletion*, you selectively pay attention to certain dimensions of your experience and exclude others. In *Distortion*, you turn into someone who guesses and gives meanings to events that may not be true or a mind-reader where you infer something that isn't actually being said. In *Generalisation*, you assume that if a specific example of a situation is true, then every example of it is also true, as in 'always' and 'everything', 'all of the time'.

All these processes are valuable linguistic devices. Without them you'd be swamped by a deluge of words! So just pay attention to these processes and challenge them when it's useful to get more detail.

Delving into the Deep Structure

Through the use of questioning, the Meta Model offers a way to dig down through the surface of the words someone uses into the deeper structure of what he's really experiencing. In this section, we take a close look at the linguistic process of generalisation in action. Specifically, we dig into the three categories of generalisations, which are:

- **Modal operators of possibility** – as in *I can't*. The modal operator of possibility refers to what you consider to be possible or not.

- **Modal operators of necessity** – as in *I have to*, *I should*. The modal operator of necessity refers to what you think is necessary for you to do.

- **Universal quantifiers** – as in *everything, everybody, always, never*. The universal quantifier is a statement that you hold to be universally true.

A negative modal operator is the linguistic equivalent of a barrier: the resistance that you put up that can constrain you simply by how you talk about a given situation.

John's role as a project manager in a large corporation makes him responsible for the efficient running of the computer systems that support customer service centres around the world. It's July and the time when the schools are out, so some of his colleagues across Europe with families are taking the opportunity to have some well-deserved holidays. However, projects still need to be delivered and customers kept happy. If you were standing behind John at the coffee machine in his office, you'd hear him tell his colleague: '*Every time* we try to get something done around here, there are weeks of delays, *I can't* get *anything* done, *no one* is helping. The *whole* of *Europe has to* close down in July and *we should* be telling people *they ought* to stagger their holidays. It's *always* the same this time of the year.' In one disgruntled moan to his colleague, John demonstrates the full power of generalisation in language – the black and white thinking style.

Notice John's modal operator of possibility in the words 'I can't.' His modal operators of necessity include 'we should', 'Europe has to', and 'they ought to', while his universal quantifiers are 'anything', 'no one', 'whole of', and 'always.'

In the following sections we further unpack these more detailed patterns so you can listen out for them and work around them in your own communication.

Expanding possibilities

The NLP approach encourages you to expand possibilities and empowers you to be more flexible in your thinking by challenging the barriers imposed by modal operators. The key lies in switching the thinking to an alternative view, by asking 'what if' type of questions. So when you hear yourself or others say 'I can't do this', begin to ask questions that challenge any limitation. For example, ask: 'What would happen if you do?' or 'What needs to happen before you do?'

A belief, such as 'I can't do this,' is an example of a generalisation. Your thoughts translate into your behaviour. (That statement is itself an example of a generalisation!)

One of Kate's breakthroughs in her own behaviour came as she was writing this chapter. She set herself the goal of being able to stand on her head in her yoga class. Noticing that she was surrounded by people of all shapes, sizes, and ages in her class who could stand on their heads, she was increasingly conscious that she really wanted to do this and frustrated at her inner fear of falling which kept getting in her way. Once she shifted her thinking to 'I can do this,' it became a matter of picking the right moment and just doing it. Once she had challenged her own belief about what was possible for her, she enlisted the help of people around her to give helpful safety tips and encourage her on. After standing on her head the first time, it became easy to repeat time and time again, knowing that it was now possible for her to do something that months before she had considered impossible. She began to practise more and got better at it. Then she wondered what the fuss was about.

Where do you hear yourself saying: 'I can't do that?' In worksheet 14-1 you check out how you talk and see how you may shift your thinking into action. Begin by listing some of the things that you say you can't do right now. Choose positive things that you may like to do in the future or that other people you admire can do. Perhaps you'd like to improve your driving on the golf course, your skills at some computer software, or your ability to hold down a relationship. Perhaps you see others giving entertaining speeches and don't think you can do that. Or you struggle to stick to a healthy regime while you're working. You'll have your own list.

Ask yourself what stops you and what would improve for you if you did do something positive from your list? It may be that you're fearful of looking foolish, you need to free up time to practise a skill, or could do with asking for help. Write down any ideas that come to mind of the barriers you see in your way. Begin to visualise what success would look like for you and how that would feel. Just behaving 'as if' you were already successful can change the way you come across to others and feel inside so that you attract support to you to realise your dream.

After you've completed the exercise, highlight the actions you'd like to make for change. For example, it may be time to set some new goals for yourself. Make sure you have well-formed outcomes – see Chapter 3 if you need any reminders on this.

Or perhaps you need to change the self-talk in your head? When you catch yourself saying something that limits you, choose a new, more positive way of speaking to yourself. A simple change to make is to write the opposite of what you can't do in your worksheet under the section 'What I want to do differently' and keep revisiting it. If your example is 'I can't speak in public', replace that with 'I want to speak well in public' and identify some ways in which you can practise this skill.

Worksheet 14-1	Opening Up Possibilities
I can't:	
What stops me:	
What three things would improve for me if I did this?	
What I want to do differently:	

Challenging necessity

NLP JARGON ALERT

When you catch the words 'have to', 'should', 'ought to' then you're tuning in to *modal operators of necessity*, which may create limitations for you.

Are you one of those who puts her life on hold because you haven't won the lottery, married a rich film star, or paid off the mortgage? Do you live life according to 'ought to' and 'should'? For example, do you feel you 'ought to' hang out with certain people or 'should' do things that you don't really want to do? Maybe your job's not brilliant or you're bored with your hobbies, but fear the consequences of doing something different.

Take a look at Vernon's statements about what he should, have to, or ought to do in Worksheet 14-2 and notice the rules he has created for himself.

Worksheet 14-2	**Vernon's Shoulds, Have To's and Ought To's**

I ought to phone my aunt Sara.

I should cold call five contacts every day.

I have to go to the gym three times a week.

I have to mow the lawn and clean the car before I meet my friends.

I should be able to run 5k in less time than Jackie.

I ought to paint the window frames this summer.

I have to iron all my shirts before Monday morning.

I ought to get the central heating boiler serviced.

I have to take my team out for a party at Christmas (even though I hate going).

I have to do my business expenses in my own time.

Now it's your turn. In Worksheet 14-3 brainstorm activities that you feel you have to, ought to, or really should do. Pick a mix from different areas of your life. You may like to revisit your wheel of life from Chapter 3.

Worksheet 14-3	**My Shoulds, Have To's and Ought To's**

_____

_____

_____

_____

You may be living with rules that no longer serve you well. The second stage of this exercise is to take each item on your list in turn and ask yourself the question: 'What would happen if I didn't?' In this way, you check whether the item on your list is as important to you as it may have first seemed.

Now it's time to ditch any items that aren't a priority for you so that you create a list of things that you actually want to do. In Worksheet 14-4, sift through your list from Worksheet 14-3 and create a revised list replacing the words 'should', 'have to', and 'ought to' with 'choose to' for those things that are truly important to you.

Worksheet 14-4	**My Choices From Now On**

I choose to:

When you change your language from 'should', 'have to' and 'ought to' into words of choice, notice what a difference it makes to your attitude. You will find that you have more choices of action than you had previously.

Shifting the universals

Remember that a universal quantifier is a statement that you hold to be universally true. To give you some examples, if you had a difficult encounter with builders, you may say that 'all builders are a problem', or if you've had troublesome relationships at home or work you may say that all women/men/teenagers/bosses are a nuisance and so on. The key words to listen out for (in your head as well as spoken out loud) include words like *all things, all the time, never, always.*

Universal quantifiers often come to the fore when people are grumbling and blaming others. This can be the stuff of prejudice and judgemental thinking especially when people are getting heated about political goings-on – whether the running of the local playgroup committee, the reorganisation of a company, or the leadership agenda for the country.

Of course, there are positive universal qualifiers too, as in: 'I always look on the bright side of life,' 'It's all good,' 'We always deliver the best you can get anywhere,' 'He always comes up smiling.'

In Worksheet 14-5 record the universal qualifiers you hear and read. Listen to conversations with people around you, and news presenters. Include statements you read in e-mails, marketing literature, and newspapers. Just get curious about the details of language and you can hear the meaning behind the words.

Worksheet 14-5	Universal Quantifiers I Hear Around Me
Terms I hear	*From Whom*

Look at your list and notice whether any one person or group has a strong tendency to generalise and whether that language serves you well. Are you listening to TV programmes or reading newspapers that make you feel good or bad? If so, then make informed choices about what you read and listen to so that your thinking doesn't narrow as well.

You can ask various questions to challenge the generalised thinking you hear around you and also challenge yourself. In this way you will expand someone's mental model – including your own. If for example you hear TV presenters regularly making universal quantifiers with no evidence to back them up, you may not be able to challenge them personally, but you can decide that their programmes are too biased to be worthy of your time. The questions you ask can include:

✔ Is that always the case? Every time? Never?

✔ Present an exception to the rule that you've heard beginning with the question: 'What if?' (For example, 'What if you found a politician who championed your cause? What would you say about this political party then?' 'What if you got served quickly – would you then say the checkout queues are always too long?)

Reading the Distorted Patterns

Recognising the subtle distortions that happen every day can transform your thinking and your life. Distortion is rather like looking in the mirror and seeing something that isn't there, such as a fat person when you're slim – changing the facts in some way.

On the positive side, distortion can aid creativity. It's the stuff that fantasy, dreams, and entertainment are made of. On the downside, your ability to distort reality can lead you to invent catastrophes, misinterpret facts, and wreck your self-confidence.

As NLP coaches, Romilla and I work with many people to give a new perspective on the thinking that doesn't serve them well in achieving the life and work they really want. Whether you're a young 'soon-to-be married' suffering wedding nerves or a chief exec panicking about the financial results, your natural ability to distort facts can lead to sleepless nights.

Some types of distortions are:

- ✔ **Complex equivalence:** Two experiences are interpreted as synonymous. For example, 'If you roll your eyes, that means you don't believe me.' Or: 'If you don't come to the company meeting, you don't value your job.'

- ✔ **Mind reading:** Assuming to know what someone else is thinking. For example, 'You really like this, don't you?' and 'She wouldn't want to come.'

- ✔ **Cause and effect:** When you operate at cause, you take full responsibility for your actions and the results you get. When you're at effect, you're likely to be taking the role of helpless victim. A clue to noticing when someone's at effect is in language such as: 'He made me do it.' The principles of cause and effect are explored in detail in Chapter 2.

Janice was working as a new teacher at a primary school in an inner-city community. She was feeling particularly stressed and anxious about the test results of some of her young pupils. At the end of a long parents' evening in the winter term, she turned to her colleague to say that she was definitely not cut out for teaching, as she knew for sure that neither parents nor pupils liked or respected her. Fortunately her colleague was a wise, experienced soul who took the young teacher off for a drink and challenged her, saying: 'Come on, what are the facts here?' Within half an hour, Janice realised she was taking on not just the educational responsibility for her pupils, but also getting overwhelmed by the larger social issues some of them faced in their home lives that affected their chances of learning and attendance. She was being unreasonably tough on herself.

Separate out the facts of what is actually said from your feelings about a situation. Notice the distorted meaning you may have made of the situation.

When people are under pressure, they can often distort reality. In Worksheet 14-6, Sean revisits a memory of when he experienced difficulties at work. By examining his thoughts, the way he talked to himself and others, and feelings around that time, he finds examples of the three distortion patterns of complex equivalence, mind-reading, and cause and effect. These patterns were demonstrated in things he said at the time about the project and his colleagues. From analysing this experience he learns what he can choose to do differently in the future.

Worksheet 14-6	Sean's Uncovered Distortions
Situation:	On the consulting project with the ABC bank where the users got angry about the new system.
Mind-reading by me or others:	I thought that the project manager didn't want me on that project even though nothing was actually said to my face. Everyone else came from a larger consulting firm, so I assumed they thought I wasn't as clever.
Complex equivalences:	If I wasn't invited to all the progress meetings, that meant they thought I was useless.
Was I at cause or effect?	I was completely at effect. I felt miserable for two months and thought I did a very poor job and this had a knock-on effect so I went to the pub most nights and drank several beers. I was also grumpy with my friends and other people around me.
Changes I can make in future:	I will get clarification of my role to find out what specific details are under my remit, and what other people are taking responsibility for, and who those people are. If I get another assignment like that, I will ask for weekly feedback meetings so everyone can see what is going well and where the risks are. In those meetings, I'll challenge people who are vague.

In Worksheet 14-7, revisit a memory of a time when things went awry for you. Choose a situation when you had some unpleasant feedback from an individual, an argument, or a misunderstanding that you would rather have avoided. Record examples of the three distortion patterns of complex equivalence, mind-reading, and cause and effect you recognise.

Worksheet 14-7	My Uncovered Distortions
Situation:	
Mind reading by me or others:	
Complex equivalences:	
Was I at cause or effect:	
Changes I can make in future:	

Deleting the Missing Parts

A conversation in which deletion is at play is like reading the headlines in a newspaper and not having the body text. The headlines alone don't reveal the full story.

For example, if your manager at work tells you, 'You did a good job,' how would you know how to do a good job again tomorrow? You may have to do some mind-reading unless you ask for more information to shift from the big picture to specific details. Or if you were to tell your boss, 'Communication isn't working,' what would he or she need to do to put it right? Is that about installing a new phone system, publishing a newsletter, or putting up directional signs in the car park?

Table 14-1 shows deletion patterns, examples, and questions you can ask to recover deleted information.

Table 14-1	Deletion Examples	
Type of Deletion	*Sample Statement*	*Sample Questions to Clarify the Deletion*
Simple	I'm scared.	What are you scared about?
Unspecified verbs	She beat me.	How did she beat you? What did she beat you with/at?
Comparisons	She's a better person.	Who is she better than? What is better?
Judgements	You don't care.	What specifically do I not care about and how specifically do I not care?
Nominalisations	Communication is tough.	Who is it that finds communicating tough and what is it tough to communicate about?

An *unspecified verb* is a verb that has an ambiguous meaning that's open to misinterpretation. A *nominalisation* is created by turning a verb into a noun. It represents something intangible such as a relationship or communication.

When information is missing, it's easy to jump to conclusions, make the wrong decisions, and sell the wrong product. Imagine you're a doctor treating a sick patient. If the patient says, 'Doctor, I have a pain,' and you reach to prescribe a drug instantly, your clinical competence may be at risk for making a diagnosis with insufficient information.

The key questions to ask in any situation where you lack sufficient information to be sure of the meaning are:

- Tell me more...
- What, when, where, who, how specifically?

Raj wants to be able to communicate better with his niece Mandy about her job searching, but talking to her is hard when she deletes information and gives him little to work with. In Worksheet 14-8 Raj makes a note of what he hears Mandy say so that he can ask questions that open up the conversation in more detail.

Worksheet 14-8	Raj's Uncovering Deleted Information Worksheet
Person and context:	My niece Mandy who needs a job.
Her statements:	Work is rubbish. I don't have time. It's all lousy pay. I do badly at interviews.
Questions to challenge the deleted information:	What specifically is it like when it's not rubbish? How much time do you need? What is lousy pay? And what isn't? What specifically do you do at interviews?

Notice that the patterns of speech join up so that you can find deletions, distortions, and generalisations all merging into one knot to unpack! This is how you can tie yourself up in anxious thoughts.

Find somebody you'd like to communicate better with who is a person of few words or who tends to delete information in a particular situation. Use Worksheet 14-9 to dig out his or her deletions.

Worksheet 14-9	My Uncovering Deleted Information Worksheet
Person and context:	
His or her statements:	
Questions to challenge the deleted information:	

Chapter 15

Adapting Language with the Milton Model

· ·

In This Chapter

▶ Talking about trances

▶ Forming language to get your message heard

▶ Linking to the Meta Model

· ·

As a child at a party, you were probably held spellbound by a magician adroitly performing ingenious tricks for your entertainment. Well, now we're going to show you some magic – using hypnotic language to keep the conscious mind occupied or overloaded, while at the same time giving you the opportunity to talk directly to someone's unconscious mind. In NLP this conjuring trick is called the *Milton Model technique*. Hypnosis has moved a long way from being a thrilling theatrical performance to a respectable tried and tested therapy, thanks to the work of Milton Erickson. Richard Bandler and John Grinder, the co-founders of Neuro-linguistic Programming, found that Erickson used 'artfully vague language' to put his clients into an altered state of consciousness – a trance, in other words. Richard and John distilled Milton Erickson's use of language giving us the Milton Model patterns, which are techniques for helping you 'en-trance' people by your use of words. Using the Milton Model patterns can help you send a person off into a light or a medium trance or indeed into a full-blown deep hypnotic experience, making the person receptive to your message directly.

Being able to spot whether Milton Model patterns are being used makes you aware of what is happening and allows you to choose the way you behave and respond to people.

In this chapter we show you how to build Milton Model patterns into your everyday speech, making the words you use compelling and irresistible.

Easing into Hypnosis

Despite the fact that you're reading this chapter, have you perhaps not fully committed to the idea of learning about hypnosis because you've been put off by people being made to look silly by stage hypnotists?

In this chapter, you find at least four reasons why it would be useful to put your doubts aside for a while and read with an open mind. So if you would like to

✔ Overcome your suspicion of hypnosis

✔ Recognise when a person is using hypnotic language patterns

✔ Connect with the other person's unconscious mind

✔ Find some really useful lessons that you can use to ease your way through life, and who knows, even find ways of helping other people when your paths cross

then try putting aside any doubts you have about hypnosis and concentrate on reading this chapter with an open mind. Of course, if, after going through the chapter you still decide that your original beliefs were correct, please feel free to stand back and let it all go until the time is right for you to recognise the value of Ericksonian hypnosis.

Distinguishing between direct and indirect hypnosis

Direct hypnosis is when the hypnotist takes control over the client, giving commands such as, 'Your eyes are getting heavy now'. Direct hypnosis may not work for everyone.

Indirect hypnosis is the form of hypnosis practised by Milton Erickson. Milton used deliberately vague language and allowed his clients to access experiences and resources they may not otherwise have been aware of consciously.

The idea is that because the language is vague, and the client hasn't been given precise instructions, she searches for her own experiences and while searching, her unconscious mind enters into a trance state, making it easier for her unconscious to accept the therapeutic message.

Using the Milton Model language to put your audience – whether one person or a group – into a gentle trance is a great way to get your message accepted. People in trance are more receptive to suggestions because you've side-stepped any resistance that the conscious mind can put in your way. That is not to say that people will do whatever they are told, especially if it violates their deeply held ethics. The aim of using trance is to direct people's attention to what you want them to notice. For example, if you want someone to stay aware of what's going on in her environment, you might say, 'As you sit here, noticing the feel of the chair supporting you, the sun lighting up the room, and the drone of the cars outside, you know that your senses are heightened and you're aware of everything around you.'

By filling in Worksheet 15-1, you can put into words any unconscious misgivings that you may be harbouring about hypnosis. Bringing your doubts into your consciousness allows you to explore the benefits of utilising the Milton Model patterns for hypnosis, adapting your language accordingly, and putting you in the driving seat. We go into detail about Milton Model patterns in the later section 'Captivating Your Audience with the Milton Model'.

Until Saira learned Ericksonian hypnosis on her NLP course, she was very uncomfortable around anyone who 'might be able to put me under'. Once she took Milton Erickson language patterns on board, she was much more comfortable and was able to use hypnotic language to build rapport with her boss and the rest of her team.

Worksheet 15-1	My Thinking on Hypnosis
My current beliefs about hypnosis are:	
I'm reading this chapter because:	

Recognising everyday trance

Have you ever:

- ✔ Driven to a destination and not remembered how you got there?
- ✔ Been so deeply engrossed in a conversation or a book that time simply flew by?
- ✔ Carried on a conversation with yourself?
- ✔ Had a daydream?

If you answer yes to any of the questions, you know what a non-chemically induced trance feels like and that's really good news because if you're reading this chapter, it means that you want to find out about the Milton Erickson way of hypnosis. (Talking to yourself can be a bit dodgy – you're probably the only person who knows what you're on about, so be careful: people do love to eavesdrop!)

A *trance* can be defined as being in a state of altered consciousness. In a trance, you can lose conscious awareness of what is going on around you, like when you're deep in thought, focusing intensely, or experiencing a state of hypnosis. Trance is a perfectly normal phenomenon; people can move through several trance states during the course of a day.

Being in an altered state can be beneficial, such as when entering into a trance during meditation, which helps you to relax your body and mind. But being in a trance can be unproductive too. For example, you may be in the habit of responding to what someone does or says by getting into a conversation with yourself along the lines of, 'I know he doesn't love me. If he did, he'd have bought flowers when he went shopping. He's bound to leave me.' This is an example of an unproductive, negative self-talk trance. Negative self-talk is a trance because your focus on the negative alters your state of consciousness.

A common trance that people in an office environment can find themselves in is getting caught up in whinging about a colleague, a boss, or unfair working conditions. One person starts moaning about how she feels and before you know it, the negative thought virus has spread across the whole department and morale starts falling along with productivity and, crucially, camaraderie. The altered state of consciousness in this case is that people focus on the negative aspects of their environment and don't see any of the positive.

If you find yourself sliding into a less-than-useful trance, you can consciously change the focus of your thoughts. So instead of thinking about the negative, you can actively remind yourself of what is good. For example, 'He loves me because he saved me having to go for the shopping', or 'I'm lucky to have a secure job that I enjoy despite what the others say'. Try taking time out to daydream about when you last felt positive, happy, or were riding the crest of a wave. As you daydream, step right into the picture and relive the event, or allow yourself to go into a meditative state by focusing on your breathing.

You may find yourself experiencing some trances at particular times, such as when you get that hollow feeling at 11 a.m. and all you can think of is a latte and a doughnut. Other trances can happen regardless of the time, such as when you're listening to someone droning on about a boring subject, or fleetingly, when you see a bird land on the windowsill or see the breeze blow through some leaves. You may experience an altered state of reality when you suddenly feel a rush of love as you see your child running towards you, arms outstretched, and all you can focus on is that little human; or overwhelming compassion as you associate into the pain of an injured pet looking to you for help.

While reading this section you may well find yourself drifting off into a daydreaming trance! One thought leads to another and Hey presto!, you're in a full-blown daydream with your thoughts far away from buckling down to Worksheet 15-2. A daydream is a gentle trance because it's an altered state of consciousness.

Use Worksheet 15-2 to list the trances you experience most often. Describe the trance and when you find yourself going into it, and then tick the box to indicate whether that trance is productive or unproductive. You may well be surprised to discover how often you go into an altered state of awareness.

Worksheet 15-2	My Everyday Trances	
Trance, Time, and Description	*Productive*	*Unproductive*

After identifying an unproductive trance, you can take corrective action to change your unproductive trance to a more productive one.

Taking the soft focus route to trance

You can assist people into trance simply by using the Milton Model language patterns. A lot of patterns exist, as you can see in Table 15-1, and the way you discover how to use them elegantly is by consigning them to your unconscious by practising different combinations and eventually using the Milton Model without having to think about how you're using the patterns.

You know the saying 'laugh, and the world laughs with you', so with rapport being a two-way process, the best way of knowing how to get a person into an altered state is to go into a trance yourself, which will allow you to use the Milton Model patterns easily and powerfully. You can use the process of peripheral vision, described here, for a quick way of going into a light trance:

1. **Focus on a spot a few feet in front of you and slightly above eye level.**

2. **Staying focused, soften the muscles around your eyes and allow your awareness to stretch out, either side of your eyes.**

Notice the feeling inside you change to one of relaxation.

As you get more practised at going into peripheral vision and being in a light trance you find you acquire the skill of doing two things at the same time – for example, using elegant hypnotic language patterns while you hold a team meeting.

Going into peripheral vision is a great way to relax. So, when you're feeling tense or under pressure, allow your eyes to soften as they focus above eye level. You may even find yourself expressing yourself more fluently as you allow your unconscious mind to become more active.

It is harder to be really truly elegant consciously, so trust your unconscious and stay entranced with the Milton Model.

Captivating Your Audience with the Milton Model

Movies are a truly powerful medium for sending out influential messages. Each person watching the film constructs her own meaning of what the film is saying but at the same time stays caught up in the story. Likewise, you can captivate your audience by using language that has more than one possible meaning, allowing your listeners to interpret what you're saying according to their own experiences, allowing your message to be accepted.

The *Milton Model language patterns* are a set of sentences that, because they are deliberately unclear, direct the listener to discover the meaning of what you're saying by forcing her to explore her own experiences. As the listener goes inside her head to look for the meaning, her conscious mind is distracted and you're able to communicate with her unconscious, reducing resistance to your suggestions and increasing your ability to influence individuals with, say, achieving their goals, getting on with a colleague, having more confidence.

As you're here, reading, let your mind gently drift to one of your favourite places – because when you think of it, it makes you feel really good – and as you see this place and let the image float slowly through your unconscious, look to your right and you see a woman who is wearing a green dress and yellow slippers! Whoops! Was that too much detail for you? Did it pop you out of your trance?

This example shows you how using vague language allows you to go into a trance by letting you use your imagination. Giving detailed instructions breaks the trance as the unconscious mind says, 'There's no woman there', or 'She's not wearing yellow slippers'.

Using terms to entrance

We now get down to showing you the mechanics of using the Milton Model patterns to get your message across. This section helps you identify the language that makes this possible.

The ideal way to weave the Milton Model patterns together is to think of the message you want to deliver and make the patterns relevant to the message and the context in which you're delivering it. When you're trying to get a team pumped up to win a paintballing competition, it may not be effective to say, 'As you sit here, listening to me, hear your heart; breathing slowly and calmly; you're feeling at peace, in harmony with nature and each other.'

The more you practise with the Milton patterns, the more you can adapt them to your personality and the more you can hold your audience enthralled with a long string of Milton Model patterns blended into a story that gets your message across.

Pretend that the Milton Model patterns are notes on a piano and learn to go up and down as you play a medley and invent your own chords!

The Milton Model patterns are about keeping your language vague in order to side-step the conscious mind. The person you're talking to goes into a trance searching for her own examples, experiences, and meanings because you haven't actually said anything specific. While your listener's conscious mind is occupied, you're able to speak directly to that person's unconscious mind – for example, to install a positive behaviour. Installing positive behaviours isn't simply the domain of therapists. Parents have a responsibility to do this. Coaches and managers can also help in the process of installing a behaviour, although only after they have permission from the person whom they're trying to help.

Because most habits and behaviours are carried out by the unconscious mind, you get quicker results by instructing or speaking to the unconscious mind directly without getting caught up in the arguments that the analytical or conscious mind presents.

The reason for the terms given to the different Milton Model patterns is to allow people to communicate about the analysis of language So be aware that the terms exist but focus on how to use them to distract someone's conscious mind and to set the listener's thoughts going in a desired direction or to make suggestions that will help the listener.

Table 15-1 gives you a complete list of the Milton Model patterns in alphabetical order. The italicised patterns that aren't in bold are a subset of Ambiguity and Modal Operators.

Table 15-1	Milton Model Patterns		
Pattern	*Explanation*	*Example*	*Words to Listen For*
Ambiguity	What you say may have more than one meaning.		
Phonological	*Homonyms,* words that sound the same, and sometimes have the same spelling, but have different meanings.	Hear/Here Sea kelp/Seek help, Serial/Cereal, Knows/Nose	
Scope	Needs clarity in order to work out which bits of a sentence belong together.	Those wicked girls and boys. Speaking to you as a parent. He is a practising doctor.	

Pattern	Explanation	Example	Words to Listen For
Syntactic	The function of a word is not immediately understandable from the context.	They are telling tales. Flying kites can be frightening. Growing children can cost a fortune.	
Punctuation	The sentence is usually grammatically incorrect and is made up of two separate sentences connected by a common word. The connecting words are in bold and italics in the example.	He has a big ***nose*** what you mean. When morning ***dawned*** on us finally. He gave her the ***push*** the boat out.	
Cause and Effect*	The implication is that one thing causes or results in something else.	As you're here reading this, you now understand the Milton Model. Because you're understanding the Milton Model, you're obviously focusing your attention. Breathing results in you relaxing.	Makes, Causes, Results in, If, Then, Because, So, And, As
Complex Equivalence*	One thing is interpreted as meaning something else.	Your having got to this chapter means that you're one of the 10% of people who actually reads a book they buy. You're late again. So, you really aren't committed to this relationship. You're reading this book, therefore you're opening your mind to more possibilities.	Means, So, Therefore
Comparative Deletion*	Omitting one side of a comparison so that it isn't clear whether the comparison is being made with a person or a thing because the compared person or thing is deleted.	He's richer. You're so much happier. Can you walk faster? She's a better person.	Good, Better, Best, Worst, More, Less, Most, Least

(continued)

Table 15-1 (continued)

Pattern	Explanation	Example	Words to Listen For
Conversational Postulates	Asking a yes-or-no question in such a way that the person agrees to the request almost automatically. This only works for something that can be done immediately. It gives the listener an implied choice without being too bossy.	Could you bring me a glass of water please? Could you just answer my question? Can't you just imagine a quiet night in? Is that an aeroplane? (Has everyone looking up, searching for a plane in the sky.)	
Double Binds	Giving the listener the illusion of a choice when in fact both choices point her in the direction you want her to take. The essential ingredient of a double bind is that the person does what you want.	Would you like to start your homework now or in ten minutes? Will you start tidying your room this afternoon or will you have it finished by tomorrow morning? Only you can decide whether you go into a light, medium, or deep trance, quickly or slowly.	
Embedded Commands	Sandwiching commands in the middle of a conversation to bypass the conscious mind and speak directly to the unconscious mind.	I wouldn't dream of telling you to *stick to eating healthily* and there's absolutely no way that I'd suggest that *you can change easily* so I promise, everything I say, *you will want to hear,* which means you can *let down your guard* and *relax* as you *let me help you* achieve your goal.	
Extended Quotes	Leading the conscious mind along twisting and turning lanes so that the conscious mind switches off and you're able to slip the real message through to the unconscious.	I was speaking to Kate this morning and she told me that she heard her friend Sue had attended David's NLP practitioner course when he started to reminisce about having *listened* to Tad talk about the *importance of indirect hypnosis, which* of course is *very important.*	

Pattern	Explanation	Example	Words to Listen For
Lack of Referential Index*	Using nouns or verbs that don't specify a particular person or thing.	Clearing out is good. And everyone piled in. They went.	
Lost Performative*	Making a value judgement without revealing who made that judgement.	Each day is a new learning experience. It's okay to let your mind wander. It's good to believe. Care must be taken. Thinking takes time.	
Mind-Read*	Claiming to know the thoughts and feelings of a person without stating how you came to know those thoughts and feelings.	I'm aware that you know the answers to my questions. I know your curiosity is growing by the second. It's obvious to me that you're enjoying yourself. I can see what you're thinking.	
Modal Operators*	These are words that indicate whether you're operating from a position of choice or of necessity.		
Necessity	Words indicating the rules that the speaker believes in.	You have to experience being in a trance in order to explain the state. I'm not saying that you have to but you must understand why it's important.	Must/ Mustn't, Will/Won't, Have to, Should/ Shouldn't
Possibility	Words useful for overcoming resistance in a person, simply by opening up avenues of possibility.	New driver: 'I can't learn to drive'. Instructor: 'Just supposing you can.'	Can/Can't, Will/Won't, Would, Could, Might

(continued)

Table 15-1 *(continued)*

Pattern	Explanation	Example	Words to Listen For
Nominalisation*	Here a verb has been turned into a noun. A verb is normally associated with movement of some sort – relating, communicating (movement back and forth between people). When the verb is turned into a noun, it effectively becomes 'frozen' and loses the movement. The idea is to move a person from a state of stuckness by unfreezing the word and introducing movement back. This can be done by adding an 'ing' to the verb and asking how, what, or when someone would like to do the verb+ing. A nominalisation is a noun that can't be put in a wheelbarrow – for example relationship, communication, life.	Relationship (verb: relate). Knowledge (verb: to know). Communication (verb: communicate). 'Our relationship is lousy' is a stuck statement because it's a statement of someone's perceived fact. Asking, 'How would you like to be relat*ing*?' puts the movement back by giving the person a choice of behaviour. 'My communication is terrible' can be opened up with 'How would you like to be communicat*ing*'. 'I have a terrible life' can get movement by asking, 'How would you like to be liv*ing*?'	
Pacing Current Experience	Stating someone's current experience in a way that the person cannot deny. The person's unconscious mind is going 'Yes I'm reading this chapter', 'Yes, actually, I'm holding this book', and 'Yes, my breathing is rhythmic' so that when these statements are followed with an instruction, the person goes 'Oh! Okay! I am learning'.	While you're sitting here reading this chapter, you're holding this book, and there's a rhythm to your breathing, which means that you're learning.	
Presuppositions*	Making linguistic assumptions. A sentence that presupposes something, such as the ability to go into trance, write, or feel sad, happy, or angry creates that state of being because a person has to go inside her own head to discover that she has had the experience of going into trance, writing, or feeling sad, happy, or angry.	And you can go into trance, can't you? People who can write well can also tell great stories and you know how to write well. And you're so much more. When you feel sad. When you feel angry.	

Pattern	Explanation	Example	Words to Listen For
Selectional Restriction Violations	Anthropomorphism, giving animals and inanimate objects human characteristics.	The walls have ears. The car's feelings got hurt. The cushion loves being cuddled. The cat cried pitifully.	
Tag Question	A means of softening a person's resistance by implying the answer in the question. Usually used at the end of a statement.	You don't really believe that, do you? You mean you can't? (Very powerful if said in a puzzled voice!) You did say you'd come to dinner? (With an implied 'didn't you?')	
Universal Quantifiers*	Words that generalise an experience.	'All the world's a stage, And all the men and women merely players'. You never listen. You always nag.	None, All, Everyone; Every, Each, Everything, Never, Always
Unspecified Verbs *	A statement that leaves out the person doing the acting or omits the verb that would clarify how someone did or would do something. For example, 'It's all your fault' can be clarified by saying 'It's all your fault because you kept me waiting.'	You don't care about me any more. You made it happen. It's all your fault.	
Utilisation	Making use of an unexpected occurrence.	A person is in a trance and a noisy lorry thunders past and the therapist says, 'As the sound of the lorry gets softer and softer, you go deeper and deeper into a trance.' Client says, 'I can't let go' and the therapist says, 'That's right, you can't *let go now*.'.	

* Indicates a 'Meta Model Violation'. For an explanation please see the section on 'Relating the Milton Model to the Meta Model' later in this chapter.

Notice similarities between some of the Milton Model patterns:

✔ The difference between Cause and Effect and Complex Equivalence is that of time, no matter how brief, separating the Cause from the Effect. For example, 'You make me angry when you don't do the dishes' has a gap between noticing the dirty dishes and feeling the emotion. Whereas in the Complex Equivalence, 'Not doing the dishes means you don't love me' doesn't need or have the separation as both parts of the statement are emotionally connected.

✔ The only difference between Lack of Referential Index and a Lost Performative is that the Lost Performative has an element of passing a judgement. For example, 'They went away', is a lack of Referential Index as no judgement is being made. 'It's good to read' is a Lost Performative, as someone has given a positive judgement to the act of reading.

✔ Depending on the construction of a sentence, there is a similarity between Comparative Deletions, Lack of Referential Index, and Lost Performative: 'It's good to be rich', 'It's better to be richer', 'They're richer'.

Turning to key patterns

Entire books have been written about the Milton Model patterns. We just don't have the space in this chapter to cover all the Milton Model language patterns in the detail we'd like. We've chosen a few, at random, to explain the Milton Model patterns and illustrate how you can use them in your day-to-day life.

Now try your hand at using the following Milton Model patterns to help you to communicate effectively. As you get more confident build in other patterns, a few at a time, from the list in Table 15-1.

Judging the lost performative

A *lost performative* expresses a value judgement without revealing who made that judgement. By not specifying who's making the statement, you give your listener the opportunity to make her own interpretations about what the value judgement is, and who is likely to have made it. The process of interpreting the value judgement causes your listener to enter into a trance, allowing you to make a helpful suggestion or give a specific instruction while the conscious mind is occupied.

Examples of Lost Performatives:

✔ Each day is a new learning experience

✔ It's a good thing to let your mind wander

✔ And it's good to believe

✔ Care must be taken otherwise there may be problems

✔ Thinking gives time

If a person is feeling particularly cantankerous, she may well say, arms akimbo, 'Oh yeah? Who says?' But, if you've piled on enough Milton Model language, she'll already be in a trance and won't be in a position to be difficult!

Use Worksheet 15-3 to come with up with at least six examples of Lost Performatives that you recognise in your own or other peoples' speech. You may want to make a note of one or two that you would like to build into your everyday speak.

Worksheet 15-3	My Examples of Lost Performatives

_____

_____

_____

_____

Making the most of mind-reading

Mind-reading is where a person claims to know the thoughts and feelings of someone else, without stating how she came to know. Examples of a mind-read:

✔ I'm very aware that you know the answers to my questions

✔ I know your curiosity is growing by the second

✔ It's obvious to me that you're enjoying yourself

✔ I'm aware that you're feeling inquisitive

✔ I can see what you're thinking

The three main benefits in knowing about mind-reading are

✔ Being able to recognise when someone is mind-reading and the mind-read leads to a misunderstanding, so that you're itching to get involved and wanting to sort out the error. Understanding can lead to solutions instead of conflict.

✔ Finding yourself reading someone's mind allows you to check whether your assumptions are correct.

✔ You can pretend to mind-read in order to plant suggestions or make someone aware of an experience. For example, 'I know you can sense we are in tune and I can see that makes you happy' can be an indirect way of asking a person to consider whether she is in tune with you and also to help her recognise that she is happy.

Only use mind-reading to make suggestions when you're confident you're enjoying a great rapport with someone. Otherwise, your suggestions may lead to disharmony if the person responds with, 'No I'm not in tune, or happy'.

Take care when mind-reading! Even the most innocent remark can lead to mayhem. The following dialogue illustrates how an innocuous remark can be explosive if the person on the receiving end of the remark is feeling edgy and fails to read the other person's mind. The background to this story is that Colleen has been attending Italian classes on a Saturday morning, while Driks plays golf. However, there aren't any classes through the summer so Colleen gets to have a lie in, a cup of coffee, and time to read and think. She really enjoys the peace and quiet. Driks is a DIY aficionado and one Saturday morning is drilling in the adjacent bedroom on his return from golf. Because there's someone around to have a chat with, Colleen strolls in to see Driks.

> Colleen: 'You know how much I love my Saturday morning Italian classes. But it's lovely to be able to have time to sit and have a quiet think now that classes are over.'
>
> Driks: 'Tsk! I've only just started drilling for goodness sake. I can't stop now.'
>
> Colleen: 'Why do you want to stop?'
>
> Driks: 'Because you said so.'

Colleen: 'I did? What did I say?'

Driks (Getting ready to throw a tantrum): 'You said you wanted me to stop drilling.'

Colleen: 'I did? Oh, I thought I was just sharing my feelings about having time to chill out and think.'

Ooops! Are you wincing because you can identify with Colleen and Driks? Never mind, you can use Worksheet 15-4 for working through the times you've done a mind-read, got it wrong, and the lessons you've learned. Or perhaps if you've snapped at someone for misunderstanding you, can you decide what you might say or do differently next time?

Hanging onto your emotions just keeps you trapped and doesn't allow you to grow. Release the hold that an experience has on you by taking on board the lessons learned that helped you to release the emotions.

Worksheet 15-4	Driks's Mind-Reading Example
Describe what happened:	I was busy drilling in the bedroom and Colleen came in and started talking. Because I was concentrating, all I heard was 'peace and quiet' and thought she wanted me to stop drilling.
What was the result of the misunderstanding?	I got irritated and snappy.
What did you learn?	I need to change my strategy for responding when I'm interrupted.
What might you do differently?	If I can't stop, I'll ask Colleen to 'give me a minute' before listening. If I feel like snapping, I'll flash up a picture of when we were in Venice, having our photo taken. That's when I remember how fabulous it was to be together and how lucky I was to have Colleen in my life. That memory always makes me feel warm and loving.

Use Worksheet 15-5 to record your experience of mind-reading. Your experience can relate to an event that had an amusing or happy outcome.

Worksheet 15-5	My Mind-Reading Example
Describe what happened:	
What was the result of the misunderstanding?	

What did you learn?	
What might you do differently?	

Perhaps at this moment you're sitting and wondering while holding this workbook – and that's okay because sitting and wondering are good – thinking over how you might use Milton Model patterns in your home or your work life. Use Worksheet 15-6 to record some examples of mind-reading statements that you can build into your life, right now. Because you know you can, don't you? Think of situations where you might want to use mind-reads. A workplace example may go something like, 'I'm sure you've noticed that it's a good time to take a break and have a coffee.' Even if the person doesn't realise that she needs a break, she'll probably go, 'Oh! What a good idea.'

Worksheet 15-6   My Opportunities for Using Mind-Reading Statements

Statements	*H-Home life* *W-Work life*

Pacing Current Experience

Pacing Current Experience is about stating the experience a person is currently having in such a way that the person can't deny the experience. The statement doesn't have to be true, but it does have to be believable. When the person's unconscious goes, 'Oh! Yeah, that's true', you're in a position to get the person agreeing with any of your following statements. Here are examples of Pacing Current Experience:

✔ An author may write something like, 'As you are sitting here reading this chapter, you're holding this book, and there's a rhythm to your breathing which means that you are learning.'

The reader isn't able to deny the statements, so her unconscious mind is going 'Yes I am reading this chapter', 'Yes, actually, I am holding this book', and 'Yes, my breathing is rhythmic', and when you follow the person's statements with an instruction, you go 'Oh! Okay! I am learning.'

✔ A therapist might be saying, 'While you are sitting here, listening to my voice, you may be thinking about something to do with why you're here or something else, and you feel the chair supporting you, which means that you are beginning to relax and recognising that you have a solution.' To which the client thinks, 'Yes I am hearing her voice', 'Nooo, I'm not thinking about why I'm here' (starting to come out of trance), 'Oh yes, I'm thinking about something else' (dropping back into trance), 'Oh yes, the chair's supporting me', 'Okay, I'm relaxing' and buys into the assumption that there *is* an answer to her issues and that she is going to come up with the solution.

The more statements you make that your listener can't deny, the more chance you have of that person accepting your suggestion.

Worksheet 15-7 gives you an opportunity to build on the Pacing Current Experience examples and to plan suggestions you want to make to the person with whom you're communicating – whether you're going to be speaking face to face, on the telephone, or e-mailing. This exercise is great for discovering just how many undeniable statements of experience you can come up with.

Worksheet 15-7	My Opportunities for Pacing Current Experience

My opportunities:

_____

_____

_____

_____

Possible statements I can use:

_____

_____

_____

_____

Using utilisation

Utilisation is making use of an unexpected occurrence to enhance the current experience. For example, if a mother is trying to put her child to sleep and the phone rings, she can say, 'and as you hear the phone ringing and listen to my voice, you know you're safe, we love you, and you're getting really sleepy'. Mum can enhance the effect by yawning.

Tricia, feeling frazzled, was having a heated 'discussion' with her teenage daughter, Freda, about the untidy state of Freda's room. Freda stormed out, slamming her door with such force that a favourite ornament fell off the wall. Tricia, perhaps unwisely, yelled after Freda, 'and take that as divine retribution'. Tricia makes the connection that the ornament falling off the wall is a message from above and utilises the ornament falling as a way of making the point that the powers above don't approve of Freda's behaviour either.

Katherine, an NLP trainer, and Jill, a therapist, were chatting and Katherine was telling Jill about Tim's cat, Herbie, which was being bullied by a new boy on the block, with the result that Herbie had taken to comfort eating. Herbie was getting horribly overweight and rather too cuddly. And Katherine felt that Tim needed to take responsibility for his cat's health and cut down on Herbie's eating. At this point Jill said, 'Do you know, I was having trouble thinking of a metaphor for one of my less than sylph-like clients and now I can tell him about Herbie.' To which Katherine said, 'By the way you do know that's called Selectional Restriction Violations, giving human characteristics to animals. But more to the point, you've just done what's called Utilisation, by turning our conversation into something that can be used usefully by you, and now by me.'

We're not suggesting that getting the opportunity to practise Utilisation only happens by chance – unless of course you set the intention and create it at a metaphysical level. But, keeping your feet on the ground, do you know anyone who has an irritating habit such as coughing loudly down the telephone at you? If you do, you can say something like, 'Oh! Thank you, that just reminds me I must get some cough drops.' Allowing you to utilise the cough and let the cougher know how annoying the coughing is hopefully leads the person to take the hint to cover her mouth when she needs to cough in future.

Just in case you can't think of any examples, use Worksheet 15-8 to note down your ideas on utilisation to train your unconscious mind to notice opportunities.

Worksheet 15-8	My Thoughts on Utilisation

Relating the Milton Model to the Meta Model

In Chapter 14, we make the point that linguistic patterns, called the Meta Model, allow you to reach levels of understanding about your problems by drilling down for specific meanings. Some of the Milton Model patterns that we talk about in 'Captivating Your Audience with the Milton Model' draw on the Meta Model for a similar purpose – for example, by putting a person into a trance – but this is done by using a Meta Model pattern in a very vague way. This is referred to as a *Meta Model violation* because the vague use of the Meta Model pattern 'violates' the specificity of the way it would normally be used.

The 'Meta Model violations' are marked with an asterisk (*) in Table 15-1. To find out all about the Meta Model refer to Chapter 14.

The Meta Model uses a question or a series of questions to get to the bottom of the problem by uncovering the deletions, distortions, and generalisations that people use in their language. (To brush up on deletions, distortions, and generalisations look at Chapter 5 'Recognising How You Filter Your Thinking'.) So, if a husband says to his wife, 'You don't love me anymore', she may respond with, 'What do I do to make you feel unloved?' The reply 'You never buy me chocolates any more' opens up the dialogue by starting to uncover how the husband is feeling unloved, allowing the wife to understand what her husband is feeling, challenge his assumption, or do something about the situation.

Using language that can have more than one meaning can send you off into a trance, allowing you to chew over what is being said. So the wife, in the preceding example, could have gone off into a trance of her own, or chosen to work out the issue by unravelling her husband's 'I'm unloved' trance.

Table 15-2 shows how a statement can be analysed using the Meta Model. The first column shows the actual statement that allows the listener to shift into a trance state as she goes inside her head to interpret what has been said. The second column illustrates the Meta Model pattern being used, and the third column shows you the questions that can unearth the mental processes leading to the statement.

Don't let the labels such as 'cause and effect violation' and 'mind-read' get in the way of the real reason for using the questions; which is to help someone shift a trance in which she finds herself. For example, if you say, 'You make me feel angry', the altered state of reality or trance is that someone has power over you and can make you feel angry. Asking you, 'What do I do when you choose to feel angry?' might make you *more* angry but it does shift your awareness to the fact that you have a choice over whether to feel angry or not.

Table 15-2	Linking the Milton Model with the Meta Model	
Statement	*Meta Model Pattern*	*Response to Draw Out the Real Meaning of the Statement*
You make me feel angry.	Cause and Effect violation	What do I do when you choose to feel angry?
I know you're excited.	Mind-read	How precisely do you know I'm excited?
He's so much better.	Comparative Deletion Lost Performative	Better than whom? Who says? At what? How do you know?

Using the appropriate language pattern is really effective because it gives you the power to make yourself heard. So you need to think about the message you want to deliver.

Pulling the Patterns Together

This chapter covers the Milton Model patterns in some detail, but in order to give you an in-depth understanding of the patterns, we have used quite a number of different patterns as examples. Now we are going to show you how to pull the patterns together and use them purposefully in your workplace and personal life.

Following is an example of the sort of statements a trainer or a teacher might say to her students:

> And as you're listening you may decide to learn slowly or quickly . . . you will all hear here everything that is said . . . It's great to think what might happen by taking all your learnings on board . . .

Now take a look at the models and patterns contained in the trainer's short statement:

✔ And as you're listening: An example of 'Pacing Current Experience' in which you're speaking to someone sitting and listening to you.

✔ You may decide to learn slowly or quickly: This 'Double Bind' tells the students that they don't have a choice in what they learn; their only apparent choice is in whether they learn quickly or slowly.

This statement also demonstrates a 'presupposition' in assuming that the listener will learn.

✔ The students hear here everything that is said: *Hear/here* demonstrates a 'Phonological Ambiguity'. *They, all,* and *everything* are 'Universal Quantifiers', which are generalisations about a noun, without specifying the noun exactly.

✔ It's great to think what might happen by taking all your learnings on board. This 'Lost Performative' implies that it's great to think about learning without identifying the person making that judgement.

Asking the students to think about what might happen uses a Modal Operator of 'Possibility'.

The verb 'to learn' has been turned into a noun, a thing – *learnings*.

And finally, *all* is another 'Universal Quantifier'.

A line manager, speaking to a member of her staff who is about to give an important presentation, may say:

I have heard good things about you and it's great, so while you may be nervous, you're also confident and relaxed because you can see beyond your presentation to feeling so good about it having been brilliant.

This manager's statement breaks down like this:

✔ The manager doesn't actually say who says the good things but does give the statement a positive slant, using a 'Lost Performative'.

✔ There are examples of mind-reads in the manager's statement: 'while you may be nervous', 'you're also confident and relaxed', and 'you can see beyond'.

✔ The 'presupposition' or assumption that the presentation will be brilliant ends the manager's pep talk.

Now use Worksheet 15-9 to generate a message full of Milton Model patterns to deliver to your audience while they are in a trance-like state. For example, you may want to deliver your message in the context of an NLP training or coaching session.

Worksheet 15-9   **Mixing and Matching Milton Model Patterns**

The context for my message:

_____

_____

_____

The message I want to deliver:

_____

_____

_____

What I am going to say:

_____

_____

_____

We have given you a tremendous amount of information in this chapter and you may find some bits of it intimidating. Please remember to take things in small chunks and chew well before taking action. You must decide whether you start having a load of fun now, or later on, discovering how to absorb the Milton Model patterns naturally and effortlessly into your everyday speech.

Chapter 16

Storytelling Magic

In This Chapter

▶ Seeing the story of your life

▶ Composing stories

▶ Telling your stories

▶ Finding your origin story

*P*erhaps you think of storytelling as that very last job of the day – another reading from *Thomas and Friends* before tucking up your children in bed and saying goodnight – or perhaps it's you being the life and soul of the party, recounting that hilarious anecdote with your listeners hanging onto your every word. But have you thought about stories having practical uses as well as being pure entertainment? Stories are a way of communicating your values, passing on your wisdom, and helping you to view choices, make decisions, and achieve your well-formed outcomes (refer to Chapter 3 for more on well-formed outcomes).

Storytelling is a favourite NLP tool used for developing rapport. With your knowledge and experience of life, you have a natural ability for storytelling. So, every time you hear a story, you discover something new that adds richness and meaning to your life.

Everyone loves hearing and telling a story. You access the left side of your brain to process the words and the sequence of the plots and the right side of your brain for imagination, visualisation, and creativity. In this chapter, you get to focus on creating your own stories from your own experience.

Looking at Your Life in Storytelling

A lot of your day-to-day activities involve telling stories. For example, when describing a project you're working on to your colleagues, you're conveying information and giving an account of your actions. Similarly, when talking passionately about your absorbing pastime, you connect with a lot of (like-minded, or not!) people. Think about your storytelling as descriptions about characters and events that your audience will find interesting, rather than simply trying to impress.

Seeing structure in stories

Sit back for a moment and think of a story that caught your attention recently – an everyday situation like the tale you heard about a job interview, that family celebration, a sporting triumph, or something that happened to friends during a trip to New York. Or, maybe somebody called you this morning ranting and raving about poor customer service he's paying heavily for. What is it about your particular story that makes it memorable and interesting? Was there some kind of problem that the key players faced and how did they resolve it? Were you intrigued by a description of a place or the people? Now fill in Worksheet 16-1 by taking a look at the key ingredients that make up an engaging story.

Worksheet 16-1	Key Ingredients of My Everyday Tale
The overall story – what is it about? Then, briefly what is the storyline – what happens in sequence from the beginning through to the end?	
What emotions are expressed by the storyteller or aroused in you? (For example, fear, anger, joy, curiosity, guilt, contentment.)	
Who are the people being talked about or who appear in the story, and what roles are they playing?	
What are the issues (for example, a moral dilemma or physical challenge that the characters face) and what is the outcome, the resolution at the end of the story?	
What other points or details make the story interesting to you?	
How have you connected with the story? What does the story show and what lesson have you learned?	

Breaking down your story into key ingredients allows you to put together a story that wins the ear of your listener. However, including all of the key ingredients may not suit your storyline. Perhaps you prefer to adapt just a few elements, making them your own and emphasising one or two details to illustrate a point?

Get into the habit of capturing interesting stories you hear, rather as you do when taking photographs, so that you can bring your stories out when the time is right.

Telling tales of your own experience

'Help, I'm not a storyteller', you may argue. Like a writer, you're suffering from *storyteller's block* and are struggling to release your natural talent. Help is at hand: the list in Worksheet 16-2 gives you ideas for topics when you're at a loss to think of engaging stories you can tell.

Your real life experiences are the basic ingredients for your stories. When using your own experience as the subject for your story, you can adapt your language by playing with the Meta Model and Milton Model tools from Chapter 14 and Chapter 15 to alternate between being specific and generalising. From Worksheet 16-2, choose a few subjects to talk about for a couple of minutes to a friend. But begin by reading through the list and ticking the topics that strike a chord, to start building your storytelling muscles.

Worksheet 16-2	My Experiences for Potential Story Material

I have experience of:

❏   Having a partner, spouse, parent, brother, or sister

❏   Going on a train journey

❏   Being shocked by something

❏   A trip to the beach or mountains

❏   Eating out at a café or restaurant

❏   Customer service

❏   Financial dilemmas

❏   Giving a party

❏   Great memories

❏   Having a bad haircut

❏   Having an unusual job

❏   Enjoying a hobby

❏   Hearing an interesting anecdote

❏   Memories from school or college

❏   Meeting a strange or eccentric person

❏   Playing tennis/golf/football/rugby or another sport

❏   Receiving unwelcome presents

❏   Riding a bicycle

❏   Being on the scene of a crime

❏   Watching a TV programme

❏   Suffering from delays

❏   Visiting a supermarket

❏   Being woken up in the night

❏   Something I want to talk about

Passion is an essential ingredient in storytelling. So review each item you ticked and think about which of the experiences had a strong impact on you. For example, have you given a party that was a truly wonderful occasion surrounded by people you care about? Or have you ridden a bicycle and felt the pain of falling off and hurting yourself?

In Worksheet 16-3 make a note of the times when your emotional reaction was at a peak from the topics you ticked in Worksheet 16-2. Notice the good times. Choose an event when you were on a high, you were at your most optimistic, and all was right with the world. For example, giving your partner that surprise birthday party. Just thinking about it brings a smile to your face. Notice the bad times as well. Find an event when you were at a low. Things were bad and you were at your most pessimistic. You felt distressed, angry, or unhappy. For example, you cringe when you remember singing a song at the Christmas party and you shudder when you recall just how much alcohol you drank. Choose a mix of experiences that impacted on you and aroused a strong reaction in you.

Worksheet 16-3	My Peak Experiences for Storytelling
Good Times	*Bad Times*

When you start to notice the good and bad times when your emotions are heightened, you access issues and situations that you feel passionate about. These times can form the basis of stories around your personal experiences that enable you to connect with an audience.

Writing your story

When Kate coaches budding authors in her 'Passion to Publication' workshops, she sets the kitchen timer and gets her students to write on any topic they choose in seven minutes flat. So here goes. You can do the same in Worksheet 16-4 or write your story on a separate sheet of paper.

This seven-minute exercise is to allow whatever comes into your head to be put down on paper without judging the quality of your writing or refining what you've written. Imagine you're telling a friend about one of your peak experiences of good or bad times from Worksheet 16-3. Now pick up your pen and write. Keep writing, letting the words flow forwards for seven minutes. When the timer pings, stop.

For the moment, forget about placing the story in the future. Don't worry that at the moment you don't know what the outcome will be. Just concentrate on getting your story down; you can find a way later of weaving what you have written into a conversation or a more formal storytelling session.

Worksheet 16-4	My Seven-Minute Story

_____

_____

_____

_____

_____

_____

_____

_____

_____

_____

_____

_____

_____

_____

_____

_____

_____

Congratulations, you now have the first draft of your story, and it's written from the heart. When you're ready to refine your story and retell it as a written or spoken story, you can follow the formula in the next section to give your story spontaneity.

Following the Formula for Creating Stories

Here's a list of tried and tested points for you to take into account so that your readers or listeners are fully engaged in your story. Ask yourself, 'Does my story:

- ✔ **Connect with emotions.** The emotions that you express in your story need to be infectious. Give your audience the chance to feel the emotions you're experiencing.

- ✔ **Introduce different characters.** Telling the story through a series of characters adds interest and brings your story to life.

- ✔ **Develop a storyline.** Does your story have a beginning, middle, and end?

- ✔ **Raise issues and offer resolutions.** Introduce a problem or challenge that your characters face and tell your listeners or readers how they solve the problem.

- ✔ **Introduce details.** Give some interesting details without boring your audience with too much description.

- ✔ **Enable the reader or listener to make connections.** People naturally make their own connections based on their own experiences – so you don't need to try explicitly to point out the connections for them.

Before using the points in the list, sit back and read this story from master storyteller Charlie Badenhop, bearing in mind that NLP is about modelling excellence. As you read Charlie's story, consider how he naturally sticks to the points in the formula, even though he wasn't aware of them before he began writing his story.

Self-Hypnosis and The Human Spirit

Over time my stories about my ex-wife's grandmother have proven to really touch people's hearts. I hope what I write today will help you to have greater faith in your own ability to persevere in difficult situations.

Grandma's ability to enter into a self-hypnotic trance state likely saved her life during World War II. Her ability to enter into a self-hypnotic trance state when telling a story made her a treasure to be around.

One evening I asked grandma what WWII was like for her. Here's what she said:

'Much of Tokyo was destroyed by US fire bombing during the end of World War II. It was very dangerous, because fires would rage nightly and spread rapidly.

'It was devastating to lose all one's worldly possessions and the very house you lived in in a few minutes time. But it was even more devastating to hear the screams of those writhing in pain as they got trapped in-between fires and had no way to escape the inferno.

'The safest place to be during the fire bombings was on the grounds of a neighbourhood temple. With only two buildings on the large property the bombers did not target the area. Most importantly though, there was a large pond on the grounds. If you submerged yourself in the pond up to your chin, you could protect yourself from the flying sparks coming from the many wooden buildings on fire.'

'Going in that pond every night took a bit of strength,' she said. 'It was winter time after a while, and the air and the water were cold. Some people didn't have the fortitude to stay in the pond until the bombers left. But staying alive was more important than comfort, so getting out of the pond early was not an option for me.'

'What I did,' she said, 'Is this . . . I wore several layers of clothes to help keep my body heat in. Once I got to the pond I would quickly immerse myself up to my chin. I felt it was very important to not slowly suffer through this process.'

'Next,' she said, 'I would look for the largest blazing fire in the distance and make believe it was one of the large fires built during one of the summer festivals. I would imagine myself getting a bit too close to the fire and needing to cool off by immersing myself in the pond. I would then look at the sparks flying everywhere and imagine they were the famous Tokyo summer fireworks display. Remembering vividly how hot it was at that time of year, it felt great to cool off in the pond.'

At this point she stopped talking and we looked at each other while also looking off into the distance.

'On January 1st for the last number of years, you've come with us when we go to the temples in the old neighbourhood to pray. Now you know the story of the one temple we always visit last. While there, I give thanks for being spared and I pray for the souls of all those who departed during the bombings, asking that their pain be erased from their souls.'

'Now,' she said, 'we have come full circle. You are American, and you have married my granddaughter. I pray this means the suffering of WWII is being transformed into friendship and love.'

'Japan is a very different country as a result of the war,' she said. 'Perhaps such terrible suffering was necessary, to bring about such great change.'

We both sat there for about a minute while saying nothing. In telling her powerful story with such a wonderful gentle intensity, the two of us had slipped off into a lovely state of self-hypnosis. It took a bit of time to travel back into the present, and find ourselves sitting in the safety of her living room. Powerful stories are often magical in that way.

Permission and source: Charlie Badenhop is the originator of Seishindo, an Aikido instructor, NLP trainer, and Ericksonian Hypnotherapist. For more of Charlie's stories visit www.seishindo.org/ newsletter.html.

Worksheet 16-5 shows the outline of a story that Gordon created to help him give an account at his next team meeting of a piece of academic research on what motivates people at work.

Worksheet 16-5	**Gordon's Story Development Worksheet**
Connect with emotions: What emotions do you want to express or bring out in your audience?	I want my audience to feel a strong sense of curiosity about their personal motivation at work.
Introduce characters: Who are the people appearing in the story?	The factory workers who were the subject of the Hawthorne experiments in the 1920s and the researchers from Harvard Business School.
Develop a storyline: What is the storyline – what happens from beginning to end?	A bunch of researchers set out to study how the physical and environmental factors in the Hawthorne Plant affected the productivity of the workers. The study moved into examining psychological aspects at play and at work, and went on for five years. The work had a lasting influence on management theory that is still referred to 80 years later.
Raise an issue and offer a resolution: What is the issue and how is the issue resolved?	The issue is how do you improve performance at work and the answer is that this is more complex than choosing the people with the right skills. The researchers came to view the workplace as a social system and the studies looked at the interrelationships between people and how group norms were arrived at.
Introduce details: What other points or details make the story interesting to the audience?	Changing the light bulbs. The researchers found that workers responded when the brightness was raised. However they were also motivated when the light levels were dimmed. The 'Hawthorne effect' is generally used to refer to how people get motivated just by others showing an interest in what they do.
Allow the reader to make connections: What connections do you want your audience to make? What lesson do you want your audience to take away?	That simply being interested in other people can be motivational and that what makes other people motivated is more complex than financial reward.

In Worksheet 16-6 you have a template to create an outline of your story. You have a choice here: to build on the work you've started in Worksheet 16-3 and Worksheet 16-4, or you can begin again with a new subject. When you have finished the exercise you have an outline of your story serving as a prompt so that you can tell your story quite naturally.

Just now you may have no idea of when you'd like to tell your story. That's fine. Just the very act of putting your ideas onto paper means that your unconscious mind will be beavering away in the background keeping your story ready for using at some point in the future.

Worksheet 16-6	**My Story Development Worksheet**
Connect with emotions: What emotions do you want to express or bring out in your audience?	
Introduce characters: Who are the people appearing in your story?	
Develop a storyline: What is the storyline – what happens from beginning to end?	
Raise an issue and offer a resolution: What is the issue and how is this resolved?	
Introduce details: What other points or details make the story interesting to the audience?	
Allow the reader to make connections: What connections do you want the audience to make? What lesson do you want your audience to take away?	

In Worksheet 16-7 reflect on what the exercise in Worksheet 16-6 tells you about your storytelling ability. Think of some different ways of telling your outline story.

Worksheet 16-7	Reflections on My Outline Story
Who might be interested in hearing my story?	
What family and friends can I practise with?	
What upcoming events have I got planned – a team meeting or a social gathering – where I may be able to tell my story?	
Is my story best written or spoken?	

Developing Your Storytelling Skills

Despite leading a busy life, find the time to develop new habits and build on your storytelling skills. Here are some tips:

- Buy yourself a really good-looking notebook that's a joy to write in. Every time you get an idea for a story, spend seven minutes capturing the essence of the story and then refine it later using the six-point formula outlined in the section 'Writing your story' earlier in the chapter.

- Find a time and place where you feel happiest writing – maybe out in the garden or at your favourite café. Fix a certain time of the day, or day of the week, for getting down to writing.

- Collect stories you've read or heard others tell. Make a list of the stories, when and where you heard them, keeping the information on your PC, laptop, or what works for you. Adapt a story by changing names and details, making the story your own.

- Make a point of sharing your stories with other people. Stories need to be told! Decide what opportunities you have that lend themselves to your storytelling. Are you going to send your stories out by e-mail or by post? Are you going to relate your stories to friends or workmates?

- When you're struggling to achieve your life or work goals and plans, ask yourself whether you have a story that can offer you a lesson here. Go back over and reread the story to discover the connections.

- When a friend asks for advice, find a story to share illustrating the situation. A story can be a powerful way of resolving a problem rather than you giving advice upfront which is rarely acted on.

- Cultivate the art of using your voice and body language to good effect by practising telling stories to groups. Take voice coaching or presentation skill training if you want to become more professional in your delivery.

Plotting Your Own Story

As an NLP coach, Kate is passionate about building self-confidence in her clients, colleagues, and friends in their daily lives and at work. When Kate first trained in NLP, she set herself a well-formed outcome (for more about achieving well-formed outcomes, look at Chapter 3) to raise confidence in others as well as in herself. Several years later, this led Kate to co-authoring *Building Confidence For Dummies*, running workshops, and creating a set of online self-confidence resources at www.yourmostconfidentself.com. Kate's stories reflect real-life challenges she comes up against.

Throughout this book you work on the outcomes that are important to you in your own life and focus your energy on getting what you want. Consider for a moment where your source material comes from, your *origin story,* the part of your own life story that has influenced your thinking most strongly, that has made you who you are today, your own account that you would really like to tell.

✔ What is the story that gets you passionate, the story that tells who you really are and what you really care about? For example, has a health setback made you determined to turn over a new leaf and look after yourself properly? Have you been angered by the ill-treatment of animals and are you now keen to set up a sanctuary? What was the trigger that stirred you and brought your story alive?

✔ What is the legacy that you'd like to leave for others once you're gone? How do you want to make a difference in the world? Have you, for example, been blessed with a happy childhood and want to make sure other children experience the same? Do you have a talent for woodwork and want to leave your grandchildren beautiful handmade toys to treasure?

✔ What are the wider issues you believe in, that go far beyond private and personal aspirations?

Use Worksheet 16-8 to put into writing the story behind your passion. It doesn't matter if your story is left untold or rests in your journal unread by the world. Go ahead and write your story anyway and when the time is right, you can develop it using the tips that follow Worksheet 16-8. Who knows, your story may be the basis of a book, a public talk, or just a one-to-one conversation at a later date.

Worksheet 16-8	My Origin Story

To keep your listeners involved in your story, be sure your narrative contains:

- **Characters:** Include people or animals that are capable of action. Make these characters memorable.

- **Scenes:** Imagine each scene in your story as a film set. Where do things happen? Who is there? What are the props?

- **Details:** Include a few subtle details drawing your listener into the story, without overloading on description.

- **Actions:** Tell the story through the characters' actions rather than just describing the persons who are involved. For example, you can have your main character looking back over his life to where he is now.

- **Sequence/plot:** What happens first, what follows, then what's next? Once you know the sequence, you may choose to tell the story out of sequence to create more tension and interest.

- **Dialogue:** Dialogue is more powerful than description to reveal the story – especially with the written word.

As a final tip, before you launch into your story, make sure your audience is in a receptive mood. If you try telling your 'once upon a time' moments to an audience that has gone deaf, no one lives happily ever after.

Part V
The Part of Tens

The 5th Wave   By Rich Tennant

"Oh, I understand completely, and let's just say
I'll ignore all the words you're not using."

In this part . . .

In true *For Dummies* tradition, here's your useful quick references for hubs of information on NLP, as well as proven, practical ideas to blend NLP into your life for true success. You have tips on ways to keep learning and practising, as well as ideas to make NLP industrial strength in the workplace. Have fun.

Chapter 17

Ten Ways of Bringing NLP into the Workplace

In This Chapter

▶ Building your NLP skills at work

▶ Solving difficult problems faster

NLP is a well-established therapy for helping people feel good about themselves and bringing about great relationships. So you won't be surprised to hear that NLP has also been proving its value in the corporate world for more than 30 years. In this chapter we show you how you can apply NLP tools in your business or workplace in a workmanlike way.

As you go through this chapter, think about where an NLP concept or exercise technique is applicable in your place of work. For example, if you're a boss, manager, or supervisor and need the full co-operation of your employees and colleagues to get the job done, ask yourself: 'How can I build rapport with my colleagues?' 'How do my colleagues take in information – as visual images, presentations, or written reports?' 'What are the common outcomes we share at work?' 'How can I be flexible in my approach and get the results I want?'

Set the Business Strategy

Whether you're setting up a new business or realigning an existing one, NLP can help you to get a clear picture of where your business is today, where you're heading, and your best way of getting there.

NLP refers to goals as outcomes. The NLP well-formed outcome model is the basic tool for setting smarter than SMART goals. Go back to Chapter 3 and apply the principles to remind yourself of the key steps in adopting the well-formed-outcome approach for getting results in any aspect of your business. Here is a reminder of the key seven steps to follow:

1. State your outcome positively: What do you want to achieve?

2. What is the evidence for having achieved your outcome? How will you know specifically when you have arrived at your desired outcome?

3. Is your outcome self-initiated and being followed through? Can you control your strategy?

4. Is your outcome set in context? Define the specific markets and audiences you're addressing.

5. Identify the resources needed: budgets, personnel, equipment, and facilities. What time, money, and energy do you need?

6. Check if your outcome is ecological: 'What do I stand to lose?'

7. What is your first step?: Plan the action and make a commitment to it.

Then, along with time line theory (outlined in Chapter 13), you can visualise achieving your strategic objectives.

Start with Yourself: Be an Example

Mahatma Gandhi is famous for coining the statement: '*You* must be the change you wish to see in the world.' Gandhi was at the time referring to championing human rights, making the point that if you want things done differently, you must initiate change by setting an example yourself. Take Gandhi's advice into your workplace: make yourself responsible for change by setting an example. Hiding behind others and the system can be oh so tempting – the kind of thinking that says: 'I have to do this because everyone else is.' 'The system doesn't allow me to do it differently.' 'I can't change things round here, that's how it is.'

If you're working in an environment where people have slipped into the habit of blaming others when things go pear-shaped, take the opportunity to stop and ask yourself : 'Am I at cause or at effect here? (Chapter 2 explains how to view being 'at cause' and 'at effect'.) For example, in your office the coffee is dispensed in plastic cups that are environmentally unfriendly, choking up the landfill. Or, you feel embarrassed at leaving work on time when others work long into the evening. Or, worse, you've seen some less-than-honest dealing with the company's customers.

You can bring about change by making a stand, starting with how you yourself behave. Stop and think about your own values, what's really important. If health is important to you, make sure you allow time to exercise during the working week. When you honour your own values and stick to them, you earn the respect of your workmates, giving others the chance to follow your example.

Unpack the Tough Stuff

Running a business is about delivering results. Performance on the 'bottom line' of the company accounts is what the investors are looking for. Sadly, achieving performance targets is not just about being nice to people at the coffee machine (unless you just happen to be the coffee shop barista). You'll face times when the going gets tough. When sales are down, jobs will be on the line, because customers pay your salaries. If you work in sales, you know that your head will be the first to roll if you don't meet targets, unlike your colleagues working in safer jobs a few steps removed from the front line. When things get tough in a business, that's when underlying negative emotions like fear and anger surface in undesirable behaviour. Ever seen a stressed out colleague lose her temper?

NLP can help you to develop the mental resilience to ride the tough times. Learning how to anchor your best state allows you to be the one who bounces back fastest if the company goes bust. (We talk about anchors in Chapter 9.) Having an anchor puts you 'at cause' (you may want to go back to Chapter 2 to check up on being 'at cause'). You realise that the person at the end of the phone who is being nasty to you has her own reasons for being in that state – she is wrapped up in her own needs rather than yours. If you're wearing your sales hat because your work involves cold calling, tell yourself you're in the business of acting a role for your company – you are not the role.

When the going gets tough, mentally take yourself off into the skies and from your helicopter up above your time line looking down on your office, be reassured that things are going to be different in a week, month, or year from now.

Step into Your Colleagues' Shoes

Your workplace is likely to be full of a wonderful assortment of characters selected to perform together in the same play. You may not be responsible for hiring the people you work with, yet you're going to need to connect amicably with your fellow players if you want to stay in that particular job. In the workplace you have the amazing opportunity to work alongside a variety of people with different interests, upbringings, and talents: Especially true if you work in a multicultural team.

So get curious about what makes your colleagues tick. (Chapter 5 helps you to look at how you filter your own thinking about yourself and other people.) Imagine what it's like to be in your colleagues' shoes. Ask yourself what you can learn from and about your colleagues. Choose someone who's very different to you, perhaps someone you admire, or someone who frustrates you. What are your similarities and differences? What advice can your colleague give you about things you'd like to do better? If you're at loggerheads with a colleague, is it because she's the one mirroring your shortcomings? Maybe she's the one with the vision, while you're stuck on detail. Perhaps you see that she's good at connecting with people whereas you're introverted and not looking for change.

Create Your Own Workplace Culture

Many companies have marvellous mission statements embracing high-flown values, but where do you fit into the company culture? Are you working in, or do you visit an office where the sign on the wall says: 'Customers come first,' and the parking spaces at the front are for the Chairman and Directors only, while customers have to park half a mile away? How about the managers who say they have family-friendly policies and then insist on you attending meetings that regularly go on late into the evening? Or the employees who demand more responsibility, yet continually blame 'them' when there's a problem.

Take some time out with your team to get clear about your own operating principles. (See Chapter 11 and the logical levels model worksheets to help you check for alignment of behaviours with the espoused culture.) Find out what's important to each person in your business and how you want and can work together. Draw up an agreed charter and check in each month to see how you're doing, what is working, and what is not. Continually check whether your business truly reflects the values you've set down in your charter and if your actions don't match up, then change them.

Build Rapport with Stakeholders

Being successful in business isn't just about being the best administrator, accountant, trainer, or technician. Business is about people, and it's your business to talk to people and have people talk to you. If you lack the social skills to connect with people effectively, then you're likely to quickly come up against a blank wall in your career and business. NLP offers you practical guidance on achieving rapport with your colleagues and business associates through listening at a deeper level to what's interesting and important to them, instead of what's most interesting and important for you. (Chapter 7 has great tips on building rapport.)

In the workplace, getting things done is not always about influencing people in senior roles in the organisation. For example, the most valuable person you need to build rapport with may actually be the personal assistant who is gatekeeper to the director's diary or the receptionist who books parking spaces for employees. Rapport isn't something you switch on and off according to whom you consider is the most important person in the company. Aim for building great rapport with all your colleagues, clients, and business associates.

Here are two quick questions to ask yourself before getting started:

- ✔ Who are the people I'd like to have better rapport with?
- ✔ What can I do to build up and maintain rapport in my business?

Own Your Career Development

With NLP tools at your fingertips, you're in a great position to take ownership of your career and the professional development of those working for you. Do you come across colleagues drifting along aimlessly, staying too long in one job because they're worried about making a change? Then one day the decision is made for them. The company gets bought out or restructured, and employees get made redundant or shifted to a new project or new organisation. Change happened anyway.

To actively manage your career development, the trick is to take time out from the hurly burly of everyday tasks, and step back and view your career objectively. Use the logical levels exercises in Chapter 11 to help you bring vision and purpose into your career. Having a plan 'B' allows you to decide what your criteria are in your career and whether your talents match your chosen criteria when considering change and shifting to a new environment. NLP firmly encourages you to honour your values and your beliefs to reflect your personal identity and sense of purpose in your chosen career.

Awaken Your Senses

When you come face to face with your VAK preferences (Visual, Auditory, and Kinaesthetic), a whole new world of communication choices opens up for you. Once you tune into the idea that people have different communication preferences, you can match their preferences to the way in which you speak, write, and make presentations so that you communicate more effectively and achieve rapport faster with your colleagues and clients. (We go through the VAK preferences in Chapter 6.)

Now that you're getting skilled in using NLP, take time to listen more closely to how people speak or write their e-mails, as well as noting the content of what they say. Underline the visual words such as *see, picture, vision,* and *clarity*; the auditory words such as *talk, hear,* and *listen*, and the kinaesthetic words and phrases about feelings and actions such as *like, hate, open up,* and *take forward*. Make sure your language matches the preferences of your colleagues, clients, or even that young lass in your office you fancy asking out for a date! If you're doing a presentation, writing a report, or bidding for new business, you won't necessarily know your audience's preferences so take care to cover all three systems of VAK and so be fully prepared to speedily connect with your audience.

Marketing with Metaprograms

For any of you working in marketing or sales, the NLP metaprograms offer those 'Aha!' moments that help you understand how customers tick so that you can adjust the way you communicate to suit your client. (Chapter 8 explains metaprograms.)

Listening out for the metaprograms of your potential customers allows you to customise advertising, Web sites, proposals, and presentations accordingly.

Try applying metaprograms to your sales and see what results you get. As with all business interactions, it pays to listen carefully to what is being said in terms of content and also the way it is being said – the structure of the language.

Find the Difference that Makes the Difference

NLP focuses on modelling excellence, based on the deeply held NLP belief that if anyone excels in any field, that excellence can be reproduced by others. If you spot colleagues, clients, and/or business associates getting the kind of results you would like, then start to model their behaviour. (Chapter 12 gives you all the information you need to get you modelling.) Get really, really curious about what your model does and how she thinks. Observe her in action as well as talking to her, because she may not be consciously aware of what she is actually doing or how. If you'd like to be successful at cold calling but get defeated by rejection, find your most persistent salesperson and hang out with her. Try her behaviour on for size and notice if you get the same results. Find out what really makes your salesperson tick, what her core values are, her beliefs about what she does, and why she does it. Isolate those essential details that make the difference between doing a satisfactory job and an excellent one.

Chapter 18

Ten (Or So) Ways of Keeping Your NLP Skills Alive

In This Chapter

▶ S-t-r–e—tching yourself further

▶ Putting NLP into practice in your daily life

*T*his chapter is all about working at making NLP an essential part of your daily life in a very purposeful way. Soon after discovering NLP, you find that:

✔ You can never know enough.

✔ Practice makes perfect.

NLP can change your life, so think carefully about where you want to take your NLP learning. This chapter offers you ten ideas to keep NLP working for you.

Setting Your Intent

Start with the big picture before getting down to detail. Do you want to apply your NLP skills to a particular area of your life? For example, do you want to use NLP at work to increase rapport with your colleagues, or to take NLP to the next level to help you become a top salesperson in the company? Perhaps you want to reopen the lines of communication with your teenager who can only grunt at you?

Using NLP with purpose begins with setting your intent and letting your unconscious mind flag up your NLP opportunities. You can do this by thinking about your current level of expertise and where you might want to take it; perhaps you admire someone's capability and want to get to his level. This is setting the intention to be as good as someone who has already got where you want to get. OK! So you may decide to be even better when you get to the level of expertise you can only dream about, but it's a great start. Keeping an NLP diary also helps to keep your mind focused on your intention to become more proficient at NLP. Chapter 1 explains more about setting your intent.

Use Worksheet 18-1 to outline your thoughts on how and when you're going to apply your NLP skills. Or perhaps you want to lay out a really detailed plan with a timescale. You may decide to attend a course. You can write down some of the topics you discover from this book – for example submodalities, strategies, or rapport – and dedicate a month to work on each of them. You can read around the topics, surf the Internet for information, or listen to NLP CDs.

| Worksheet 18-1 | My Plan for Applying My NLP Skills |

_____

_____

_____

_____

Keeping an NLP Diary

Keeping a record of your progress is invaluable, so we recommend keeping an NLP diary. Start with what you're aware that you don't know. Record your schedule for what NLP topics you plan to focus on. Then, at bedtime, write down:

- ✔ What you're going to practise tomorrow.
- ✔ Whether you were on track for today and what lessons you had learned by the end of the day.
- ✔ Your successes and failures.
- ✔ What you'll do differently tomorrow as a result of what you've learned today.

Remember that everything you do is a learning experience. Consider the NLP presupposition: 'There's no failure – only feedback'. Use feedback to bring about change. (Refer to Chapter 2 to check out NLP presuppositions.)

Worksheet 18-2 gives you the opportunity of getting the hang of keeping a diary. To start you off, we give you an example of the type of entry you can put in your diary.

Worksheet 18-2	My NLP Diary		
My Practice Focus	*What I Hope To Achieve*	*Successful/Needs Adjustment*	*What I Learned*
EXAMPLE: I want to discover whether [person's name] has a Visual, Auditory, or Kinaesthetic preference.	Make spotting VAK preferences second nature.	I find I can't always hear the Auditory words being spoken.	I need to maintain eye contact with the person, watching for cues while listening to the words he's saying.

Going Back to Basics

Even fully trained NLP practitioners need to go back to basics periodically to update their NLP skills. This means revisiting notes you made when you started learning NLP or rereading books you haven't picked up for a while, perhaps deciding to focus on an NLP topic again and applying the tools to listening to radio or watching TV with a 'new ear'. Going over old material with hindsight can help take you to a different level of expertise. As you become more and more skilled in NLP, find new ways of utilising the NLP tools. Be proactive in your learning and follow the dieticians' advice of 'little and often'. Build on what you learned from the previous day.

Using Worksheet 18-3, pick six NLP topics from this book (we've suggested one topic to get you started), giving yourself a score from 0 (don't understand at all) to 5 (good grasp) of how much you understood about the topic, noting any issues arising from your chosen topic. If you fully understand the topic, write down how you'd explain it to someone new to NLP.

Worksheet 18-3 My Understanding of the NLP Concepts in This Workbook		
NLP Topic	*Score 0-5*	*Issues/Explanation*
Example: The Meta Model	2	I forget the patterns and sometimes get the Meta Model confused with the metaprograms.

Staying Curious

Actively work at keeping your mind open to new ideas and taking on board the other person's point of view. Looking at things from another angle can be an amazingly useful skill if you ever find yourself completely off course when reading someone's mind.

Jonah was getting really upset with his boss, Keith, who was being extremely irritable. Jonah was convinced he was going to get the sack and his productivity began to slide, making Keith even more irritable. Things were going from bad to worse until Jonah, deciding he had nothing to lose, took the bull by the horns and literally marched into Keith's office, telling him that he felt their relationship could be better and asking how he could help. A weight seemed to lift off Keith's shoulders as he opened up to Jonah telling him about his messy divorce.

Next time you find yourself getting cross or upset with yourself or someone else, ask what's going on to make you or the other person behave that way.

Handling the NLP Tools

NLP offers a powerful toolkit for changing your thinking and behaviour. However, you need to use the NLP tools sensitively, for your own benefit and for the benefit of others.

When meeting someone who's going through a crisis, such as a divorce, or being fired from a job, ask yourself which NLP tool you can use to best ease the person's situation. If the person is feeling weighed down by it all, and only if he's receptive to it, you can help him change the submodalities of his feelings to get him moving forward (Chapter 10). Or you can work through a well-formed outcome (Chapter 3) to help him decide on a job he'd really like.

Make sure that the person you want to help really wants or needs your help. Nothing's more annoying or distressing for someone who's indulging in idle chat with you if he makes a mildly negative remark and you seize upon it, and whoosh! the person finds he's being harangued by an NLP evangelist.

Looking for NLP in Everyday Situations

A great way to stay aware of NLP in everyday situations is to thank the difficult people that stray into your life. Whether you choose to have someone as a friend or not, you can learn from him. Examining why a person can shake your equilibrium gives you valuable insights into your own thinking processes. By understanding how he does what he does, you can adapt your behaviour and experiment with using different techniques to develop a better relationship with him. The end result is that your flexibility of behaviour helps you gain mastery over your NLP skills and, who knows, unexpected friends.

Other everyday situations are watching television or listening to the radio, both of which give you a wonderful opportunity to hone your NLP skills:

1. **Choose which NLP skill you want to practise.**

2. **As you watch television or listen to the radio, make a list of how someone is using the technique that you want to spot.**

Politicians make brilliant subjects. See if you can spot the mannerisms that show they're being economical with the truth!

Watching TV with the sound turned off allows you to practise reading body language. You may also find yourself learning lip-reading, but that's a side benefit.

'People watching' is another fun activity, opening up endless opportunities for becoming an NLP expert. Likewise, listening to the words people use and their tone of voice. You can also learn a lot from eavesdropping – assuming you're a naturally nosy person who doesn't have any qualms about listening in to other people's conversations.

If you want to take your NLP skills to the next level and you enjoy a good relationship with your four-legged friends, cats and dogs can teach you a lot about sensory acuity because they're so receptive to scents, sounds, and noises. (Chapter 6 explains all about sensory acuity.)

Checking Your Habits

Habits are, well, they're just habits – day-to-day actions that have become second nature. For example, eating every last scrap on your plate even though you're full, or automatically coming out with the excuse that you're *much too busy to meet up* with a friend you no longer want to have as your pal. By implication, a habit is an unconscious behaviour. Only by consciously unpicking a habit can you decide whether to keep that behaviour unchanged or to adapt it to make it more effective, before consigning the habit to the care of the unconscious once again. So if you find you're getting results you don't want, break down what you do to help you change your habit and your result. For example, if cleaning your plate equates to eating too much, resulting in a cuddlier you, you can modify the habit by perhaps using a smaller plate, or smaller portion, or simply giving your leftovers to the dog.

Scripting Your Communications

When you're putting across information, keep the following four basic questions in mind:

- ✔ Who is my audience?
- ✔ What is the outcome that I want to achieve?
- ✔ What is the message I want to deliver?
- ✔ What is the best way of conveying my message?

Using these four points, you can *storyboard* (make a few rough sketches) what you want to say or achieve in each point, framing the points within NLP language and techniques. For example, you can take on board VAK (Visual, Auditory, Kinaesthetic) preferences, metaprograms, hypnotic language, including tone of voice and gestures – anything that you think helps your audience to grasp your message. (Chapter 6 introduces you to VAK preferences and Chapter 8 to metaprograms.)

You can practise your NLP messaging techniques in front of a mirror, and after you've got over feeling like a total idiot, you may well get the message that you're a whizz at communicating.

Teaching Others

A brilliant way to discover what you know, or indeed, what you don't know, is by teaching. The process of planning what you want to say to others and then speaking it out loud engages the conscious mind and gives you the reassurance that you're on track with your NLP learning. Pretend that your sole purpose in life is to share what you know about NLP with your captive audience. So talk to your friends and colleagues, and circulate the NLP wisdom that you hold.

Choosing a Model of Excellence

If you want to discover how to be successful at something, find a role model who has achieved fame and fortune in your chosen field. Remember, however, success isn't necessarily about money. Look out for the very best person you can think of who displays the sort of temperament you admire and would like to adopt. (Chapter 11 helps you to identify characteristics you desire in a role model.)

You can find out more about your role model, living or dead, by reading his biography or articles in the press and magazines, listening to him on radio and CDs, or watching him on TV.

Joining a Practice Group

Have you ever started a course of study and quickly given up because you felt that learning in isolation was too much effort? Well the answer to your NLP learning is to join a practice group. You only have to search the Internet to find your nearest local NLP group.

And, hey, if you can't find an NLP group to join, *start one*. The setup can be as flexible or as rigid as you want. You can invite speakers, in which case you may need to have a membership fee, or you can ask a member to prepare a talk on an aspect of NLP, following up the talk with discussion. Working in a group gives you a terrific opportunity to practise presentation skills in a safe environment, and at the same time reassuring your group members that they're truly getting to grips with NLP.

Chapter 19

Ten NLP Resources

*Y*ou can find a wealth of information on NLP once you get interested. This chapter offers you some resources to tap into, and each link takes you a step further in your NLP quest.

Seek Out NLP Organisations Online

If you search online for NLP resources, you're be spoilt for choice. Here's a selected list to simplify your surfing.

✔ Association of NLP, based in Hertfordshire, UK: www.anlp.org

✔ Professional Guild of NLP, based in Lancashire, UK: www.professionalguild ofnlp.com

✔ American Board of NLP, based in Honolulu, USA: www.abh-abnlp.com

✔ Canadian Association of NLP (CANLP): www.canlp.com

✔ International NLP Training Association (INLPTA), based in Virginia, USA: www.inlpta.co.uk/index.html

✔ British Board of NLP: www.bbnlp.com

Read More Widely about NLP

A good starting point for getting into NLP, if you haven't already read it, is *Neuro-linguistic Programming For Dummies*. You can also find part of *Neuro-linguistic Programming For Dummies* in *Personal Development All-in-One For Dummies* together with chapters on hypnotherapy and cognitive behavioural therapy (both titles published by Wiley). Anglo-American Books, based in the UK, offers a range of books, CDs, and DVDs on NLP and related subjects, and also operates a video library at www.anglo-american.co.uk.

Real People Press, based in Colorado, published the first widely available books on NLP by Bandler and Grinder in 1979 (*Frogs into Princes*, *Reframing*, *Trance-Formations*, and *Using Your Brain: For a Change*) and continues to publish new NLP books, CDs, and DVDs. Go to www.realpeoplepress.com.

You can find more books, tips, and tools about NLP at www.nlpco.com and at www.nlpanchorpoint.com. Check out the NLP Wikipedia at www.nlpwiki.org/ and more NLP organisations and NLP professionals at www.nlpcomprehensive.org. The NLP Research and Recognition project Web site is at www.nlpiash.org/DNN/Default.aspx?alias=www.nlpiash.org/dnn/research.

Go to a Conference

In the UK, Jo Hogg's NLP conference attracts international speakers. Jo's Web site is at www.nlpconference.co.uk.

Talk to the Authors

Based in the UK, we – Kate Burton and Romilla Ready – offer personalised coaching and workshops that integrate NLP. Contact us via our main Web sites at www.kateburton.co.uk and www.readysolutionsgroup.com.

Explore a Related Field of Personal Development

Charlie Badenhop is the originator of *Seishindo*, a discipline of human potential designed to create emotional balance, enthusiasm, compassion, and sense of belonging in the world. He is also an Aikido instructor, NLP trainer, and Ericksonian hypnotherapist. For Charlie's stories, sign up for the Seishindo newsletter at www.seishindo.org/newsletter.html.

Check Out the NLP Encyclopaedia

The NLP expert Robert Dilts's Web site is at www.nlpu.com and is home to the freely available *Encyclopaedia* – a truly generous resource which is also available for sale at www.nlpuniversitypress.com.

Find an NLP Training Course

You're spoilt for choice when it comes to NLP training courses – the field is enormous and growing daily. Do your research well to find the best provider for you. Before booking on a full 20-day Practitioner training course, aim to experience a short course with any training organisation you're considering and speak to other delegates who have attended. Check out the trainers' experience and profile.

Get clear about what you want to achieve from the training and how it meets your needs. Come up with your selection criteria. For example, if you're keen to run training yourself, look at whether the company teaches you how to teach others. Check the curriculum carefully to see who it's aimed at – some courses focus on NLP for personal development, others have a bias to business, education, sport, and health fields. If you're keen to mix with people from other countries and cultures, consider a course with one of the larger providers in a city such as London or New York. If you want to be sure of having a local network of NLP practice buddies, choose a training company that attracts people within easy reach of where you live or work.

Join an Online Community

The www.nlpconnections.com Web site is a growing community of NLP followers. For Master NLP Practitioners, check out the NLP Executive Coaching Community Yahoo! group by emailing NLPExecutiveCoachingCommunity-owner@yahoogroups.com.

Seek Out an NLP-Trained Therapist

For long-term one-to-one therapeutic support, you can find skilled therapists or hypnotherapists at:

- ✔ UK Council for Psychotherapy, www.ukcp.org.uk
- ✔ British Association for Counselling and Psychotherapy, www.bacp.co.uk
- ✔ The General Hypnotherapy Register, www.general-hypnotherpy-register.com

Hire an NLP-Trained Coach

Find a professional coach via the International Coach Federation at www.coach federation.org, or via www.anlp.org which is an independent organisation promoting high standards, professionalism, and good practice in NLP.

Index

Notes

Notes

FOR DUMMIES®

Do Anything. Just Add Dummies

UK editions

...ving and Selling a Home

Renting Out Your Property

Buying a Property in Eastern Europe

...-0-7645-7027-8   978-0-470-02921-3   978-0-7645-7047-6

...ONAL FINANCE

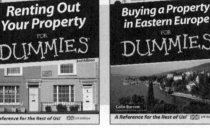

...nvesting

Personal Finance & Investing ALL-IN-ONE

Bookkeeping

...-0-7645-7023-0   978-0-470-51510-5   978-0-470-05815-2

...NESS

...arting a Business

Marketing

Business Plans

...8-0-7645-7018-6   978-0-7645-7056-8   978-0-7645-7026-1

Answering Tough Interview Questions For Dummies (978-0-470-01903-0)

Being the Best Man For Dummies (978-0-470-02657-1)

Body Language FD (978-0-470-51291-3)

British History For Dummies (978-0-470-03536-8)

Buying a Home on a Budget For Dummies (978-0-7645-7035-3)

Buying a Property in Spain For Dummies (978-0-470-51235-77)

Cognitive Behavioural Therapy For Dummies (978-0-470-01838-5)

Cricket For Dummies (978-0-470-03454-5)

CVs For Dummies (978-0-7645-7017-9)

Detox For Dummies (978-0-470-01908-5)

Diabetes For Dummies (978-0-470-05810-7)

Divorce For Dummies (978-0-7645-7030-8)

DJing For Dummies (978-0-470-03275-6)

eBay.co.uk For Dummies (978-0-7645-7059-9)

Economics For Dummies (978-0-470-05795-7)

English Grammar For Dummies (978-0-470-05752-0)

Gardening For Dummies (978-0-470-01843-9)

Genealogy Online For Dummies (978-0-7645-7061-2)

Green Living For Dummies (978-0-470-06038-4)

Hypnotherapy For Dummies (978-0-470-01930-6)

Life Coaching For Dummies (978-0-470-03135-3)

Neuro-linguistic Programming For Dummies (978-0-7645-7028-5)

Parenting For Dummies (978-0-470-02714-1)

Personal Developmet All-In-One For Dummies (978-0-470-51501-3)

Pregnancy For Dummies (978-0-7645-7042-1)

Retiring Wealthy For Dummies (978-0-470-02632-8)

Self Build and Renovation For Dummies (978-0-470-02586-4)

Selling For Dummies (978-0-470-51259-3)

Sorting Out Your Finances For Dummies (978-0-7645-7039-1)

Starting a Business on eBay.co.uk For Dummies (978-0-470-02666-3)

Starting and Running an Online Business For Dummies (978-0-470-05768-1)

The Romans For Dummies (978-0-470-03077-6)

UK Law and Your Rights For Dummies (978-0-470-02796-7)

Writing a Novel & Getting Published For Dummies (978-0-470-05910-4)

FOR DUMMIES®

Do Anything. Just Add Dummies

HOBBIES

Poker FOR DUMMIES
978-0-7645-5232-8

Knitting FOR DUMMIES
978-0-7645-5395-0

Drawing FOR DUMMIES
978-0-7645-5476-6

Also available:

Art For Dummies
(978-0-7645-5104-8)

Aromatherapy For Dummies
(978-0-7645-5171-0)

Bridge For Dummies
(978-0-471-92426-5)

Card Games For Dummies
(978-0-7645-9910-1)

Chess For Dummies
(978-0-7645-8404-6)

Improving Your Memory For Dummies
(978-0-7645-5435-3)

Massage For Dummies
(978-0-7645-5172-7)

Meditation For Dummies
(978-0-471-77774-8)

Photography For Dummies
(978-0-7645-4116-2)

Quilting For Dummies
(978-0-7645-9799-2)

EDUCATION

Psychology FOR DUMMIES
978-0-7645-5434-6

The Koran FOR DUMMIES
978-0-7645-5581-7

Anatomy & Physiology FOR DUMMIES
978-0-7645-5422-3

Also available:

Algebra For Dummies
(978-0-7645-5325-7)

Astronomy For Dummies
(978-0-7645-8465-7)

Buddhism For Dummies
(978-0-7645-5359-2)

Calculus For Dummies
(978-0-7645-2498-1)

Cooking Basics For Dummies
(978-0-7645-7206-7)

Forensics For Dummies
(978-0-7645-5580-0)

Islam For Dummies
(978-0-7645-5503-9)

Philosophy For Dummies
(978-0-7645-5153-6)

Religion For Dummies
(978-0-7645-5264-9)

Trigonometry For Dummies
(978-0-7645-6903-6)

PETS

Puppies FOR DUMMIES
978-0-470-03717-1

Dog Training FOR DUMMIES
978-0-7645-8418-3

Cats FOR DUMMIES
978-0-7645-5275-5

Also available:

Labrador Retrievers For Dummies
(978-0-7645-5281-6)

Aquariums For Dummies
(978-0-7645-5156-7)

Birds For Dummies
(978-0-7645-5139-0)

Dogs For Dummies
(978-0-7645-5274-8)

Ferrets For Dummies
(978-0-7645-5259-5)

Golden Retrievers For Dummies
(978-0-7645-5267-0)

Horses For Dummies
(978-0-7645-9797-8)

Jack Russell Terriers For Dummies
(978-0-7645-5268-7)

Puppies Raising & Training Diary For Dummies
(978-0-7645-0876-9)

Available wherever books are sold. For more information or to order direct go to www.wiley.com or call 0800 243407 (Non UK call +44 1243 843296)

FOR DUMMIES®

The easy way to get more done and have more fun

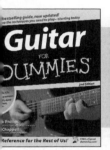

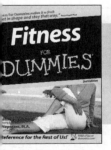
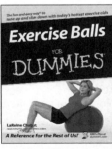
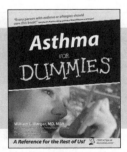

FOR DUMMIES®

Helping you expand your horizons and achieve your potentia[l]

INTERNET

978-0-7645-8996-6

978-0-471-97998-2

978-0-470-08030-6

Also available:

Building a Web Site For Dummies, 2nd Edition (978-0-7645-7144-2)

Blogging For Dummies For Dummies (978-0-471-77084-8)

eBay.co.uk For Dummies (978-0-7645-7059-9)

Video Blogging FD (978-0-471-97177-1)

Web Analysis For Dummie[s] (978-0-470-09824-0)

Web Design For Dummies 2nd Edition (978-0-471-78117-2)

Creating Web Pages All-in-One Desk Reference For Dummies (978-0-7645-4345-6)

DIGITAL MEDIA

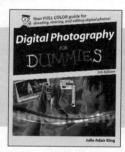

978-0-7645-9802-9

978-0-470-04894-8

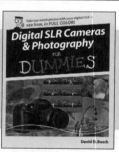

978-0-7645-9803-6

Also available:

BlackBerry For Dummies (978-0-471-75741-2)

Digital Photography All-In-One Desk Reference For Dummies (978-0-470-03743-0)

Digital Photo Projects For Dummies (978-0-470-12101-6)

iPhone For Dummies (978-0-470-17469-2)

Photoshop CS2 For Dummies (978-0-7645-9571-4)

Podcasting For Dummies (978-0-471-74898-4)

Zune For Dummies (978-0-470-12045-3)

COMPUTER BASICS

978-0-7645-8958-4

978-0-470-05432-1

978-0-471-75421-3

Also available:

Macs For Dummies, 9th Edition (978-0-470-04849-8)

Windows Vista All-in-One Desk Reference For Dummies (978-0-471-74941-7)

Office 2007 All-in-One Desk Reference For Dummies (978-0-471-78279-7)

Windows XP For Dummies, 2nd Edition (978-0-7645-7326-2)

PCs All-in-One Desk Reference For Dummies, 3rd Edition (978-0-471-77082-4)

Upgrading & Fixing PCs For Dummies, 7th Edition (978-0-470-12102-3)

Available wherever books are sold. For more information or to order direct go to www.wiley.com or call 0800 243407 (Non UK call +44 1243 843296)